Catholic Theology

'Doing Theology' introduces the major Christian traditions and their way of theological reflection. The volumes focus on the origins of a particular theological tradition, its foundations, key concepts, eminent thinkers and historical development. The series is aimed at readers who want to learn more about their own theological heritage and identity: theology undergraduates, students in ministerial training and church study groups.

Titles in the series

Catholic Theology, Tracey Rowland
Anglican Theology, Mark Chapman
Reformed Theology, Michael Allen
Methodist Theology, Kenneth Wilson
Baptist Theology, Stephen Holmes
Lutheran Theology, Steven D. Paulson

Catholic Theology

Tracey Rowland

Bloomsbury T&T Clark
An imprint of Bloomsbury Publishing Plc

B L O O M S B U R Y
LONDON · OXFORD · NEW YORK · NEW DELHI · SYDNEY

Bloomsbury T&T Clark

An imprint of Bloomsbury Publishing Plc

Imprint previously known as T&T Clark

50 Bedford Square	1385 Broadway
London	New York
WC1B 3DP	NY 10018
UK	USA

www.bloomsbury.com

**BLOOMSBURY, T&T CLARK and the Diana logo are
trademarks of Bloomsbury Publishing Plc**

First published 2017
Reprinted 2017 (five times)

British Library Cataloguing-in-Publication Data
A catalogue record for this book is available from the British Library.

ISBN: HB: 978-0-5670-3438-0
PB: 978-0-5670-3439-7
ePDF: 978-0-5676-5766-4
ePub: 978-0-5676-5767-1

Library of Congress Cataloging-in-Publication Data
Rowland, Tracey, 1963- author.
Catholic theology / Tracey Rowland.
New York : Bloomsbury Academic, 2017. |Series: Doing theology ; 3
LCCN 2016052848| ISBN 9780567034380 (hb) |ISBN 9780567034397 (pb)
LCSH: Theology–Study and teaching–CatholicChurch. | Catholic Church–Doctrines.
LCC BX900 .R69 2017 | DDC 230/.2–dc23
LCrecord available at https://lccn.loc.gov/2016052848

Series: Doing Theology

Typeset by Deanta Global Publishing Services, Chennai, India
Printed and bound in Great Britain

Contents

Acknowledgements

Much gratitude is due to Sebastian Condon for compiling the Appendices on the Documents of the Second Vatican Council, the Papal Encyclicals and the Christological heresies.

Christina Kennedy assisted with the Appendix on the Doctors of the Church and Natasha Marsh skilfully proofread various drafts.

I am also very grateful to my academic colleagues Rev Dr Scot Armstrong, Dr Adam Cooper, Rev Dr Paschal Corby OFM Conv, +Peter Elliott, Anna Krohn, Dr Michael Lynch, Dr Jolanta Nowak, Dr Gerard O'Shea, Dr Colin Patterson, Dr Anna Silvas, Dr Wanda Skowronska, Dr Conor Sweeney, Dr Matthew Tan, Owen Vyner and Rev Dr Joel Wallace for their collegial friendship which has contributed to the quality of this work. Further, none of this would have been possible without the managerial support of Lieutenant Colonel Toby Hunter of the Royal Marines who serves as the Institute's Registrar.

This work is dedicated to Stuart for his quarter-century of chivalrous fidelity to an academic wife and to my mother Pauline who saw to it that I had a Catholic education.

The Dominican Monastery,
Dubrovnik, June 2016.

Introduction

At the beginning of the twenty-first century there is no one particular Catholic approach to the study of theology, though there are guard rails in the form of doctrinal principles that ought not to be violated. Different Catholic theologians will have their own methodologies and Catholic academies themselves get associated with particular schools and theological trends depending on the scholars they employ and the preferences of those who fund the particular academy. In some cases, when a theological institution is under the governance of a bishop, if the bishop himself is not intellectually inclined, and many are not, the bishop may simply appoint people on the basis of availability and economic factors (clergy are cheaper than lay lecturers) and he may not be at all interested in the preferred theological methodology of candidates for teaching positions. In such circumstances theology students often find themselves in a position where they are taught by different scholars following different methods and often reaching different conclusions. This can be quite daunting for undergraduates and young seminarians who innocently expect that their teachers will all be singing from the same hymn sheet, as it were.

A similar problem confronted humanities undergraduates in the 1970s and 1980s when it seemed as though every second academic was a different species of Marxist. To navigate one's way through the ideological thicket one needed a map depicting all the sub-species of New Left intellectuals and their favourite doctrinal principles. One needed to be able to distinguish a Leninist from a Trotskyite and both from Maoists and Euro-communists. Marxist feminists were particularly complex since some believed that patriarchy was a more evil social force than capitalism, while others thought that the problem of patriarchy could only be resolved *after* the destruction of capitalism. Writing essays in the 1970s and 1980s for submission to Arts faculties was an art form that required a preliminary knowledge of the Marxist ideological fault lines. Today an extensive knowledge of postmodern philosophy is similarly required.

A major difference, however, between contemporary Catholic theology academies and the typical university Arts Faculty after 1968 is the operation of the 'don't mention the war' maxim. Whereas on the university campuses of the 1960s and 1970s it was common for students to listen to public lectures where ideological opponents would debate the issues of the day, in the contemporary Catholic theological academy the proponents of different methodologies have a tendency to avoid open intellectual warfare. In place of what Antonio Gramsci called 'the war of manoeuvre' (direct confrontation) there is a preference for a 'war of position', a quiet, behind-the-scenes attempt to improve one's position through the acquisition of bureaucratic power, giving one authority over future appointments and curriculum development. This makes it somewhat harder for the average undergraduate or seminarian to understand why what they learn in the morning lectures may not in fact sound anything like what they hear after lunch. The whole territory of Catholic theology is highly fragmented and there is little agreement about methodological principles and issues that are classified as central to the subject of 'Fundamental Theology'. The conflict at the Synods on the Family (2014 and 2015) was symptomatic of this. Foundational fault lines include the understanding of the relationship between nature and grace, faith and reason, history and dogma, *logos* and *ethos* and the correct principles to be applied to biblical hermeneutics. There is also the issue of 'conflicting metanarratives' or alternative intellectual histories that seek to account for the rise of secularism in the formerly Christian countries of the Western world. Different metanarratives are associated with different choices in the field of Fundamental Theology and prescribe different solutions to the ideology of secularism.

Therefore a short answer to the question of how Catholics *do theology* is: 'It depends on what species of intellectual Catholic one is!' This means that to write a book on how Catholics do theology is quite a challenging exercise since whatever one says is open to the criticism that some particular approach has been omitted, some sub-species of Catholic theologian has been left out of the line-up, or alternatively, unjustly privileged.

However, there is also the important fact that, unlike versions of Christianity that arose in the sixteenth century, Catholic scholars operate within an ecclesial community where there is the office of the papacy and the Congregation for the Doctrine of the Faith (CDF). While the CDF accepts that there is more than one valid approach to the task of intellectually unpacking Christian Revelation, it also holds that there are invalid approaches or, in premodern parlance, heretical ideas, which fall outside the boundaries of legitimate theological pluralism. It is not the case that anyone who happens to call themselves a Catholic theologian can legitimately claim to be doing 'Catholic theology'.

With an introductory text, the best that an author can hope to achieve is to give students an overview of the most significant approaches and fault lines and allow them to gradually fill in the details and nuances as they progress in their studies. Accordingly, many of the chapters have the quality of a broad-brush exposition of the current state of play. They seek to answer the following questions: Who are the most significant theologians? What are they saying? In what tradition are they operating? What are the hallmarks of their particular approach to the study of Catholic theology? The following chapters are, in short, efforts to summarise the *status quaestionis* for those at the beginning of their theological studies and to highlight the most significant conflicting metanarratives.

The first chapter is addressed to perennially important issues in Fundamental Theology as they have been set out in documents of the International Theological Commission. Included here is an overview of some significant 'critical couplets' such as Christ and the Trinity, Nature and Grace, Faith and Reason, Christology and Mariology, Scripture and Tradition, and *logos* and *ethos*. This chapter cannot possibly cover every particular construction of these relationships in Catholic intellectual history. It will, however, direct students to the most contemporary material and magisterial interventions on these relationships; from there they can dig deeper into the historical debates.

The chapter on the foundational principles and critical relationships is followed by a chapter on Thomism (the most systematic of all the theological schools), which seeks to profile the many different appropriations of Thomist thought throughout history. This is the longest chapter because there have been so many different Thomist projects. Students are often quite confused when finally they master one school of Thomism only to run up against a lecturer who represents a different school. They then find themselves in a position of having to learn about an alternative reading of some particular aspect of Thomist thought. In the Anglophone world there is also a tendency for millennial generation students who survey the contemporary intellectual life of the Church and find it a mess to want to 'reboot the system' to 1961. The Thomist chapter should make it clear that even in 1961 there was no unified approach to the appropriation of medieval scholarship, although a unified approach was regarded as an ideal.

The Thomism(s) chapter is followed by an account of the theological method(s) of the founders of the *Communio* journal, namely Hans Urs von Balthasar (1905–88), Henri de Lubac SJ (1896–1991) and Joseph Ratzinger/ Benedict XVI. In contrast to the Thomists, these theologians are not tightly systematic. They are much more synthetically oriented. They take ideas from the entire intellectual treasury of the Church and do not therefore confine themselves to the ideas of a single Church Father or Doctor. Their philosophical range is also much broader than that of the classical Greek philosophy that undergirded so much Thomist theology. When they do appropriate Thomist ideas, they approach Aquinas as the great synthesiser of the Patristic heritage. They read Aquinas through the lens of his Patristic antecedents, not through the lens of his commentators, of whom they are quite critical. They are in fact especially critical of interpretations of Aquinas that flow from the seventeenth and nineteenth centuries, the so-called 'Baroque' or 'Suárezian Thomism' and 'Leonine Thomism'.

De Lubac and Ratzinger were both *Periti* (expert theological advisers) at the Second Vatican Council (1962–5) and the *Communio* circle of theologians to which they belong has become associated with the 'hermeneutic of reform' approach to interpreting the documents of the Second Vatican Council. There is however another stream of scholarship offering a different interpretation from scholars in the *Communio* circles and from the magisterial teaching of Paul VI, John Paul II and Ratzinger/Benedict XVI. Those representing the other interpretation are often described, in shorthand terms, as the '*Concilium* stream'.

Philip Trower has described the intellectual battle between the two different interpretations of the Council as presented in the pages of the competing journals *Communio* and *Concilium* (the latter included Karl Rahner SJ (1904–84), Edward Schillebeeckx OP (1914–2009) and Hans Küng on its editorial board) as a 'theological star wars' played out over the heads of the faithful.[1] In other words, what people in parishes received as the 'teaching of the Council' was often the residue of ideas floated by the former Vatican II *Periti* in one or the other of these journals.

The conflict between the two interpretations may be explained by what Ratzinger described as the most severe theological crisis for the Catholic Church in the twentieth century, namely, coming to an understanding of the mediation of history in the realm of ontology.[2] To the perennial critical relationships (such as Christ and the Trinity, nature and grace, Scripture and Tradition, faith and reason), there was added in the twentieth century the history–ontology relationship. This is, in part, the Heideggerian 'being in time' issue. Some scholars have gone so far as to describe the Second Vatican Council as an attempt to Heideggerise Catholic theology by reconciling the timelessness of the faith with the contemporary interest in history, culture and hermeneutics. Precisely how theologians construe the relationship between faith and history, in particular how they view the mediation of history in the realms of ontology and Revelation, will have a deep impact on their overall theological vision. Here there is a spectrum of positions, with some species of Thomists occupying one end and the *Concilium* theologians, especially those in the tradition of Edward Schillebeeckx, occupying the other, with the *Communio* theologians located somewhere between the two. Since there is strong agreement (across the spectrum) that Ratzinger is right in his judgement that the history–ontology relationship was *the crisis issue* of twentieth-century Catholic theology, the fourth chapter is devoted to the projects of the *Concilium* scholars and, in particular, their ways of interpreting Vatican II and construing the history–ontology relationship.

With the transition from the papacy of the Bavarian Benedict XVI to that of the Argentinian Francis, Latin American issues have risen in prominence and Liberation Theology (which waned in Europe after the fall of European Communism in 1989) is back in fashion. For this reason the fifth and final chapter seeks to provide an overview of the theological methodology of the intellectuals within this movement and to situate Pope Francis in relation to the school of Liberation Theology and other approaches discussed in earlier chapters.

Appendices are offered at the end listing (i) the Christological heresies, (ii) the Documents of the Second Vatican Council, (iii) all the papal encyclicals from Leo XIII to Francis and (iv) the Doctors of the Church.

Dates of authors are listed in brackets after the first mention of their name, no dates are given if the author is still living. This has been done for the sake of younger readers who may be hearing about an author for the first time and have no idea of whether, for example, Erich Przywara was a medieval Franciscan or a twentieth-century Jesuit.

A number of the scholars to be mentioned have names with a nobiliary particle – von, van and de – and the etiquette of only including the particle if the surname is preceded by the Christian name(s) – thus, Hans Urs von Balthasar or simply Balthasar – has generally been followed. However, exceptions have been made for Henri de Lubac and Augustine Di Noia since they are almost universally described in the academic literature as de Lubac and Di Noia rather than simply Lubac or Noia. A theologian's religious post-nominals have also been inserted after the first mention of their name for the sake of younger readers who may not know, for example, that Karl Rahner was a Jesuit ('SJ'), or that Edward Schillebeeckx was a Dominican ('OP'). This is because knowing a person's religious family can provide insights into the spiritual context in which his or her theological work was undertaken. Finally, the use of the symbol + before a surname will indicate that the theologian cited is either a bishop or an archbishop.

The American writer Anthony Esolen has compared the Catholic Church in the first decades of the twenty-first century to a sleeping dragon, snoring on top of his horde of gold.[3] This book is written for those who want to get to the gold, to mine the wealth of the Catholic intellectual patrimony, while the dragon sleeps and snores. As such it belongs to the same literary genre as James V. Schall SJ's *Another Sort of Learning*, subtitled *How to Acquire an Education while still in College or Anywhere Else*. This is a 'How to do Catholic Theology' even if one is bored stupid in a seminary or in any other ostensibly Catholic educational institution under the jurisdiction of snoring dragons.

Fundamental Issues and Building Blocks

The International Theological Commission ('ITC') is a body established under the authority of the Papacy and the Congregation of the Doctrine of the Faith, consisting of some thirty theologians, drawn from different regions of the world and with different areas of academic expertise. Every five years the Commission produces three documents on contemporary theological 'hot issues'. These documents do not carry the weight of magisterial authority, but they are a useful guide to mainstream Catholic thinking in the areas they cover and a number have been devoted to the subject of theological method. They are a good place to begin one's forays into the world of doing Catholic theology.

The first of these, entitled *The Unity of the Faith and Theological Pluralism*, was published in 1972. In this document the ITC members acknowledged that there is a plurality of legitimate Catholic approaches to the study of theology, but they also outlined some fifteen general principles to which each and every theologian, of whatever stripe and colour, would reasonably be expected to adhere in order to merit the appellation 'Catholic'.

The mystery exceeds any system

The first of these principles is that 'unity and plurality in the expression of the Faith have their ultimate basis in the very mystery of Christ that ... goes beyond the possibilities of expression of any given age and thus eludes exhaustive systematisation'. This principle might sound quite prosaic, even boring, but in fact it relates to one of the most hotly debated issues in contemporary Catholic theology from the first half of the twentieth century to the present. Put differently it is the tension between 'Mystery' and 'System'.

Before the Second Vatican Council Catholic theology was so highly systematic that scholars complained of having to work within a conceptual straitjacket. The Tridentine enthusiasm for systemisation was the subject of much criticism. The Russian Orthodox theologian Vladimir Lossky (1903–58) wrote:

> Theology as *Sophia* is connected at once to *gnosis* and to *episteme*. It reasons, but seeks always to go beyond concepts. Here a necessary moment of the *failure* of human thought breaks in before the mystery that it wants to make knowable. A theology that constitutes itself into a system is always dangerous. It imprisons in the enclosed sphere of thought the reality to which it must open thought.[1]

Lossky warned against the tendency to replace the 'mystery lived in silence' with 'mental schemata easily handled, certainly, and whose use can intoxicate, but which are ultimately empty'.[2] A Catholic statement expressing the same concern may be found in the observation of de Lubac that 'Catholic truth will always exceed its own conceptual expression, and even more so, therefore, its scientific formulation in an organised system'.[3]

De Lubac was complaining about the condensation of the faith to a basket of formulae, rather like the way that the Chinese Communist Party produced Mao Tse-Tung's *Little Red Book* of Marxist maxims, which was distributed to millions of Chinese people during the Maoist era (1949–76) for indoctrination purposes. As +Rudolf Voderholzer has explained, de Lubac was not critical of the existence of dogma itself but of the 'reduction of faith to a free intellectual assent to propositions about the object(s) of faith – without any (faith-generated) interior insight'.[4] De Lubac's statements on this issue were an early articulation of what became the first principle on the list of the ITC's 1972 document.

Thomas Weinandy OFM, a member of the 9th ITC, convened in 2014, has expressed the same principle in the following terms:

> Some Christian systematic theologians today, having embraced the Enlightenment presuppositions and the scientific method that it fostered, approach theological issues as if they were problems to be solved rather than mysteries to be discerned and clarified. However, the true goal of theological inquiry is not the resolution of theological problems, but the discernment of what the mystery of faith is. Because God, who can never be fully comprehended, lies at the heart of all theological inquiry, theology by its nature is not a problem-solving enterprise, but rather a mystery-discerning enterprise.[5]

The difference between Weinandy and de Lubac is that de Lubac was critical of a one-eyed focus on dogma to the exclusion of the mystery (typical of pre-Conciliar theology), while Weinandy is critical of a post-Conciliar tendency to reject any part of the Catholic intellectual tradition that cannot be defended by reference to the principles of the scientific method. From a different and even opposite angle, this common post-Conciliar academic practice results in the same occlusion of the mystery.

Notwithstanding this concern that the mystery not be occluded or domesticated, it is nonetheless the case that all kinds of erroneous ideas can develop if people are not aware of how decisions taken in one field of theology will have a consequence in another field of theology. For example, one's understanding of Christology will have flow-on effects in theological anthropology, moral theology, sacramental theology, ecclesiology and soteriology, to name but the most obvious areas to be affected. While a rigidly tight system is problematic and certainly produced a 'back-lash' response after the Second Vatican Council, a lack of a panoramic vision or ignorance of the broad contours of the 'big picture' can lead to all kinds of distortions and ultimately a collage of half-truths.

Thus this first principle on the ITC list should not be interpreted as a criticism of doctrine per se. This first principle is simply making the claim that Catholic theology is not something as narrow as a compilation of doctrinal formulae. Even the popular nineteenth-century compendium on Catholic doctrine known in academic shorthand as 'Denzinger' or 'Denzinger-Schönmetzer', which is itself the closest thing to a handbook of doctrines, acknowledged this principle in the following terms:

> Reason enlightened by faith, when it seeks piously and soberly, by God's gift, can reach a certain understanding of the mysteries. ... Yet it will never be able to penetrate them as it can the truths that are in its own domain. Because the divine mysteries, by their very nature, transcend the created mind, so, despite revelation and the pious acceptance of it, they still remain enveloped by faith in darkness as by a cover during our pilgrimage in mortal life far from the Lord. We walk by faith and not by sight. (DS 3016)

More recently, Martin X. Moleski SJ addressed the relationship between doctrine and theological study using metaphors drawn from the world of information technology. As he put it:

> Dogmatic theology has a real but limited value in this love affair between Jesus and the believer. The rigidity and formalization of theology plays exactly the same role in carrying the message of God's love to his people as does a communications protocol in delivering messages over the tangled web of the internet. Unless there are strict rules of interpretation about how to transmit and receive, there will be

no communication from one computer to another. All of the elements of the message will fall into disarray and be lost in the noise and confusion of the environment. From time to time, when the message is deteriorating, someone has to trace the circuits and determine why the transmission is being corrupted. When someone is downloading a new piece of software from the internet, for example, they do not want the intermediary computers to add or subtract a single byte from the original. Personal or random reinterpretations of what is sent would destroy the functionality of the program and prevent it from performing as it was designed to perform. Furthermore, the person seeking the new software generally does not want to receive the communications protocol itself. They want the software, not a set of rules and regulations that describe how software may be sent and received. If the rules did not exist, the transmissions could not take place, but the rules are no substitute for the files transmitted by the rules.[6]

This is a helpful description of why doctrine is indispensable, while at the same time it is not the whole file, not the whole faith. There do need to be strict rules of interpretation about how to transmit and receive; otherwise personal or random reinterpretations of what is sent would destroy the functionality of the entire programme. One would end up, not with Christianity, but with some ideology with Christian influences.

All metaphors however have their limitations and it is important to note here that while some doctrines work as mere boundary markers in the process of transmission and reception, guiding the very principles of the transmission, others, especially those that have been defined to be dogmas of the faith (i.e. beliefs derived directly from Revelation), are part of the actual deposit of the faith, part of the files to be transmitted, in other words. They are a file in their own right and not a mere rule of transmission. They are usually studied under the umbrella of 'Dogmatic Theology'.

The unity–duality of the two Testaments

Secondly, the ITC document asserted that the 'unity-duality of the Old Testament and New, as the fundamental historical expression of the Christian faith, provides a concrete point of departure for the unity-plurality of the same Faith'. This means that the Old Testament is not to be dismissed as mere history that ceases to have theological significance after the Incarnation of Christ. Rather, the principle is that the whole of salvation history is encompassed by the books of both Testaments. The work *Lovely Like Jerusalem: The Fulfilment of the Old Testament in Christ and the Church* by Aidan Nichols OP covers this principle in depth.[7] There is also a reflection on this subject delivered as an address by Pope John Paul II to the Pontifical Biblical Commission in 1997. In this address John Paul II observed:

> Since the second century A.D., the Church has been faced with the temptation to separate the New Testament completely from the Old, and to oppose one to the other, attributing to them two different origins. The Old Testament, according to Marcion, came from a god unworthy of the name because he was vindictive and bloodthirsty, while the New Testament revealed a God of reconciliation and generosity. The Church firmly rejected this error, reminding all that God's tenderness was already revealed in the Old Testament. Unfortunately the Marcionite temptation is making its appearance again in our time. However what occurs most frequently is an ignorance of the deep ties linking the New Testament to the Old, an ignorance that gives some people the impression that Christians have nothing in common with Jews.[8]

John Paul II went on to assert that 'it is impossible fully to express the mystery of Christ without reference to the Old Testament'.[9]

In a parallel statement, in his essay *Daughter Zion: Meditations on the Church's Marian Belief*, Joseph Ratzinger argued that 'all consequent Marian piety and theology is fundamentally based upon the Old Testament's deeply anchored theology of woman'.[10]

The faith and reason relationship

Thirdly, the ITC members stated that while faith is not the same thing as a philosophy, it must, like philosophy, be presented in rational terms. John Paul II's encyclical, *Fides et Ratio* (1998), addressed this principle in the following paragraph:

> Theology is structured as an understanding of faith in the light of a twofold methodological principle: the *auditus fidei* [hearing or receiving the faith] and the *intellectus fidei* [making sense of the faith so received]. With the first, theology makes its own the content of Revelation as this has been gradually expounded in Sacred Tradition, Sacred Scripture and the Church's living Magisterium. With the

second, theology seeks to respond through speculative enquiry to the specific demands of disciplined thought.[11]

The relationship between faith and reason is one of the perennial subjects in the intellectual life of the Church. The Australian theologian, Neil Ormerod, began a paper at a conference to celebrate the promulgation of *Fides et Ratio* with the statement that 'the problem of the interrelationship between faith and reason is complex and tortuous'.[12] He further noted that from a theological perspective 'the faith-reason debate is subsumed within the grace-nature issue' and that the difficulty is always one of how to overcome a false dichotomy between the two while recognising the distinction. This difficulty lies at the heart of the debates about how to relate faith and reason. Aidan Nichols surveyed the many attempts to deal with the difficulty of the false dichotomy in his *Faith and Reason: From Hermes to Benedict XVI*. He began with a summary of the ideas of Georg Hermes (1775–1831) – a kind of 'Catholic Kantian' – and combed through the positions of Anton Günther (1783–1863), Louis Bautain (1796–1867), Gregory XVI (1765–1846), Pius IX (1792–1878), Leo XIII (1810–1903), Joseph Kleutgen (1811–83), Étienne Gilson (1884–1978), Maurice Blondel (1861–1949), Hans Urs von Balthasar, Karol Wojtyła (1920–2005) (John Paul II) and finally Joseph Ratzinger (Benedict XVI). Numerous other authorities such as Jacques Maritain (1882–1973) and Pierre Rousselot (1878–1915) are addressed in his commentary along the way and appear in the extensive footnotes.

Other helpful guides into this territory include *The Grandeur of Reason: Religion, Tradition and Universalism*, edited by Peter M. Candler, Jr and Conor Cunningham, and *Reason Fulfilled by Revelation: The 1930s Christian Philosophy Debates in France*, edited by Gregory B. Sadler.

As the title of Sadler's work suggests, the faith and reason relationship was a hot issue in French Catholic circles in the 1930s and many of the contemporary debates take the form of siding with or opposing one of the factions that came to the fore in the 1930s. Sadler's work is helpful because it offers an introductory overview of the factions along with English translations of seminal papers originally written in French. Étienne Gilson was one of the players in these debates and it has been argued that Ratzinger/Benedict XVI's preferred construction of the relationship is strongly Gilsonian while Wojtyła/John Paul II's preferred construction was at least implicitly Gilsonian.

A common complaint of both pontiffs and numerous other Catholic scholars is that in the last couple of hundred years reason has been reduced to discursive thinking alone (*ratio*) and to what is empirically verifiable, ignoring other dimensions of rationality such as intuition or *intellectus*. In his *Leisure as the Basis of Culture*, Josef Pieper (1904–97) put the problem like this:

> The medievals distinguished between the intellect as *ratio* and the intellect as *intellectus*. *Ratio* is the power of discursive thought, or searching and re-searching, abstracting, refining and concluding whereas *intellectus* refers to the ability of 'simply looking' (*simplex intuitus*), to which the truth presents itself as a landscape presents itself to the eye. The spiritual knowing power of the human mind, as the ancients understood it, is really two things in one: *ratio* and *intellectus*: all knowing involved both. The path of discursive reasoning is accompanied and penetrated by the *intellectus*' untiring vision, which is not active but passive, or better, receptive – a receptively operating power of the intellect.[13]

A problem with much contemporary philosophy, especially in Anglophone universities, is that it denigrates the role of *intellectus*.

The three most significant magisterial documents in this field are *Dei Filius* (1870) of Vatican I, *Dei Verbum* (1965) of Vatican II and John Paul II's encyclical *Fides et Ratio* (1998).

In the decades separating these documents the magisterial teaching had to contend with the issue of history. An engagement with the significance of history for intellectual judgement was missing from *Dei Filius*, though it was an issue raised by a number of the bishops in the Conciliar debates of Vatican I. An excellent article on these debates is Fergus Kerr's 'Knowing God by Reason Alone: What Vatican I never said'.[14] Vatican II's *Dei Verbum* is generally interpreted as offering a much deeper theological epistemology than Vatican I's *Dei Filius* since it recognises the historical nature of Revelation.

Cardinal Angelo Scola emphasised the significance of *Dei Verbum* for the contemporary Catholic understanding of the relationship between faith, reason and history in the following passage:

> *Dei Verbum* proposes truth as an event. This consideration is, upon close examination, the fruit of the Council's Christological focus. In fact, in the language of Vatican II, truth and Jesus Christ are identified: in this way, Vatican II frees the notion of truth from the ahistorical pre-comprehension that tends to reify it, thus restoring truth to its identity as a historical event. Truth is in fact inseparable from event; otherwise we drift into formalism. The consideration of revelation as an 'event which occurred in the past and continues to occur in faith, the event

of a new relationship between God and man', presupposes a renewed approach to revealed truth.[15]

Some account of the relationship between faith and reason and (after *Dei Verbum*) faith, reason *and history*, is thus a fundamental building block of every Catholic theology.

Orthodoxy not reductive to a system

Notwithstanding the above principle with its emphasis on offering a rational defence of the faith, the fourth principle to be mentioned by the ITC members is that orthodoxy should not be construed as a form of consent to a system. This is a variation on the first principle that the mystery exceeds the system. The exact words used by the ITC are as follows:

> The truth of the Faith is bound up with its onward movement through history, from Abraham on to Christ, and from Christ to the *parousia*. Consequently, orthodoxy is not consent to a system but a sharing in the onward movement of the Faith and so, in the Church's own selfhood that subsists, identical, through all time, and [is] the true subject of the Credo.

The two dangers to be averted here are, first, the temptation to think that the finite human mind might be able to pin God down into the confines of human conceptual packages, with faith, a theological virtue, presupposing a personal relationship with God, being reduced to a mere intellectual consent to a series of propositions, and, second, the danger of becoming so hooked on some particular theological methodology or system that one's life of faith is reduced or truncated to promoting the system.

As a generalisation it is often remarked that before the Second Vatican Council there was a tendency to think of the Catholic faith as primarily a form of consent to an intellectual system, which occludes or sidelines the mystical dimension of the faith; while after the council the intellectual dimension has in some parts of the world become so seriously weak that people no longer know what the Church teaches. The task is to see the intellectual dimension of the faith in the context of the whole life of the Church and her members. The faith cannot be reduced to a system of propositions, but the understanding of the faith does require some rudimentary knowledge of dogmatic theology, such as one finds expressed in the creeds. Theology students, in particular, do need to understand how the dogmas relate to one another.

Joseph Ratzinger has referred to the Apostle's Creed, the Sacraments, the Ten Commandments and the Lord's Prayer as the 'four classical and master components of catechesis' which have 'served for centuries as the depository and résumé of Catholic teaching'.[16] To paddle out into the waters of theology without knowledge of these 'classical and master components' could be dangerous.

The faith and history relationship

The fifth principle on the ITC list refers to the significance of history in theological study. It asserts that since the truth of the Faith is lived in an onward movement it necessarily involves its relation to the *praxis* and to the history of the Faith. However the ITC authors go on to declare that 'since Christian faith is founded on the incarnate Word, its historical and practical character distinguishes it in its essence from a form of historicity in which man alone would be the creator of his own direction'. Another way to express this principle is to say that while Catholic theology is always a reflection on Revelation in some way and that such reflections become embodied in historically embedded practices, Revelation is nonetheless something *received*, not something *constructed*. Being a Catholic means that one regards oneself as the recipient of the gift of faith, not the creator of a world view with some Christian ingredients.

It follows from the above that the Church is the comprehensive subject giving unity both to theologies and to dogmas as they arise throughout history. As Ratzinger/Benedict XVI put the proposition, 'This communion we call "Church", does not only extend to all believers in a specific historical period, but also embraces all the epochs and all the generations'.[17] Due to the work of the Holy Spirit 'it will always be possible for subsequent generations to have the same experience of the Risen One that was lived by the apostolic community at the origin of the Church, since it is passed on and actualized in the faith, worship, and communion of the People of God, on pilgrimage through time'.[18]

This principle was emphasised in the theology of Adam Möhler (1796–1838), who belonged to the Tübingen circle of scholars. The latter were particularly interested in the problem of how to acknowledge that Revelation is historical while at the same time respecting the faith as something timeless. This principle leads to the conclusion that the Magisterium (encompassing papal and episcopal authority) is the guarantor that what is passed on from one generation to another is the same faith as that of the apostolic generation and not something that has been mutated or contaminated by ideologies. These issues are addressed by the ITC document under the sixth principle.

Marks of true and false pluralism

Principle seven then addresses the issue of the discernment of true and false pluralism or what in earlier centuries was called heresy. According to this principle,

> The criterion that makes it possible to distinguish between true and false pluralism is the Faith of the Church expressed in the organic whole of her normative pronouncements: the fundamental criterion in Scripture as it relates to the confession of the believing and praying Church. Among dogmatic formulas those of the earlier Councils have priority. The formulas that express a reflection of Christian thought are subordinate to those that express the facts of the Faith themselves.[19]

Joseph Ratzinger used the labels 'fruitful pluralism' and 'disintegrative pluralism' to refer to the true and false kinds of pluralism. The second, he said, 'arises when men no longer feel themselves equal to the arc of tensions inherent in the whole of the faith. It always presupposes a previous narrowing and impoverishment, which are not reversed by the proliferation of juxtaposed partial Christianities rising and falling in succession.'[20] This is a very similar point to that made by Gilbert Keith Chesterton (1874–1936) in his book *Orthodoxy*. The idea is that disintegrative pluralism occurs when people get so hooked on one part of the Christian kerygma that they begin to lose a panoramic vision. What should be a symphonic harmony is reduced to something quite discordant because one note or melody is drowning everything else. Typically some principle or doctrine is taken out of its rightful position and exaggerated or some fashionable concept becomes a hermeneutic through which every other part of Christian teaching must pass or else be sidelined. To put this principle another way, Catholic theology is renowned for its capacity to cope with mystery and with paradox and for its similarity to Gothic architecture. Just as every small piece of a Gothic cathedral has a role to play in maintaining the balance of the opposing structural tensions, so too, in Catholic theology, there is always a delicate balance between apparently antithetical 'truths' held in tension. When this tension is lost, when one single buttress is made to bear all the weight, because this particular buttress has become a fashionable subject of reflection, then all possibility of transcendence is lost and one is left with something quite defective, destined to collapse.

Notwithstanding the fact that the Church is the comprehensive subject giving unity to both Old and New Testament theologies and to doctrines as they arise throughout history, in the 1990 *Instruction on the Ecclesial Vocation of the Theologian*, also a document of the Congregation of the Doctrine of the Faith, one finds the statement that 'theology is not simply and exclusively an ancillary function of the Magisterium: it is not limited to gathering arguments for a priori magisterial decisions. If that were so, the Magisterium and theology would draw perilously close to an ideology whose sole interest is the acquisition and preservation of power.' The document goes on to speak of two roots of theology – the dynamism towards truth and understanding inherent in the faith, and the dynamism towards love. It concludes thus:

> The truth of the faith resonates not as a mono-phony but as a symphony, not as a homophonic, but as a polyphonic melody composed of the many apparently quite discordant strains in the contrapuntal interplay of law, prophets, Gospels and apostles. The omission of one of the thematic elements of this symphony simplifies the performance but is rejected by the Fathers as heresy, that is, as a reductive selection, because the truth lies only in the whole and its tensions.[21]

In order to achieve the harmony it is helpful to keep in mind a number of baseline theological issues that are perennially important. Two such issues are the Incarnation and its meaning for creation, and the Crucifixion of Christ and its meaning for redemption. Keeping these baselines held together in tension further requires an extensive knowledge of Christology and Trinitarian theology. The early Councils of the Church are important sources of these core Christological and Trinitarian doctrines, including the definitions of various Christological and Trinitarian heresies. A summary of these appears as an appendix to this volume.

The eighth principle to be found in the ITC document on the subject of *The Unity of the Faith and Theological Pluralism* states that there are limits on pluralism and those limits are reached when doctrinal statements are 'gravely ambiguous' or otherwise incompatible with the faith. In this context, in his *Essay on the Development of Christian Doctrine*, Blessed John Henry Newman outlined seven criteria for discerning when an idea represents a legitimate development of a doctrine and where it might be incompatible with the faith. The criteria are the following:

(i) Preservation of Type. (Here Newman refers to an organic metaphor earlier used by Vincent of Lérins. A baby's limbs grow and develop but they are still the same limbs. Put negatively, young birds do not grow into fishes.)

(ii)   Continuity of principles. (The life of doctrines may be said to consist in the law or principle that they embody.)

(iii) Power to assimilate alien matter to the original idea. (The harder it is to assimilate an idea, the more likely it is to represent a corrupting influence.)

(iv)   Logical Sequence. (A doctrine is likely to be a true development, not a corruption, in proportion as it seems to be the *logical issue* of its original teaching.)

(v)   Anticipation of its Future. (The fact of early and recurring intimations of tendencies that afterwards are fully realized, is evidence that those later and more systematic fulfilments are in accordance with the original idea.)

(vi)   A conservative action upon its past. (A true development illustrates, not obscures, corroborates, not corrects, the body of thought from which it proceeds.)

(vii) Chronic vigour. (Corruption is distinguished from development by its transitory character.)[22]

While Newman's list is not itself 'Catholic doctrine', *The Essay on the Development of Doctrine,* which contains the list, is nonetheless a classic text in this field. In particular Newman's emphasis on the *organic* quality of the development of doctrine is a hallmark of much contemporary mainstream Catholic thinking in this territory.

The faith and culture relationship

Principle nine of the ITC document acknowledges that the faith may be expressed differently in different cultures but nonetheless asserts that new cultural expressions need to be in union with the universal Church of the past and present. This principle relates to a sub-branch of Catholic theology called the theology of culture or, more narrowly, 'inculturation', meaning the process of evangelisation, especially in cultures receiving the message of the Gospel for the first time. The works of Joachim Gnilka, such as his *Die Methode der Kirchenvater im Umgang mit der antiken Kultur* (The Approaches of the Church Fathers in Intercourse with the Culture of Antiquity), are examples of this field of scholarship.[23]

In his Address to the Bishops of Asia as Prefect of the Congregation for the Doctrine of the Faith, Joseph Ratzinger stated that one might be tempted to think that culture 'is the affair of the individual historical country (Germany, France, America, etc.), while faith for its part is in search of cultural expression' and thus that individual cultures would allocate a cultural body to the faith. Such an understanding would mean that faith has to live in a parasitic condition upon other cultures and that Christianity's claim to being able to unite the universal with the particular is fictitious. He rejected this analysis as Manichean: 'Culture is debased, becoming a mere exchangeable shell' and 'faith is reduced to a disincarnated spirit ultimately void of reality.' According to Ratzinger, the Church is her own cultural subject for the faithful with her own overarching form.[24]

Like Gnilka, Ratzinger regards the early Church Fathers as guides into this field of theological reflection. He specifically endorses the judgement of St Basil the Great that in encountering pre-Christian cultures, Christianity has to make a slit or wound in the pre-Christian culture in order to graft the new tree. The slit has to be made at the right angle, at the right time and in the right way. The ITC document 'Faith and Inculturation' of 1988 expressed this principle with the statement that 'the Gospel quite often demands a conversion of attitudes and an amendment of customs where it establishes itself: Cultures must also be purified and restored in Christ'. This same document also explores the significant role of the Holy Spirit in the work of evangelisation. At paragraph twenty-eight one finds the following statement of principle:

> In the 'last times' inaugurated at Pentecost, the risen Christ, alpha and omega, enters into the history of peoples: From that moment, the sense of history and thus of culture is unsealed and the Holy Spirit reveals it by actualizing and communicating it to all. The Church is the sacrament of this revelation and its communication. It recenters every culture into which Christ is received, placing it in the axis of the 'world which is coming' and restores the union broken by the 'prince of this world'. Culture is thus eschatologically situated; it tends toward its completion in Christ but it cannot be saved except by associating itself with the repudiation of evil.

This need for purification through a sometimes painful 'wounding' means that there will be some cultural practices that can never be 'baptised' or appropriated and placed at the service of the Gospel, but which must be repudiated as evil. Moreover, it means that inculturation does not legitimise syncretism. Syncretism is a practice that has resisted purification.

The dogma and history relationship

Principles ten, eleven and twelve all relate to the status of doctrinal formulations. They hold that doctrinal formulations must be considered as responses to precise questions that arise in time and that their permanent interest depends on the continuing relevance of the questions with which they were concerned. Further, while they may be expressed in the language of a particular philosophy this does not thereby bind the Church to that particular philosophy. Most significantly, these definitions must never be considered apart from the expression of the divine word in the Sacred Scriptures or separated from the entire Gospel message.

In 1989 the ITC published a document titled *The Interpretation of Dogma*, which addressed many of the hermeneutical questions that arose in the nineteenth and twentieth centuries as they pertain to the interpretation of doctrines. This document is an indispensable resource for theology students when approaching questions about the status of various doctrines and valid approaches to their interpretation.

On the Interpretation of Dogma described the relationship between truth and history as being the 'nub of the question' of how to interpret dogma. The document states unequivocally that 'Catholic theology begins from the certitude of faith that the *Paradosis* of the Church and the dogmas she transmits are authentic statements of the truth revealed by God in the Old and New Testaments', and further that Catholic theology also affirms that the revealed truth, transmitted by the *Paradosis* of the Church, is 'universally valid and unchangeable in substance'. The theological foundation for this position is expressed by the ITC in the following paragraph:

> Given once and for all through the apostles, the faith is faithfully treasured in the Church as the '*depositum fidei*' (1 Tim. 6.20; 2 Tim. 1.14). The Church is in fact Christ's Body animated by the Holy Spirit, and she has received from Christ the promise that the Holy Spirit will constantly guide her towards the fullness of truth (Jn 16.13). The Gospel of Truth (Eph. 1.13) was confided to the Church as God's people journeying on. In her life, the confession of her faith and her liturgy, she must witness to the faith before the eyes of the whole earth. She may be defined as 'the pillar and ground of truth' (1 Tim. 3.15). It is true that we now see the truth as it were in a mirror, and only in part: It is only at the end of all things that we shall see God face to face, as he is (1 Cor. 13.12; 1 Jn 3.2). Our knowledge of truth is poised in the tension between 'already' and 'not yet'.

On the Interpretation of Dogma goes on to summarise the magisterial teachings on dogma. It notes that the Second Council of Nicea (787) encapsulates the teaching of the early Church Fathers on the transmission of the Gospel in the *Paradosis* of the Church under the guidance of the Holy Spirit, that the Council of Trent (1545–63) defended the teaching and warned against private interpretations of Sacred Scripture, that Vatican 1 (1869–70) confirmed the teaching of Trent and recognised that dogma can develop without departing from the original sense and meaning, that the Second Vatican Council accepted that dogma has a historical dimension and that Paul VI, in *Mysterium fidei* (1965) insisted on maintaining the precise language of the Church. Vatican II also held that the people of God as a whole have a share in the prophetic office of the Church (*Lumen Gentium* 12) and that with the assistance of the Holy Spirit, a growth in the understanding of the Apostolic Tradition does take place (*Dei Verbum* 8).

It is axiomatic in all the above that the doctrines of the Church cannot be interpreted without faith. Accordingly the authors of *On the Interpretation of Dogma* suggest that three principles flow from this fact:

1. Dogmas are to be interpreted as a *verbum rememorativum*. They are to be interpreted as a return journey by memory, a memory-laden recall of the mighty acts of God, which the testimony of Revelation presents. For that reason, they must be brought into focus beginning with Scripture and Tradition, and be explained within and by means of those parameters. They must be interpreted within the whole corpus of Old and New Testaments according to the analogy of faith (cf. *Dei Verbum* 12).

2. Dogmas are to be interpreted as a *verbum demonstrativum*. They are not confined to the works of salvation of past times, but are meant to express salvation effectively in the here and now. They are meant to be light and truth. That is why they should be given a salvific meaning and presented in a living, attractive and stimulating fashion to the people of each and every epoch;

3. Dogmas are to be interpreted as a *verbum prognosticum*. As a testimony to the truth and reality of salvation and the last things, dogmas are anticipatory statements about the end of all. They must give birth to hope and be explained in terms of the last end, of man's final destiny and that of the universe, (DS 3016) and as a hymn of praise to God.

Further, it is a fundamental principle of Catholic theology that dogmas contain both a theological and juridical dimension. The juridical dimension refers to the 'sliding scale in the matter of obligation' (*Lumen Gentium* 25). Different dogmas hold higher or lower ranks in the 'hierarchy of truths' in Catholic teaching and their relative weights 'differ in proportion to their relationship with the mystery of Christ'.

Other fundamental principles in the field of the interpretation of dogma include the idea that dogmas must be understood analogically, which means that in any statements that refer to any similarities between God and his creation, the dissimilarity is always greater. Moreover, this analogical character of dogmas 'must not be incorrectly confused with a purely symbolic conception which would consider dogma as a subsequent objectivisation, whether of an original existential religious experience or of certain social or ecclesiastical practices'. Finally, the theological interpretation of dogmas is not an intellectual process only. It is also a spiritual process, involving the assistance of the Holy Spirit and 'purification of the eyes of the heart'. In addition to the graces of the Holy Spirit the witness of martyrs, saints and Doctors of the Church is also an aid to spiritual insight.

Appendix IV of this work contains a list of those thirty-six writers who are venerated as 'Doctors of the Church' for their contributions to Catholic teaching and the resolution of theological crises. Of the thirty-six, four are women. For a work that examines the contribution of the female Doctors of the Church to the development of the Catholic theological tradition, recourse can be had to Matthew Levering's *The Feminine Genius of Catholic Theology*.[25]

Pluralism and unity in morals

Returning to the document on *The Unity of the Faith and Theological Pluralism*, principles thirteen through to fifteen deal with the issue of pluralism and unity in morals. They hold that the unity of Christian morality is based on unchanging principles, contained in the Scriptures, clarified by Tradition, presented to each generation by the Magisterium. This is assisted by the conscience of every person, which expresses a certain number of fundamental demands.

Two ITC documents directly related to the subfield of moral theology are *Nine Theses in Christian Ethics* written by Balthasar in 1974 and *The Question of the Obligatory Character of the Value Judgments and Moral Directions of the New Testament* written by Heinz Schürmann (1913–99) and also published in 1974.

Since the Second Vatican Council the field of moral theology has been closely tied to scriptural foundations and aligned with Christology and theological anthropology. John Paul II's 1993 encyclical *Veritatis Splendor* showcases this kind of approach.

Distinctive family traits of Catholic theology

More recently in 2012, some four decades after the release of its first document on theological methodology, the ITC produced a document entitled *Theology Today: Perspectives, Principles and Criteria*. Its purpose is to identify 'distinctive family traits of Catholic theology' against the social background of so much fragmentation within the discipline. A number of the family traits classified in 2012 reiterate the principles in the 1972 document. The first is that Catholic theologians must recognise the primacy of the Word of God. They need to understand that 'theology is scientific reflection on the divine revelation which the Church accepts by faith as universal saving truth'. Secondly, 'a criterion of Catholic theology is that it takes the faith of the Church as its source, context and norm'. Thirdly, authentic Catholic theology has a rational dimension. Fourthly, theology in its entirety should conform to the Scriptures and the Scriptures should sustain and accompany all theological work. This is often expressed by the phrase 'the study of the sacred page should be the very soul of theology'. The fifth principle is that theologians must remain faithful to the Apostolic Tradition and not go off on frolics of their own. Here reference is made to the life of the Church in the early centuries when Christological and Trinitarian heresies threatened the faith and unity of the Church. It is noted that in these times the bishops meeting in the great ecumenical Councils of Nicea I (325 AD), Constantinople I (359 AD), Ephesus (431 AD), Chalcedon (451 AD), Constantinople II (553 AD), Constantinople III (680–1 AD) and Nicea II (787 AD) set forth their teaching in solemn definitions as normative and universally binding. These definitions are said to belong to the Apostolic Tradition and to continue to serve the faith and unity of the Church. In this context it is also noted that the Second Vatican Council referred to the Magisterium of the pope and the bishops of the Church and held that the bishops teach infallibly when, either gathered with the bishop of Rome in an ecumenical council or in communion with him though dispersed throughout the world, they agree that a particular teaching concerning faith or morals 'is to be held definitely and absolutely'. Moreover, the pope himself, head of the College of Bishops, teaches infallibly when 'as supreme pastor and teacher of the faithful … he proclaims in an absolute decision a doctrine pertaining to faith and morals'. The effect of this principle is that for Catholic theologians, Scripture, Tradition and the Magisterium of the Church are inseparably linked.

The sixth principle is that theologians need to pay attention to the *sensus fidelium*. This concept is so complex that in 2014 the ITC issued a separate document entirely devoted to an analysis of its meaning. Paragraph thirty-four of *Theology Today: Perspectives, Principles and Criteria* states:

> The nature and location of the *sensus fidei* or *sensus fidelium* must be properly understood. The *sensus fidelium* does not simply mean the majority opinion in a given time or culture, nor is it only a secondary affirmation of what is first taught by the magisterium. The *sensus*

fidelium is the *sensus fidei* of the people of God as a whole who are obedient to the Word of God and are led in the ways of faith by their pastors. So the *sensus fidelium* is the sense of the faith that is deeply rooted in the people of God who receive, understand and live the Word of God in the Church.

The *sensus fidelium* is described as vital to the work of Catholic theologians since it falls to them 'to critically examine expressions of popular piety, new currents of thought and movements within the Church, in the name of fidelity to the Apostolic Tradition'.

The seventh principle, found in paragraph thirty-seven, is that in 'Catholic theology the magisterium is an integral factor in the theological enterprise itself, since theology receives its object from God through the Church whose faith is authentically interpreted by the living teaching office of the Church alone, that is, by the magisterium of the pope and the bishops'. It follows from this that 'a correct theological methodology requires a proper understanding of the nature and authority of the magisterium at its various levels, and of the relations that properly exist between the ecclesiastical magisterium and theology'. In this context the Communio ecclesiology, which fosters the idea of the Church as an ensemble of believers with different but mutually supporting vocations and charisms, is recommended and the relationship between bishops and theologians is presented as symbiotic. Paragraph thirty-nine concludes with the statement 'there is indeed in the Church a certain "magisterium" of theologians, but there is no place for parallel, opposing or alternative magisteria, or for views that would separate theology from the Church's magisterium'.

Principle eight asserts that Catholic theologians need to comport themselves in a professional manner in prayerful and charitable collaboration with their colleagues. Although at first glance this principle would seem to have nothing to do with methodology, the fact that the concept '*odium theologicum*' or 'theological hatred' is in common use, testifies to the fact that theology is far from being an irenic practice and that without prayer and charity, research can become skewed away from the truth.

The ninth principle refers to the duties of theologians to 'read the signs of the times in the light of the Gospel' and to be 'aware of and understand the aspirations, the yearning, and the often dramatic features of the world in which we live'. Here it is significant that the signs of the times, usually interpreted as fashionable social and intellectual trends, are not themselves to be construed as the will of God, as if Catholics were all Hegelians; rather these trends and social realities need to be examined in the 'light of the Gospel'. The second and related point is that unless theologians are aware of what is happening in the world outside their study door, their scholarship runs the risk of pastoral irrelevance.

Principle ten is that Catholic theology should make use of reason and acknowledge the strong relationship between faith and reason so as to overcome both fideism and rationalism. In the enunciation of this principle the document gives quite a long historical overview of the understanding of reason and hence philosophy through the centuries and its different relationships to theology in recent times.

The eleventh principle holds that Catholic theologians should attempt to integrate a plurality of enquiries and methods into the unified project of the *intellectus fidei*. Interdisciplinary research is here regarded as something positive. There is no ipso facto theoretical problem with taking the scientific research of other disciplines into account since the Catholic faith insists on the unity of truth. The Catholic theologian should however pay close attention to the theoretical presuppositions upon which other disciplines have been founded. There is, for example, a wealth of scholarly material critical of the alleged theological neutrality of the discipline of sociology.[26]

The twelfth and final principle is that Catholic theologians should delight in the wisdom of God and be attentive to the Holy Spirit, especially as the wisdom of the Holy Spirit is found in the knowledge of the saints. As James Keating has expressed the idea:

> Theological method must be commensurate with the interpersonal mystery of theological reflection: the divine object that does not admit of objectification. The mysterious relationality of the Trinity disclosed in the Divine Economy dictates the specific character of relationality which ought to inform theological method: 'If theology's method is dictated by love's dynamism, then this is to say that God's own Trinitarian love should dictate the method by which God is known and loved'.[27]

In his *The Shape of Catholic Theology*, Aidan Nichols offered the following examples of different but equally legitimate theological orientations:

> The New Testament motif of the cross as the foundation for a wisdom wider than the wisdom of this world suggested to Justin Martyr a picture of theology in which revelation is presented as fulfilling and going beyond the insights of pagan sages. The theme of the up-building of the Church into the humanity of Christ, as found in the Pauline letters, lies behind Clement of Alexandria's presentation of theology as exploring the Gospel's power to bring us human and spiritual maturity ... while the pervasive metaphor of the divine glory in the

fourth Gospel inspired von Balthasar to offer a theology whose axis is the entry into this world through Christ of a beauty, *Herrlichkeit*, beyond all description. Again, the implicit model found in the narrative structure of the canon as a whole, from *Genesis to Apocalypse*, may be said to have been brought out in St Thomas's pattern of theology around the 'going forth' *exitus*, of creatures from God and their *reditus*, 'return' to him redeemed by grace.[28]

Nichols concluded that the most important question of any theologian is this: What overall perspective on Christian faith did Revelation suggest to this person?[29]

The Catholic word 'and'

A principle not mentioned in any of the above ITC documents is one that is perhaps so obvious to Catholics that it does not need emphasising though it has been the subject of comment by Protestant theologians. When addressing the important doctrinal principles that divide Catholic from Protestant theologians, Karl Barth (1886–1968) argued that it is the Catholic attraction to the word 'and' that is the most distinguishing hallmark of Catholic theology. In 1963 he wrote:

> The greatest obstacle to reunion between Protestants and Catholics is a little word which the Catholic Church adds after nearly every one of our Protestant affirmations. It is the little word 'and'. When we say Jesus, Catholics say 'Jesus and Mary'. We seek to obey Christ, our only Lord: Catholics obey Christ and his Vicar on earth, the Pope. We believe the Christian is saved through the merits of Jesus Christ. Catholics add, 'and our own merits', that is, because of works. We believe the sole source of Revelation is scripture. Catholics add 'and Tradition'. We say knowledge of God is obtained by faith in His Word expressed in scripture. Catholics add 'and by reason'.[30]

Catholic theologians try to transcend dualisms by paying close attention to the relationships between different elements of Catholic teaching. Inclusivity and relationality are typical attributes of Catholic theology, not dualisms or sharply defined either/or options. As the English theologian Stratford Caldecott (1953–2014) observed: 'The unity-in-distinction of the Trinity is the basis for an analogy that runs right through creation as a kind of watermark: the analogy of a "spousal" union between subject and object, self and other.'[31] A longer expression of the same principle may be found in the following statement of Cardinal Gerhard Müller who was appointed Prefect of the Congregation of the Doctrine of the Faith in 2012:

> The Catholic proposition has always been able to avoid extremes, extreme alternatives: either God or the world, either God or man, either the Cross or the Resurrection, either the soul or the body. Life is immanent and contains immanent purposes, but we know, too, that the ultimate, transcendental purpose is the one that crowns all existence. Communism and laissez-faire capitalism offered a paradise on earth, in opposition to the authentic heavenly paradise that every Christian aspires to. We make of our lives an attempt to achieve full harmony between things that seem irreconcilable, between the two poles, because we perceive that there is no real contradiction between them. … Instead of thinking about life in terms of oppositions, we have to learn from Christian humanism to live joyfully and harmoniously both sides of the same coin.[32]

+Robert Barron's book *Vibrant Paradoxes: The Both/And of Catholicism* offers an extensive collection of essays on this both/and Catholic mental habit.[33]

Christ and the Trinity

Of all the poles that need to be held in tension, the most fundamental is that of the divinity and humanity of Christ. In his work *Christ, the Christian and the Church*, subtitled *A Study of the Incarnation and its Consequences*, Eric Mascall (1905–93) offered the following snapshot summary of what might be called the foundation stone of the Christian faith:

> The doctrine of the Incarnation involves two mutually inter-related truths, either of which raises great problems for the human intellect, but both of which are in essence so simple that they can be stated in two English sentences of words of one syllable taken from the Gospel itself. The first is 'The Word was God', the second, 'The Word was made Flesh'. The maintenance of the former was the primary concern of the first of the four great ecumenical councils, that of Nicea; the maintenance of the second was the primary concern of the other three, those of Constantinople, Ephesus and Chalcedon. The first of these texts assures us that Christ is truly God, the second that he is truly man.[34]

There are two ITC documents addressed to the subject of Christology: *Select Questions on Christology* published in 1979 and *Theology, Christology, Anthropology*, published in 1981.

In *Select Questions on Christology* it was stated that 'the substantive and radical unity between the Jesus of history and the glorified Christ pertains to the very essence of the Gospel message'. Therefore if Christological inquiry limits itself to the Jesus 'of history', it is 'incompatible with the essence and structure of the New Testament, even before being disavowed from without by a religious authority'. Moreover, 'apart from the assistance provided by the mediation of ecclesial faith, the knowledge of Jesus Christ is no more possible today than in New Testament times'. The ITC authors state that 'outside the ecclesial context, there is no Archimedean lever'.

The point that the ITC members seek to hammer home in the first part of their document is that while historical studies can be valuable, the Christian faith, and specifically the understanding of Christ, cannot be predicated solely on historical studies.

The ITC members also address the argument that the Church's dogmatic teachings in the area of Christology are mere Hellenistic accretions unrelated to genuine biblical Revelation. They argue that, on the contrary, the thought pattern of the Greeks was totally alien to the Christological dogmas as they were developed, and that in particular the Greek philosophers found it difficult to accept the idea of a divine incarnation. Moreover, the 'Arian heresy [which denies the divinity of Christ] offers a good illustration of how the dogma of Christ's divinity would have looked had it truly emerged from the philosophy of Hellenism and not from God's own revelation'.

The Council of Chalcedon in 451 AD was particularly significant for the correct dogmatic foundations of Christology. This Council had to grapple with the issue of how to reconcile the transcendence of God (clearly evident in the Old Testament) with the immanence of God (made evident by the Incarnation). Scholars associated with the school of Alexandria tended to emphasise the unity of the divine and human natures in Christ, those of the school of Antioch tended to emphasise the distinction between the two natures in Christ. The Council of Chalcedon held that the two natures exist in Christ 'without confusion' and 'without division'. The formula can be read as a transcendence of both the Platonic emphasis on divine transcendence and the Stoic emphasis on divine immanence.

At the Third Council of Constantinople in 681 AD, under the influence of St Maximus the Confessor, the Church focused on the role played by the human will of Christ in salvation history and declared that human salvation had been willed by a Divine Person through a human will.

The ITC members note that 'as history takes its course, and cultural changes occur, the teachings of the Council of Chalcedon and Constantinople III must always be actualised in the consciousness and preaching of the Church, under the guidance of the Holy Spirit'. Within such a framework, 'the task of theologians is, first of all, to construct a synthesis in which are underlined all the aspects and all the values of the mystery of Christ. Into their synthesis theologians need draw the authentic findings of biblical exegesis, and of the research on the history of salvation.' Of particular importance are the pneumatological dimensions of Christology and the cosmological dimensions. The ITC Commissioners summarise the pneumatological dimension in the following passage:

> The Holy Spirit cooperates uninterruptedly in the redemptive deed of Christ. 'He covers the Virgin Mary with his shadow, which is why her offspring is holy and will be called the Son of God' (Lk. 1.35). When Jesus is baptised at the Jordan (Lk. 3.22), he receives 'the anointing' in order to carry out his mission as Messiah (Acts 10.38; Lk. 4.18), while a voice from heaven declares him to be the Son on whom the Father's favour rests (Mk 1.10 and parallels). From that moment on, Christ is in a special way 'guided by the Holy Spirit' (Lk. 11.20), he casts out devils; he announces that 'the reign of God is at hand' (Mk 1.15) and that it is to be brought to consummation by the Holy Spirit (Roman Missal; cf. Heb. 2.14). Finally, through his Spirit, God the father raises Jesus from the dead and fills mankind with him. Mankind thus puts on the form of humanity proper to the glorified Son of God (cf. Rom. 1.3-4; Acts 13.32-33), after having known the form of humanity proper to the servant. The glorified humanity of Christ was also empowered to bestow the Holy Spirit on all human beings (Acts 2.22). The new and eschatological Adam can thus be called 'a life-giving spirit' (1 Cor. 15.45; cf. 2 Cor. 3.17). And so, in a very real sense, the Mystical Body of Christ is animated by the Spirit of Christ forever.

The cosmological dimension is found primarily in the Pauline literature and emphasises the lordship of Christ over all creation, and His future renewal of the cosmos.

In an introductory paragraph to *Theology, Christology, Anthropology* one finds the statement that 'the context of Christology includes the human desire for and the knowledge man has of God, the revelation of the triune God, and the image of man in contemporary anthropology and in the Incarnation of Jesus Christ'. The authors observe that if these basic elements are not first treated adequately, Christology itself is placed in danger. In other words, 'Fundamental Theology' is called 'fundamental' because without it one's scholarship is rudderless.

Specifically the ITC authors state that the economy of Jesus Christ or what is usually called Christology and the Revelation of God (often designated as Fundamental Theology) must not be confused or separated – rather the complementary character of the two approaches must be maintained. Another way to express this is to talk about the relationship between Christian Theocentrism and Christocentrism. Thus, the document states:

> Christian Theism consists properly in the Triune God, and he is known uniquely in the revelation to us in Jesus Christ. Thus, on the one hand, knowledge of Jesus Christ leads to a knowledge of the Trinity and attains its plenitude in the knowledge of the Trinity; on the other hand, there is no knowledge of the Triune God except in knowledge of Jesus Christ himself. It follows that there is no distinction between Theocentrism and Christocentrism: the two terms denote the same reality.
>
> Natural theism is not the same as, and therefore is not to be confused with, either the Theism/monotheism of the Old Testament or historical Theism, that is, the Theism that non-Christians have professed in various ways in their religions. The monotheism of the Old Testament has its origins in a supernatural revelation and therefore retains an intrinsic relation to – indeed, demands – the Trinitarian revelation. Historical Theisms do not arise from a 'pure nature' but from a nature subject to sin, objectively redeemed by Jesus Christ and elevated to a supernatural destiny.

Following the above analysis, the ITC authors conclude that any kind of distinction between Christology and the Trinity is to be avoided in theology and catechetics. The mystery of Jesus Christ belongs to the structure of the Trinity and the mystery of the Trinity is Christological. An accessible overview of the central teachings in this area can be found in Aaron Riches' *Ecce Homo: On the Divine Unity of Christ*.[35]

The relationship between Christology and Mariology

Chapter 8 of the Conciliar document *Lumen Gentium* (1964) provides a doctrinal synthesis of the relationships between Mariology and Christology and Mariology and Ecclesiology and is regarded as the highest magisterial statement on these relationships. The Letter from the Congregation for Catholic Education ('CCE') on *The Virgin Mary in Intellectual and Spiritual Formation* (1988) also provides an excellent summary of all recent magisterial teaching on Mariology from the dogmatic Bull of Pius IX *Ineffabilis Deus* in 1854 through to John Paul II's encyclical *Redemptoris Mater* of 1987.

Paragraphs eighteen through to twenty-three of the CCE document address the subject of 'The Contribution of Mariology to Theological Research'. Key principles include the idea that everything about Mary is relative to Christ and referable to the mystery of the Church.

The Catholic understanding of the intrinsic relationship between Mariology and Christology was underscored in the following passage from Joseph Ratzinger's *Mary: The Church at the Source*:

> Mariology is an essential component of a hermeneutics of salvation history. Recognition of this fact brings out the true dimensions of Christology over against a falsely understood *solus Christus* [Christ alone]. Christology must speak of a Christ who is both 'head *and* body', that is, who comprises the redeemed creation in its relative subsistence [*Selbständigkeit*]. But this move simultaneously enlarges our perspective beyond the history of salvation, because it counters a false understanding of God's sole agency, highlighting the reality of the creature that God calls and enables to respond to him freely. Mariology demonstrates that the doctrine of grace does not revoke creation, but is the definitive Yes to creation. In this way, Mariology guarantees the ontological independence [*Eigenständigkeit*] of creation, undergirds faith in creation, and crowns the doctrine of creation, rightly understood.[36]

The leading centres for the study of Mariology are the International Marian Research Institute located at the University of Dayton in Ohio and the *Pontificia accademia mariana internazionale* (PAMI) based in Rome. For an excellent overview of key issues in contemporary Mariology students can have recourse to the essay 'Mariology at the Beginning of the Third Millennium' by Isabell Naumann ISSM, a member of both the Pontifical International Marian Academy and the International Marian Research Institute.[37] She concludes her magisterial summary of the principles and issues with the following quotation from Balthasar:

> Without Mariology Christology threatens imperceptibly to become inhuman. The Church becomes functionalistic, soulless, a hectic enterprise without any point of rest, estranged from its true nature by the planners. And because, in this mainly-masculine world, all that we have is one ideology replacing another, everything becomes polemical, critical, bitter, humourless, and ultimately boring, and people in their masses run away from such a Church.[38]

In Catholic theology the Church is always feminine. The Church is therefore referred to as 'she' or 'her' not 'it'. This is consistent with the idea that the

Church is the 'Bride of Christ' and the 'Mystical Body of Christ', not yet another multinational corporation.

The relationship between nature and grace

The idea that the doctrine of grace does not revoke creation, but is the definitive Yes to creation, also relates to yet another fundamental 'couplet' in Catholic theology and this is the relationship between nature and grace. This particular relationship has huge implications for the sub-discipline known as sacramental theology since it is absolutely fundamental for understanding how God relates to the human person across time and space.

In *The Primacy of Peter* Charles Journet (1891–1975) distinguished between two concepts of Christianity: one typical of Protestant theology and one typical of Catholic theology. The first he described as the mnemic concept, the second, the ontological concept. The difference between the two is presented as a difference over the way in which the presence of Christ constitutes Christianity. According to the Protestant account, Christ is only present in time by way of signs, tokens and promises – which from a Catholic point of view is a kind of nostalgic return to the Old Testament – whereas, according to the Catholic account, Christ is really and truly present in time under the guise of signs, tokens and promises. This principle lies at the foundation of the Catholic understanding of sacramentality. For the Protestant account we have a mnemic presence of Christ, a mere awareness through memory of an important event that took place once and for all in the past, 'like a meteorite which is consumed and leaves a trace only in the memory', whereas for the Catholic account there is a 'real and unbroken repercussion in time of a supremely important event which took place once and for all in the past, like a stone thrown into the water which gives rise to concentric waves which spread indefinitely through time and space'.[39] Journet suggests that Protestantism makes the error of considering the two natures of Christ side by side such that the human nature of Christ becomes 'simply an occasion of our salvation, a mere phenomenal shell, in which the invisible God made his appearance'.[40]

Thomas Guarino summarised the difference between the Catholic and Protestant accounts with the statement that for Catholics, 'the two orders, ontological and soteriological, are distinct (at least notionally) but in fundamental continuity', while for traditional Protestantism, 'a wedge has been driven between fallen and corrupted nature and the work of the Redeemer'.[41]

Martin D'Arcy SJ (1888–1976) focused on this 'wedge' in the following passage about the Calvinism of Karl Barth:

> Barth's meaning is that the Redemption has restored the world and that there are reflections of this new glory to be found in the works of man and of civilisation. But the restoration belongs to another plane and will not be revealed until the last day. Till then it is hidden in God with Jesus Christ. The best that can be seen in the world is a reflection like the light reflected on a pool or mountain-side. Culture, he says, has its own worth and dignity, but it is 'an exclusively earthly reflection of the Creation, which itself remains … lost and hidden from us'. There is 'no continuity between the analogies and the divine reality, no objective relation between what is signified and what really is; no transition, therefore, definable in terms of any progress, can be made between one and the other'. Such an inflexible verdict rules out any hope of relating heaven and earth, grace and nature. History can never be more than a pastime. When the last trumpet sounds, all the works of man will fade out; they have no bearing on what then is to be revealed.[42]

Contrary to Barth, D'Arcy argued that from the Catholic point of view 'nature and the supernatural action of God have been wedded together, and to divorce them is, however salutary the purpose, a desecration'. The task of the Catholic theologian is, therefore, 'to do justice to the marriage, while accepting the very different roles and even temperaments of each member'.[43]

Precisely how this can be done, that is, 'doing justice to the marriage while accepting the different roles and temperaments of each member' was a major point of theological debate in the twentieth century. The three most influential attempts to describe the relationship were offered by Reginald Garrigou-Lagrange OP (1877–1964), by Henri de Lubac and by Karl Rahner. These three alternative approaches to construing the nature and grace relationship will be discussed in greater depth in the following chapter. Although the three approaches have been described as generating the most bitter theological dispute of Catholic theology in the twentieth century (especially the conflict between Garrigou-Lagrange and de Lubac), there has been no magisterial document addressing this issue since the one line in paragraph twenty-six of Pius XII's *Humani generis* (1950), which simply reiterated the principle that grace, however it is construed, must always be understood as a gratuitous divine gift, not something to which any person can claim an entitlement. All the parties in the dispute would argue that their approach is consistent with this principle. The *Catechism of the Catholic Church* offers a summary of the magisterial teaching on the subject of grace in paragraphs 1996 through to

2005. The statements to be found here are referenced back to Scripture and to the works of St Augustine.

Recent works by Aidan Nichols, Thomas Joseph White OP and Edward Oakes SJ (1948–2013) have recommended the approach of Matthias Joseph Scheeben (1835–88) as a way of transcending the division between Henri de Lubac and Reginald Garrigou-Lagrange on the understanding of the nature–grace relationship. Scheeben's account of the relationship uses the nuptial imagery favoured by de Lubac, Balthasar, Scola and others in the *Communio* circles but nonetheless pays attention to the temperaments of both parties to the marriage, so to speak, consistent with Thomist priorities.

The relationship between *logos* and *ethos*

The concepts *logos* and *ethos* have been much discussed since Liberation Theology became fashionable. *Logos* tends to be shorthand for the ideas or intellectual logic behind something, while *ethos* refers to the embodiment of ideas in institutional or social practices. The standard reading of the relationship between *logos* and *ethos* has always been that the two are intimately connected. Canon law and pastoral practices are not disconnected from doctrine but flow from doctrine, and have their rationale in doctrine. They do not exist in two separate compartments or ontological spaces. All practices embody some logic, some meaning that is intrinsic to the practice itself and is not imposed on the practice by someone's mental decision to give the practice meaning Y rather than meaning Z. Our actions embody meanings. This was a common theme in twentieth-century Catholic philosophy and theology. Among the philosophers it was a central intellectual insight of Maurice Blondel, Karol Wojtyła and Alasdair MacIntyre. Wojtyła in fact developed a whole anthropology around the principle that action follows being. Among the theologians it was a recurring theme in the works of Romano Guardini (1885–1968) and Joseph Ratzinger.

Guardini was one of the Catholic scholars whose ideas fed into the deliberations of the Second Vatican Council through the German-speaking *Periti*. He was admired by Rahner, Ratzinger and Balthasar, among many other luminaries, including a young Fr Bergoglio who chose Guardini's theology as the topic for his doctoral dissertation, though the dissertation was abandoned.

Guardini was greatly concerned about the trend towards granting epistemic primacy to *ethos* or *praxis* over *logos*. He regarded this trend as a hallmark of liberal pragmatism and linked it to liberalism's rejection of metaphysics and the idea of a natural law that participates in the eternal law. Roland Millare has described Guardini's central insight as the recognition that modern culture is governed by a mechanistic and utilitarian *logos* (which lies at the root of the Liberal tradition) while an *ethos* of an authentically Christian culture is one underpinned by a Eucharistic *logos* oriented towards self-giving love. It was a central principle of Guardini's theology of culture that 'until a sacramental *logos* (which is related to an *ethos* of love as self-gift) is given its proper primacy, an *ethos* driven by lust, power, avarice, and ugliness will continue to reign.'[44]

It is not only the Liberal philosophical tradition underpinning the culture of modernity that has fostered the epistemic priority of *ethos* over *logos*, but also the Marxist philosophical tradition underpinning large swathes of the Liberation Theology movement. For Marxist intellectuals epistemology, or knowledge, is class-based – hence the Marxist concepts 'false consciousness' and the 'bourgeois mystification of knowledge'. It was for this reason that Central European intellectuals found themselves doing manual labour (like building the infamous 'intellectuals' bridge' – *Branický Most* – in Prague) after their homelands were taken over by communists. The ideas of anyone with a high middle-class education were deemed to be unsound and so persons from such backgrounds had to be employed as manual labourers to minimise their influence on social life. Such persons were barred from taking positions at the switch points of cultural power. The CDF addressed this Marxist mentality in section ten of the document *Instruction on Certain Aspects of the 'Theology of Liberation'* (1984). Paragraph one of this section states:

> The partisan conception of truth, which can be seen in the revolutionary 'praxis' of the class, corroborates this position [the challenge to the sacramental and hierarchical structure of the Church]. Theologians who do not share the theses of the 'theology of liberation', the hierarchy, and especially the Roman Magisterium are thus discredited in advance as belonging to the class of the oppressors. Their theology is a theology of class. Arguments and teachings thus do not have to be examined in themselves since they are only reflections of class interests. Thus, the instruction of others is decreed to be, in principle, false.

In a positive statement of the same principle, in *Principles of Christian Morality*, Ratzinger wrote:

> Christian *praxis* is nourished by the core of Christian faith, that is, the grace that appeared in Christ and that is appropriated in the sacrament of the Church. Faith's *praxis* depends on faith's truth, in which man's truth is made visible and lifted up to a new level by God's truth. Hence, it is fundamentally opposed to a *praxis* that first wants to produce facts and so establish truth.[45]

With reference to the debates at the two Synods on the Family (2014 and 2015), Cardinal Müller argued that 'separating life from doctrine is like trying to separate Christ as Son of God from Christ as Saviour'. He described the 'split between life and doctrine', 'justice and mercy', 'God and Christ', 'Christ as Lord and Christ as Shepherd', and the separation of 'Christ from the Church' as all cases of a Gnostic dichotomy.[46]

Closely related to the issue of the relationship between *logos* and *ethos* is the relationship between Faith and Experience. Like the principles governing the *logos* and *ethos* relationship, the general point to be made is that Faith and Experience should not be separated to create yet another Gnostic dichotomy. As Ratzinger expressed the principle: 'It is clear that faith without experience can only be verbiage of empty formulas' and 'to reduce faith to experience is to rob it of its kernel'.[47]

Just as different understandings of the relationship between nature and grace lie at the foundations of different theological projects (neo-scholasticism, Rahnerian theology and Lubacian–Balthasarian theology), so too different accounts of the relationship between Faith and Experience lie at the foundations of neo-scholasticism, *Concilium* theology (especially in the tradition of Schillebeeckx) and *Communio* theology (along the lines of de Lubac, Balthasar, Ratzinger and Scola).

The relationship between Scripture and Tradition

The modern history of the theological treatment of Tradition and its relationship to Scripture is usually taken to begin with the Reformation and in particular with the Council of Trent's decree *De canonicis Scripturis* in 1546.[48] Whereas the Protestant Reformers emphasised the *sola scriptura* principle, and treated the many Catholic religious traditions or customs as mere human constructions and often abuses of the faith, the Catholic Counter-Reformers fostered the idea that the deposit of the faith is to be found in both Scripture and Tradition.

In paragraph ten of *Dei Verbum*, the Second Vatican Council's Dogmatic Constitution on Divine Revelation, the Council of Trent's 'two sources' theory of Revelation (Scripture and Tradition) are united into one:

> Sacred Tradition and sacred Scripture, then, are bound closely together, and communicate one with the other. For both of them, flowing out from the same divine well-spring, come together in some fashion to form one thing, and move as towards one goal.[49]

Dei Verbum thereby sought to overcome the Scripture–Tradition dualism by recognising that both Scripture and Tradition flow from the same Revelation of Christ (anticipated in the Old Testament) and merge into a unity. According to *Dei Verbum* the plan of Revelation is realised by *deeds and words* having an inner unity: the deeds wrought by God in the history of salvation manifest and confirm the teaching and realities signified by the words, while the words proclaim the deeds and clarify the mystery contained in them.

In a paper delivered in 1963, Joseph Ratzinger argued that Revelation is more than Scripture. He spoke of a 'pneumatic surplus' of Revelation, which cannot be reduced to writing. Scripture, he argued, is not synonymous with Revelation but is only a part of Revelation's greater reality. He praised the Protestant scholars Karl Barth and Emile Brunner (1889–1966) for understanding this fact. As he was later to emphasise, for Christians, truth is a person. In a redaction of this paper published in 1966 in a book co-authored with Karl Rahner, Ratzinger summarised his own account of tradition in the following list of propositions:

(i) At the beginning of all tradition stands the fact that the Father gives the Son over to the world and that the Son for his part allows himself to be given over to the 'nations', as a sign. This original *paradosis*, in its character as judgment and gift of salvation, is continued in the abiding presence of Christ in his Body, the Church. To that extent the whole mystery of Christ's continuing presence is primarily the whole reality which is transmitted in tradition, the decisive fundamental reality which is antecedent to all particular explicit expressions of it, even those of scripture, and which represents what has in fact to be handed down.

(ii) Tradition then exists concretely as presence in faith, which again, as the in-dwelling of Christ, is antecedent to all its particular explicit formulations and is fertile and living, thus developing and unfolding throughout the ages.

(iii) The organ of Tradition is the authority of the Church, that is, those who have authority in it.

(iv) Tradition also exists, however, as actually expressed in what has already become a rule of faith (creed, *fides quae*), by the authority of faith. The question whether certain express affirmations were transmitted from the beginning side by side with scripture, whether, therefore, there is a second material principle besides scripture, independent from the beginning, becomes quite secondary in comparison, but it would probably have to be answered negatively.[50]

Rahner, Ratzinger and de Lubac all contributed to the drafting of *Dei Verbum*. For an in-depth analysis of their contributions a number of essays may be found in Volume III of Herbert Vorgrimler's *Commentary on the Documents of the Second Vatican Council*.

Other significant scholarly publications on the subject of the Catholic understanding of tradition are Maurice Blondel's *History and Dogma* (1903) and Yves Congar's *Tradition and Traditions: The Biblical, Historical, and Theological Evidence for Catholic Teaching on Tradition*, originally published in French in two volumes between 1960 and 1963. Blondel was a French layman, philosopher and critic of Leonine Thomism and its Baroque antecedents; Congar (1904–95) was a French Dominican similarly critical of Baroque-era Thomism, founder of the seventy-seven-volume *Unam Sanctam* series on ecclesiology, a French Army chaplain in the Second World War who spent the years (1940–5) as a prisoner of war, a Knight of the French Legion of Honour and recipient of the *Croix de Guerre* and the *Médaille des Évadés*. Most significantly from the point of view of Catholic theology, he was a *Peritus* at the Second Vatican Council. He was later made a cardinal during the papacy of John Paul II. The works of Blondel and Congar were highly significant influences on the Conciliar treatment of tradition.

The basic principles governing this territory are summarised in paragraphs 80–100 of the *Catechism of the Catholic Church*.

Principles of scriptural interpretation

The Pontifical Biblical Commission has produced two documents addressing the issue of the principles to be applied to biblical interpretation: *The Interpretation of the Bible in the Church* (1993) and *The Jewish People and their Sacred Scriptures in the Christian Bible* (2002). These documents built on principles set out in *Dei Verbum*, as well as the encyclical *Providentissimus Deus* (1893) of Leo XIII and *Divino afflante Spiritu* (1943) of Pius XII. The latter was the document in which the Church definitively accepted the use of the philological and historical method in the study of the Bible. This was in addition to the Patristic 'four senses' approach to reading Scripture – the literal, allegoric, moral and anagogical senses.

In the *Interpretation of the Bible in the Church* the historical-critical method is praised for its contribution to a deeper understanding of the 'intention of the authors and editors of the Bible as well as the message which they addressed to their first readers' and it is described as 'implying no a priori if used in an objective manner'. Words of caution are however sounded over the practice of some exegetes of hooking the method up to 'certain hermeneutical choices', which can be 'tendentious'. Reading Scripture through the lens of Marxism or Feminism are two specific examples of this practice given in the document. With respect to the particular issue of *Wirkungsgeschichte* (the study of the history of the influence of a particular text), the following observation is made:

> The mutual presence to each other of text and readers creates its own dynamic, for the text exercises an influence and provokes reactions. It makes a resonant claim that is heard by readers whether as individuals or as members of a group. The reader is in any case never an isolated subject. He or she belongs to a social context and lives within a tradition. Readers come to the text with their own questions, exercise a certain selectivity, propose an interpretation and, in the end, are able either to create a further work or else take initiatives inspired directly from their reading of Scripture.

These words of caution were echoed in *Verbum Domini* (2010), the Post-Synodal Apostolic Exhortation of Benedict XVI, which referred to the 'danger of dualism and a secularised hermeneutic'.

With reference to the dualist danger Pope Benedict wrote that to distinguish two levels of approach to interpreting the Bible (the historical-critical and the theological) does not mean that one should separate or oppose them or even merely juxtapose them but rather the two must be held together in a relationship of reciprocity. Without the theological dimension Scripture ends up being a text belonging to the past; without the hermeneutic offered by faith Scripture is often interpreted in such a way that the historicity of the divine elements is denied.[51]

A similar sentiment may be found in the work *Der Unbequeme Jesus* (The Inconvenient Jesus) by Marius Reiser. Reiser is critical of the tendency of some biblical scholars to give an epistemic priority to the historico-critical method over every other approach to exegesis:

> The attribute 'historico-critical', current within exegesis, is a tautology; for historical research is always critical insofar as it is *Wissenschaft*. Effectively, however, 'historico-critical' usually means an historical investigation with the named philosophical premises of the Enlightenment. Insofar as it concerns *Wissenschaft*, we ought finally to bid these premises adieu![52]

At the beginning of *Verbum Domini* reference is made to the fact that the expression 'the Word of God' is used in a number of ways and is a kind of 'polyphonic hymn'. While Christ's Incarnation is at the heart of Revelation, creation itself is a part of the polyphonic symphony, as are the words spoken through the prophets and Apostles as handed down in the Church's living Tradition, and of course, added to this symphony is the word of God found in both the Old and New Testaments. Paragraph seven concludes with the statement that while Catholics venerate the Sacred Scriptures, the faith is not a 'religion of the book'. Rather, following the insights of St Bernard of Clairvaux (1090–1153) and *Dei Verbum* (10) it can be said that 'Christianity is the "religion of the word of God", not of "a written and mute word, but of the incarnate and living Word". Consequently the Scripture is to be proclaimed, heard, read, received and experienced as the word of God, in the stream of the apostolic Tradition from which it is inseparable.'

A summary of the magisterial teaching in this area can be found in paragraphs 101–141 of the *Catechism of the Catholic Church*.

The relationship between the Magisterium and theologians

A subtheme of the relationship between the papacy and the *sensus fidelium* is the relationship between the authority of the Magisterium and the authority of the professional, academic theologians. The expression 'the Magisterium' refers to the teaching that is proper to the College of Bishops or to individual bishops in communion with the pope. The ITC has produced a document on the relationship entitled *The Ecclesiastical Magisterium and Theology*. It refers to a common duty of bishops and theologians as being 'to preserve the sacred deposit of revelation, to examine it more deeply, to explain, teach and defend it' for the service of the people of God and the whole world's salvation. The phrase 'to preserve the sacred deposit of revelation, to examine it more deeply, to explain, teach and defend it' is taken from an Address of Pope Paul VI to the International Congress on Theology at Vatican II, delivered on 1 October 1966.[53] In the discharge of this duty, both the bishops and the theologians are bound by the Word of God and the *sensus fidei*, as well as by the documents of the tradition and a pastoral and missionary concern for the world. The bishops, more specifically, have the task of authoritatively interpreting the Word of God, censoring opinions that endanger the faith and morals proper to the Church, and proposing truths of contemporary relevance. The theologians tend to play a mediating role between the Magisterium and the members of the Church in general.

The sixth thesis proposed by this ITC document classifies the respective authority of the bishops and the theologians in the following terms:

The Magisterium derives its authority from sacramental ordination, which 'along with the task of sanctifying confers also the tasks of teaching and ruling'. This 'formal authority', as it is called, is at once charismatic and juridical, and it founds the right and the duty of the Magisterium insofar as it is a share in the authority of Christ. Care should be taken that personal authority and the authority that derives from the very matter being proposed also be brought to bear when this ministerial authority is being put in to effect.

Theologians derive their specifically theological authority from their scientific qualifications; but these cannot be separated from the proper character of this discipline as the science of faith, which cannot be carried through without a living experience and practice of the faith. For this reason, the authority that belongs to theology in the Church is not merely profane and scientific but is a genuinely ecclesial authority, inserted into the order of authorities that derive from the Word of God and are confirmed by canonical mission.

Not all those who are honoured as Doctors of the Church can say that their contributions to the intellectual life of the faith have been 100 per cent accepted. Even St Augustine and St Thomas Aquinas had ideas that were later qualified or rejected, but aspiring Church Doctors can at least learn from the spiritual sensibilities of the great Doctors, from the above reflections of the members of the ITC and from the maxim *sentire cum ecclesia* (to think with the Church).

Hallmarks and Species of Thomism

Thomism is an intellectual tradition and arguably one of the most significant of all such traditions for the study of Catholic theology. The word 'Thomism' refers not only to the thought of St Thomas Aquinas (1225–74), the great medieval Dominican, but also to the contributions of his successors, those who have taken his ideas and developed them, and this includes the whole history of disputed questions that cause divisions or intellectual fault lines within the Tradition. A non-exhaustive summary of different varieties of Thomist thought includes Classical Thomism, Baroque (including and especially Suárezian Thomism), Leonine Thomism (all of which refer to Thomism of a particular era), Neo-Thomism (which is an expression used by some authors to refer to pre-Conciliar Thomism in general, while others use it to refer specifically to what is now more commonly called Strict Observance Thomism, one of the varieties of Thomism influential in the period between the pontificates of Benedict XV and Paul VI), Transcendental Thomism (which is shorthand for a Thomist engagement with the epistemology of Immanual Kant), Whig Thomism (which refers to various projects to synthesise elements of Thomist thought with elements of Liberal political philosophy), Analytical Thomism (which brings elements of Thomist thought into dialogue with contemporary analytical philosophy, especially the philosophy of Wittgenstein), Lublin Thomism, Fribourg Thomism, Toulouse Thomism, River Forest and/or Laval Thomism (which refer to projects that arose within particular communities of Thomist scholars), Gilsonian or Existential Thomism (which has a particular reading of Thomistic metaphysics) and Christocentric Thomism (which focuses upon the significance of the Christology of St Thomas for moral theology and theological anthropology). There are also Augustinian Thomism, Romantic Thomism and Postmodern Thomism, which are slightly different labels referring to the same disposition of keeping the theological side of Classical Thomism integral to the whole project and not severed or sidelined on the basis of a dualistic (predominately post-Kantian) epistemology and/or Suárezian ontology. The Postmodern or Romantic note is a reference to the interest of scholars in these circles to engage with typically Romantic movement and postmodern issues concerning the uniqueness of each human being. These types are united in a rejection of readings of Aquinas as Aristotle with a Christian gloss. There is also the expression 'Hillbilly Thomism' coined by the American novelist Flannery O'Connor (1925–64) to refer to her literary appropriations of Thomist ideas.

The only other scholar in Christian history who has been appropriated in so many different ways and given rise to so many different schools of thought is St. Augustine. Outside the field of theology the divisions among disciples of the Jewish philosopher Leo Strauss (1899–1973) – for example, the differences between East Coast Straussians and West Coast Straussians, first generation Straussians and second generation Straussians, the gentleman Straussians and the philosopher Straussians – are a similar intellectual phenomenon. Students of theology with Thomist lecturers should therefore ask the question, which particular school of Thomism is my lecturer representing? Confusion arises when students of one Thomist try to enter into conversations with students of another Thomist who belong to a different school and they are not aware that there are different appropriations. Some scholars do not belong to any one school, but pick and mix ideas from a number of different schools and they are called 'freelance Thomists'.

Classical Thomism

Classical Thomism is quite simply a term used to describe the original thought of St Thomas Aquinas. Of course, many of the debates internal to the Tradition are about how this original collection of texts is to be appropriated. The term signifies the original works without reference to any of the subsequent glosses or synthetic adoptions. Two helpful works for gaining access to the biographical facts about St Thomas are Aidan Nichols' *Discovering Aquinas: An Introduction to his Life, Work and Influence* and Frederick Christian Bauerschmidt's *Thomas Aquinas: Faith, Reason and Following Christ*, in which the following passage appears:

> Thomas was born around the year 1225 at his family's castle in the Roccasecca, about midway between Rome and Naples. His father, Landulf of Aquino, was a baron of Emperor Frederick II, one of the most powerful Holy Roman Emperors of the Middle Ages, whose holdings extended from Germany into southern Italy, and who was in almost constant conflict with the papacy. At some point the family's allegiance must have shifted from Frederick to the pope, for Thomas's brother Reginald was executed by the emperor and was considered a martyr by the family. Thomas was the youngest male and, as was often

the case with noble families, had been destined by his family for life in the Church, though one that befitted his noble lineage. So at the age of five he was sent to the monastery of Monte Cassino, to receive a basic education and eventually, his family hoped, to become abbot of this prestigious monastery. Thomas stayed at Monte Cassino until around the age of fourteen, when he went to Naples to pursue further studies at the university there. ... Thomas encountered in Naples the new mendicant form of *vita apostolica* represented by the Order of Preachers, who had been in Naples since 1231, and he was inspired to become a friar preacher. Thomas would spend five years in Naples, having passed from the monastic to the scholastic and mendicant worlds.[1]

The decision to opt for the *nouveau* Dominicans over the well-established Benedictines was not well received by the Aquino family and an attempt was made to dissuade the young Thomas by placing a honeytrap in his path. The plot failed and Thomas went ahead with his choice to study under the Dominicans. Nonetheless, Aidan Nichols suggests that this decision was not quite as bad as 'the son of the Duke of Buccleuch' absconding 'from Eton to become a hippie in Islington'.[2] Nichols argues that St Thomas never repudiated his Benedictine heritage and in fact cited St Gregory the Great (who had been a monk and biographer of St Benedict) almost 2,500 times in his various works.

St Thomas completed his novitiate in Paris where he met St Albert the Great who recognised his considerable intellectual gifts. St Albert took him to Cologne in 1248 to help found a new study house. In 1252 St Thomas returned to Paris and in 1256 at the tender age of thirty-one he became one of the twelve Masters of the Sorbonne. In 1261 he was deployed to the Priory of Orvieto where he began work on the *Catena aurea* (a commentary on the Gospels compiling insights from Patristic authors), the *Contra errores graecorum* (a commentary on the compatibility of the Greek and Latin Church Fathers), a commentary on the Book of Job and an edition of a liturgy for the Feast of Corpus Christi. Four years later he was moved to Santa Sabina, the Priory on the Aventine Hill in Rome where he began work on the *Summa Theologicae*. In either 1268 or 1269 he was sent back to Paris. Mirroring his own *exitus–reditus* schema for salvation history, St Thomas's life returned full circle to Naples in 1272. He died in 1274 in Fossanova while on route to the Council of Lyon. A bibliography of his works can be found in both Bauerschmidt and Nichols. Theology students are usually first confronted with the *Summa Theologiae* and for those venturing into this territory a helpful guide is Bauerschmidt's *Holy Teaching: Introducing the Summa Theologiae of St. Thomas Aquinas.*[3] This work includes extensive footnotes that explain the meaning of concepts used in the various questions and it provides some historical context. A not so easily obtainable treasure is a copy of Roy J. Defarrari's 1960 publication of *A Latin-English Dictionary of St. Thomas Aquinas*. This is useful as a handbook for those working with the primary texts in Latin.

Baroque Thomism

The expression 'Baroque Thomism' was coined by Marie-Dominique Chenu OP (1895–1990) to refer to the commentaries on the works of St Thomas produced by scholars in the late scholastic era after the first stirrings of Protestant opposition to scholasticism. It includes the commentaries of Cardinal Cajetan (1469–1534), a Dominican, and Francisco Suárez (1548–1617), a Jesuit. The expression is often used pejoratively by those who accept Chenu's criticisms of this moment in Thomist scholarship. Specifically Chenu charged Baroque scholasticism with being ahistorical. By this he meant that the scholars of the Baroque era extracted doctrinal propositions from the original work and collated them like a legal textbook without any reference to their historical or intellectual context. Daniel D. Novotný has also observed that it was in this Baroque period that the Jesuit's *Ratio atque Institutio Studiorum Societatis Iesu* (curriculum for Jesuit formation and use in Jesuit colleges) gave an institutionally codified position to philosophy as an autonomous discipline for the first time since antiquity.[4] Similarly, Frederick Copleston SJ (1907–94) concluded that 'Suárez's *Disputationes metaphysicae* mark the transition from commentaries on Aristotle to independent treatises on metaphysics and to *Cursus philosophici* in general. ... After his time the *Cursus philosophici* and independent philosophical treatises became common, both inside and outside the Jesuit Order.'[5] Novotný also notes that one of the key characteristics of this era was the interest in the systematisation of doctrines and concepts.

Not only does philosophy acquire an autonomous status in this period, but so too does the civil order vis-à-vis the realm of the sacred and human nature vis-à-vis the order of grace. With respect to the realm of the sacred the word '*saeculum*' initially meant the period of time between the Incarnation and the Second Coming of Christ, while the liturgical phrase '*in secula saeculorum*' could be translated as 'for ages and ages' or 'for all eternity'. It was a chronological concept not an ontological concept. However in the Baroque era it morphed into the notion of the 'secular' as some social space untouched by the influence of the Church.[6] Running in tandem alongside this transition or intellectual mutation was the notion of a 'pure nature'. Jean Borella diagnosed the problem with the notion of an autonomous account of human nature as an 'overemphasis on the Aristotelian idea of the natural order as a rigid system of natures complete-in-themselves, which exclude the supernatural just as the circle excludes the square'.[7] Robert Spaemann has also observed that 'all of the Thomists of the sixteenth century cite Aristotle in this context'.[8] They 'superimposed a hypothetical purely natural destiny of man, a "*finis naturalis*" onto the actual destiny given in salvation history; and the fateful construction of a "*natura pura*" came into being'.[9] Associated with what came to be known as the extrinsicist account of nature and grace (i.e. nature and grace in separate unrelated boxes) there developed in the works of Francisco Suárez an extrinsicist account of the *duplex hominis beatitudo* (twofold human beatitude). The Suárezian anthropology, in effect, opened the door to various Thomist engagements with Liberal political theory by suggesting that there might be goods of human flourishing, to use the contemporary language, connected to the *finis naturalis*, which can be detached from the final end of the human person. In sharp contrast to this intellectual trajectory, more contemporary scholars read Aquinas's account of creation as offering a thoroughgoing theological overhaul of Aristotelianism. Nicholas J. Healy has observed that in *Eschatology, Death and Eternal Life* Joseph Ratzinger shows how Thomas's theology of creation entails a 'complete transformation of Aristotelianism'.[10]

A standard criticism of Baroque-era Thomism, of which Ratzinger's position is representative, is that it failed to recognise the transformation. It is further suggested that this failure was due to the fact that the theologians of the era were focused on defending the intrinsic goodness of postlapsarian human nature against the Calvinists. In doing so, they made Aristotle not merely an ally but a kind of de facto 'Father of the Church'.

Louis Bouyer (1913–2004), a French Oratorian and one of the many critics of Baroque scholasticism, has described this period in the following terms:

> There was no lack of Christian philosophers during the late sixteenth and early seventeenth centuries. The first Neo-Thomists, such as Cajetan, the Salamanca Carmelites, or John of St. Thomas were interested in philosophy at least as much as in theology itself. Unfortunately, none of them did much more than extract their master's philosophy from its theological context, apparently without wondering whether the two elements were separable, or whether the philosophy they sought to define was not distorted in the process.
>
> The only Christian thinker of that period who had more ambitious aims was undoubtedly Suárez. Though exceptionally intelligent in the strictest meaning of the term, Suárez sought to reconcile the views of

contemporary as well as earlier thinkers through quasi-diplomatic compromise, instead of attempting a true synthesis. The result was an extraordinarily flexible philosophy, but Janus-Like, affirming with one mouth what he is simultaneously denying with the other.[11]

Not only was the Suárezian anthropology to have significant flow-on effects in the fields of soteriology and Catholic social teaching, but the contribution of Suárez was also to have a major impact on the understanding of Revelation as it was taught in seminaries. Suárez fostered a propositional account of Revelation by which Revelation does not disclose God himself so much as pieces of information about God. An in-depth account of how the Suárezian approach to Revelation is a modern (Baroque) invention can be found in an essay by John Montag SJ entitled 'The False Legacy of Suárez'.[12] Montag argues that although Suárez was working within the intellectual Tradition of Thomism as taught at the University of Salamanca, his account of Revelation is significantly different from that of Classical Thomism:

> Thomas never had cause to reify the mediation into words or propositions through which God hands over 'things to be believed'. Nor does Thomas separate the moment of belief or assent from some prior moment of apprehension. We have seen, too, that for Thomas, revelation takes place in the judgment and understanding, as part of the assent of faith. Revelation does not occur 'on its own', as if it were a thing apart, before becoming part of human thought and experience. But, for Thomas, what God reveals has precisely that quality which Luther sought to recover in his translation – that is, the intimate self-manifestation, the word which pours from the heart, and which animates faith.[13]

In their introduction to *Radical Orthodoxy* John Milbank, Graham Ward and Catherine Pickstock summarised the importance of the Suárezian reversal in the following terms:

> [It] assumes the loss in the late Middle Ages of the metaphysical framework of participation, and the concomitant loss of an intrinsic link between sign and the thing signified. As a result, the content and the authorization of revelation are prised apart, and both aspects are thought of as isolated occurrences grounded in the will rather than a necessity intrinsic to the real. Revelation is now something positive in addition to reason, precisely because a rational metaphysics, claiming to comprehend being without primary reference to God, frames all discourse, including the theological. Ironically, revealed truth becomes

something ineffably arbitrary, precisely because this is the only way it can be construed by an already intrinsically godless reason.[14]

The Suárezian account of Revelation, along with variations on Melchior Cano's (c.1509-60) account of Tradition, was widely taught in Catholic academies up until the Second Vatican Council (1962-5) and its promulgation of *Dei Verbum* (The Dogmatic Constitution on Divine Revelation) in 1965. As a *Peritus* to Cardinal Josef Frings of Cologne, the young Fr Ratzinger was one of those consulted on the drafting of this document. Ratzinger's opposition to the Suárezian account of Revelation was earlier the subject of a section of his *Habilitationsschrift* (the postdoctoral thesis required of lecturers in German universities), which had to be jettisoned when one of the examiners indicated that he would fail the dissertation because of the criticism of Suárez. The point that the young Ratzinger was making in his *Habilitationsschrift* was that the Suárezian account was a Baroque initiative that differed from the understanding of the scholastics, in particular from the account of Revelation to be found in the works of St Bonaventure (1221-74). Following the lead of Romano Guardini, Ratzinger argued that 'Revelation does not reveal *some thing*, nor does it reveal various kinds of things, but in the man Jesus, in the man who is God, we are able to understand the whole nature of man'.[15] This emphasis on the notion that Christ *is Himself* the Revelation of God the Father to humanity became enshrined in the documents *Dei Verbum* and *Gaudium et spes* of the Second Vatican Council and thereby superseded the dominance of the Suárezian approach. Bauerschmidt summarised the moment of Suárezian dominance with the following statement: 'What in Thomas was an unfolding of revealed truth became in early modern Thomism a project of construction.'[16]

While much of the scholarship on this period of Thomism has focused on the areas of nature and grace and Revelation, Matthew Levering, a leading contemporary American Thomist, has suggested that the Christology and Eucharistic theology of this era deserves attention and has been overlooked in many of the standard histories of this period.

Leonine Thomism

The expression 'Leonine Thomism' refers to the body of scholarship that sought to revive the thought of St Thomas following the publication of the encyclical *Aeterni Patris* by Pope Leo XIII (1810-1903) in 1879. Key scholars associated with this revival were Tommaso Zigliara OP (1833-93), Alberto Lepidi OP (1838-1922), Carlo Maria Curci SJ (1810-91), Luigi Taparelli d'Azeglio SJ (1793-1862), Matteo Liberatore SJ (1810-92) and

Joseph Kleutgen SJ (1811–83). Of particular importance were Kleutgen's five volumes on the theology of St Thomas, and two volumes on the philosophy of St Thomas – *Die Theologie der Vorzeit* (1853–70) and *Die Philosophie der Vorzeit* (1863 and 1870). The fact that Kleutgen divided the Thomist corpus into these two completely separate discipline classifications is itself a hallmark of Leonine Thomism. The philosophical Aquinas was treated as a different intellectual beast from the theological Aquinas since the main reason for this Thomist revival was to provide the Church with an intellectual armoury against the onslaught of various kinds of post-Cartesian and post-Kantian philosophies. The basic strategy was to cull philosophical ideas from the Thomist corpus, which could be presented as a perennial philosophy impervious to historical influence and marketable to intellectuals of any species anywhere, and then the theological top story could be added to upgrade seminarians and other committed Catholics.

   A significant effect of this revival was the production of translations of the works of St Thomas and the establishment of centres for Thomist scholarship, such as the Higher Institute of Philosophy, founded at Louvain by Désiré Mercier, later Cardinal Mercier (1861–1926), in 1889. In 1894, the Institute's review *Le Revue néo-scholastique* appeared and was to have considerable influence. Also significant was the 1882 compilation of St Thomas's collected works in Latin, known as the Leonine *Opera Omnia*.

   In his *Three Rival Versions of Moral Enquiry*, in which the third chapter is focused on the history of Leonine Thomism, Alasdair MacIntyre was critical of the Thomism of this era for its alleged misreading of the integration of Aristotelian and Augustinian thought in Aquinas. Specifically MacIntyre accused Kleutgen and others of his ilk of anachronistically reading St Thomas as if he were answering questions to epistemological problems only raised by or after Descartes. MacIntyre also argued that while Kleutgen was correct to notice that there had been a rupture in the discipline of philosophy, a modern and premodern philosophy as it were, he was wrong to see Descartes as the moment of rupture. According to MacIntyre the rupture begins with the late scholastics and is particularly acute in the works of Francisco Suárez who is 'more authentically than Descartes the founder of modern philosophy'.[17] (Descartes was Jesuit-educated and although he generally held an unfavourable judgement on that education, he was open to ideas presented in Suárez's *Disputationes Metaphysicae*.)

   Contrary to Kleutgen and others of the Leonine generation, MacIntyre argues that St Thomas's own understanding of his work was that of conceptual clarification, analysis and description, not that of epistemological justification. He [St Thomas] also regarded his works as incomplete, leaving the way open for further developments from other scholars. For Kleutgen, however, St Thomas offers the world a finished system in the manner of Suárez. MacIntyre summarises his critique of Kleutgen and the Leonine Thomism Kleutgen fostered in the following paragraph:

> It was a mark of the unusual philosophical ingenuity of Kleutgen that, having first misidentified Aquinas's central positions with those of Suárez, thus opening up a kind of epistemological question for which there is no place within Aquinas's own scheme of thought, he went on to supply an epistemological answer to that question by reading into texts in *De Veritate* an epistemological argument which is not in fact there. So by this creative multiplication of misinterpretations Aquinas was presented as the author of one more system confronting the question of Cartesian and post-Cartesian epistemology, advancing, so Kleutgen contended, sounder answers than either Descartes or Kant.[18]

MacIntyre concluded that the centrifugal effect of Kleutgen's Thomism was to foster a variety of different Thomisms in the twentieth century, depending on the preferred epistemological starting points of individual scholars. Another effect was the rise of intellectual histories of the various appropriations of the Thomist texts throughout the centuries. Those who approached the Thomist corpus from this intellectual history perspective, rather than from a perspective of ransacking everything St Thomas wrote for propositional bullets to fire at philosophical enemies, laid the foundations for many different, but often quite compatible Thomist projects, later in the twentieth century.

Lest MacIntyre's criticism be marginalised as idiosyncratic, similar conclusions have been reached by other scholars, including +Augustine Di Noia OP. Specifically Di Noia is critical of the intellectual habit of reading Aquinas's account of the existence and nature of the triune God (*Summa theologica* 1a. 2–26) as a philosophical preamble to the ideas presented in the *Summa theologica* (1a. 27–43) as a theological appendix. He describes this habit as 'profoundly mistaken' and 'a glaring instance of the difficulties posed by treating the philosophical components as independent of the overarching theological argument'.[19] Di Noia suggests that 'there is an alternative way to construe the philosophical component in Aquinas's theology, one that avoids the impression that his theological positions are largely parasitic upon a philosophical system derivable from his thought'.[20] Di Noia outlines his alternative reading of the relationship between philosophy and theology in the works of Aquinas in the following terms:

> Philosophical analysis and construction are moments intrinsic to theological thinking in the *Summa*, that is, to the ordered and

progressive explication of the doctrines of the faith in such a way as to exhibit their intelligibility. The interweaving of philosophical analysis and construction in the web of theological argument in the *Summa* is in the service of properly theological affirmation. The outcome is not a theological/philosophical system, but a highly ramified complex of interrelated dialectical arguments, always open to embracing or engaging alternative positions that can be rationally justified. The principle of unity and coherence is supplied by the mysteries of the faith in their own interconnection and intelligibility, itself rooted in the *scientia divina*.[21]

According to this reading, 'coherence and integration are seen to be functions of an overarching theological vision rather than a philosophical system' - 'the more conspicuously philosophical components have their logical home in an overarching theological argument'.[22]

A more specific criticism of those readings of Aquinas that seek to separate the philosophical components of his synthesis from the theological is offered by Mark D. Jordan in his *Rewritten Theology: Aquinas after His Readers*. In the chapter titled 'Thomas's Alleged Aristotelianism or Aristotle among the Authorities', Jordan argues that Aquinas 'never pretends to be producing a copy of Aristotle's philosophic project', 'he never identifies himself as a "peripatetic" much less a proponent of "neo-Aristotelianism" (the very form of the term would have puzzled him)'.[23] According to Jordan's reading of Aquinas, Aristotle is merely one highly respectable pagan author whose 'texts can be brought into helpful constellation with other authorities'.[24] St Thomas did 'not regard Aristotle as a block of doctrine to be carried in whole'.[25] Jordan acknowledges that some species of Thomists 'may have thought they were in a war against the Enlightenment, Kant or Hegel, but they had already absorbed the enemy's vocabulary and table for the organisation of knowledge'.[26]

Other scholars who have examined the relationship between philosophy and theology in the works of Aquinas and who are critical of reading the corpus in such a way that the philosophy is an independent element include Michel Corbin SJ, O. H. Pesch OP (1931–2014), Thomas Hibbs, Victor Preller (1931–2001) and Brian Marshall.

Fergus Kerr has also drawn attention to the work of Gerald Vann OP (1906–63) who insisted that the more mystical Pseudo-Dionysian dimensions of Classical Thomism should be kept in the synthesis with the Greek philosophical elements.[27] Vann's reading of the Aristotelian ethic as 'essentially changed' by Aquinas's understanding of the primacy of the beatific vision later became a hallmark of the moral theology of Servais Pinckaers OP (1925–2008).

Whether one wants to separate the theological Aquinas from the philosophical Aquinas or read the philosophical components within the context of an overarching theological argument is thus a highly significant intellectual baseline decision for aspiring Thomist scholars. Many of the fault lines or divisions that have arisen within the Tradition of Thomism after the nineteenth century have their source in this methodological choice.

Neo-Thomism

The term 'Neo-Thomism' is the most nebulous of all the labels. It tends to refer to the Thomism of a particular time period (the sixty years between the death of Leo XIII in 1903 and the beginning of the pontificate of Paul VI in 1963) and also to the variety of Thomisms that arose during this period, some of which were proceeding along the lines laid by Kleutgen's Leonine Thomism while others were not.

In this sixty-year period three dominant streams emerge. The first stream is one that continues in Kleutgen's trajectory, gives priority to epistemological issues and mines the Baroque commentators for bullets to fire at an assortment of philosophers with 'bad' ideas. Chenu and others with an interest in history accused those in the first stream of relying too heavily on the Baroque commentaries and not paying sufficient attention to primary sources and historical contexts. In other words the Stream One-type Thomists were not into what is today called the Cambridge school of ideas. Alasdair MacIntyre explained the methodological principles of the Cambridge School when he wrote that when interpreting the work of any scholar one needs not only to pay attention to the words on the page (which might mean something quite different in the era in which they were composed from what they mean today), but also to consider the historical context in which the ideas were forged. For example, he writes:

> With Aquinas's texts, as with those of many philosophers, a crucial question is always: Against whom is he writing here? Within what controversy is this or that particular contention to be situated? Philosophers characteristically invite us not simply to assert p, but to assert *p* rather than *q* or *r*, and we will often only understand the point of asserting *p*, if we know what *q* and *r* are.[28]

The important hermeneutical principle is thus to know something of the social conditions of the times in which works were composed and something of the author's interlocutors, his or her audience, benefactors, patrons and religious superiors as well as friends and enemies, especially intellectual opponents. The habit of cutting and pasting propositions appeals to the legalistic mind and to the mathematical mind that wants to keep things conceptually tidy but it can get in the way of a true understanding of the intentions of the author and it hides from vision any insight into the author's methodology or general approach to a problem.

A second stream of Neo-Thomism takes on board elements of Kantian epistemology and seeks to synthesise these elements with aspects of Thomist thought. This becomes known as Transcendental Thomism because of its appropriation of the Kantian transcendental method (see its principal characteristics in its own section below).

A third stream is interested in the study of Thomist ideas in their historical context and this gives birth to Existential Thomism, the hallmark of which is an interpretation of *esse,* which includes the notion of existence and is thus *not* a neo-Aristotelian account of *esse.*

The historical research of this third stream fuels passionate debates over the nature of the classically Thomist understanding of the relationship between grace and nature, faith and reason, theology and philosophy. These debates broke out in the 1930s, reached a searing level in the 1940s, then got closed down in the 1950s only to reemerge with a vengeance at the Second Vatican Council. Indeed, one approach to reading the documents of the Second Vatican Council is to consider them as the end product of debates that take place on the Council floor and in committee meetings between proponents of one of these three streams of thinking. Most of the leading *Periti* belonged to either the second or third streams.

The reason for the fireworks is that proponents of Streams Two and Three accuse Stream One advocates of misconstruing the Classical Thomist presentation of these key relationships. Before Alasdair MacIntyre appeared on the scene in the 1980s and argued that the Leonine Thomists got the relationship between Aristotelian philosophy and Patristic theology wrong, Chenu, de Lubac, Étienne Gilson and others had already argued that the Thomists who took for granted the accuracy of the Baroque commentaries got the nature and grace relationship wrong. To this list of indictments one can add the conclusion of a young Fr Joseph Ratzinger that Thomists who were influenced by Suárez got Revelation wrong. The charges do not however end here. Leonine and Stream One Neo-Thomists have also been criticised for reading the classically Thomist notion of substance through post-Lockean glasses (a parallel criticism to MacIntyre's about reading Aquinas with post-Cartesian glasses), for wrongly assuming that it is possible to extract the so-called proofs of God's existence that come early in the *Summa Theologicae* from their theological context and then serving them up in philosophy of religion courses (Di Noia's point above), thereby suggesting that atheism is a mere malfunction of the intellect rather than a complex problem involving the whole human person – a consequence of neglecting the love and reason relationship – and finally, Stream One Neo-Thomists are indicted on the charge of being so neurotically obsessed with the problem of historicism as to deny any role for history or personal experience in theological work. In addition to all these criticisms there was the pedagogical complaint that there was something quite academically unsound about the tendency of the Stream One Neo-Thomists to cut and paste doctrinal propositions from the Thomist corpus and then serve these propositions up to seminarians for rote learning without any reference to the intellectual or historical context from which they were extracted. The whole approach to theological study, especially in the context of the formation of seminarians, was to present students with a series of twenty-four philosophical theses, which were consumed over a three-year period. To these philosophical theses there were later added another layer of theological propositions, all culled from Aquinas or Thomistic commentators and repackaged in manuals on different topics. While the diet was not uniform across every seminary in the world the philosophical theses and teaching from manuals were the standard fare.

In his *Twentieth Century Catholic Theologians* Fergus Kerr made the sociological observation that all the greatest theologians of the Second Vatican Council and post-Conciliar era were in some way in rebellion against the straitjacket of this kind of seminary teaching and that the greatest rebel of all, Hans Küng, had been subjected to a full seven years of it. Hans Urs von Balthasar, another rebel, famously went to classes on Stream One Neo-Thomism wearing earplugs. Meanwhile, a young Joseph Ratzinger was known to have remarked when leaving a lecture on the subject of how God is the *summum bonum* that 'a *summum bonum* doesn't need a mother'.[29] It would seem that what the young Ratzinger found unattractive here was not the proposition itself, with which he would no doubt agree, but the dry conceptualism. Alfred Läpple, his Prefect of Studies, was later to write that 'scholasticism wasn't his [Ratzinger's] beer'.[30] He preferred reading Augustine or John Henry Newman or even the Jewish philosopher Martin Buber.

Thomas O'Meara OP has summed up these negative characteristics of the first stream of Neo-Thomism or what is often called Strict Observance Thomism as 'a lack of sophistication in method, a questionable arrangement of disciplines, an absence of history, [and] a moralistic interdiction of other theologies even when based upon scripture and tradition'.[31] Similarly, Serge-Thomas Bonino OP has used the expression 'Fundamentalist Thomism' to describe the following mentality:

> This variety of Thomism is easily recognisable on account of its visceral reaction against the historical approach to the Thomistic corpus [what has been called Stream Three above] and is easily irritated by what it

considers to be the excessive attention given today to the historical and cultural conditionings of the intellectual life. True, in its aversion to historicism it does have the benefit of defending the trans-historical value of concept and truth, but it does so by forgetting that the absolute of truth is given only in the contingency of history. ... This position holds up the work of St. Thomas as some sort of timeless Koran, guaranteed by magisterial sanction and containing the definitive expression of theology and philosophical wisdom, formulated once and for all as immutable theses.[32]

Frederick Bauerschmidt has also noted that Stream One-type Thomists had a different understanding of what theology is from the Stream Three-type Thomists. Speaking specifically of Chenu (the groundbreaker for Stream Three-type Neo-Thomism), Bauerschmidt observed:

For Chenu, what Thomas offers his modern-day confreres and the Church as a whole is not a timeless system, but 'a body of master-intuitions, which are only embodied in conceptual frameworks on the condition that they there retain their living light and are submitted to an ongoing confrontation with an always-richer reality'. This always-richer reality is what he calls 'the revealed-given' (*le donné révélé*) – a reality that is given to human beings in the economy of salvation and therefore accessible not through metaphysics but through exegesis and historical inquiry informed by faith. By conceiving of theology as faith *in statu scientiae* and by focusing on the historical and cultural contingencies shaping the character of that *scientia*, Chenu sought not only to distinguish philosophy from theology, but also to re-join theology to spirituality. Chenu sees theological systems as expressions of the master-intuitions underlying Traditions of spirituality.[33]

John Milbank has similarly drawn attention to the difference between Chenu's reading of the relationship between philosophy and theology and that of the more Aristotelian (Stream One)-type Thomists:

As Chenu explained, Aquinas taught that what revelation involves is a heightened participatory access through simultaneous event and illuminated interpretation of event to those inaccessible first principles which are God himself, such that *sacra doctrina* is in continuity with the mystical *lumen fidei* (S.T. I q.1.a.7 resp. and ad 1). Aquinas's theory of 'quasi-subalternation' in this way takes Aristotle's account of scientific foundations, which involves the nesting of one science within another, back within the 'enchanted' orbit of participatory theories.

For while subordinate sciences take their principles from a higher science according to Aristotle, in the case of theology, argued Thomas, this means that the human science of God – and all things under the aspect of God – takes its principles (which are also its 'object' – thereby, as Chenu points out, disallowing any autonomous terrain for the subordinated science, as in the normal Aristotelian scheme) not, as for Aristotle, from a higher humanly-known science, but from the divine science which is the knowledge that God has of himself (ST 1 q.1 a.2).[34]

Milbank concluded that Chenu's Aquinas 'much more rendered science as Augustinian wisdom than he rendered wisdom as Aristotelian science'.[35]

In summary, the debate between Stream One-type Neo-Thomists and Stream Three-type Neo-Thomists over the nature of theology is fundamentally a debate about how Aquinas related the Aristotelian components of his synthesis to the Patristic and the merit of modern conceptions of so-called scientific rationality. It is, in other words, a debate about how theology and philosophy are related, and what philosophy(ies) make the best 'handmaids' to theology. It is also a debate about how nature and grace are related, since for the Stream Three types, while grace and nature are distinct concepts, 'Catholic nature' is not synonymous with 'Aristotelian nature'. These are baseline questions that influence the whole understanding of the Thomistic theological enterprise and theology in general.

At the beginning of the twenty-first century support for Strict Observance or Fundamentalist Thomism is rarely found in established academic circles, though it remains popular in Traditionalist circles where an attitude abides that all was perfect before the Second Vatican Council and one should simply ignore the documents of the Council and the magisterial theology of subsequent papacies and hold out for a thoroughgoing restoration of the pre-Conciliar intellectual order. In effect this means that Traditionalists have no answers to the barrage of intellectual assaults that have been made on the universality of Christian Revelation from those with an interest in hermeneutics and the history and dogma relationship. This stance fosters a ghetto-culture in which efforts are made to live as though the Second Vatican Council did not happen. The tragedy is that the Traditionalists are arguably correct in their understanding that the truths of the faith are best mediated by a culture that is in form and substance Catholic, not a culture that is in form and substance post-Christian or a mutated Christianity (as the culture of modernity is judged by most intellectual historians to be). The Traditionalists are also correct in their judgement that different liturgical forms embody different theological meanings or at least that the theological accents are differently placed in alternative liturgical forms. However the insight that the

Traditionalists miss is the Strand Three-type Thomist argument that elements of the Tridentine theological framework, including significant components of Strand One-type Thomism, are actually already *modern*. In other words, if modernity is your enemy, then seventeenth-century Salamanca Thomism is not your best ally; indeed, as the Strand Three argument goes, it should also be your enemy.

The superhero or star exhibit for the Strict Observers is Reginald Garrigou-Lagrange OP who was famously described by the French author François Mauriac (1885–1970) as the *monstre sacré* (sacred monster) of Thomism. Less poetically he has also been called 'Reginald the Rigid'. He held the position of professor of Dogma and Mystical Theology at the Pontifical University of St Thomas in Rome (the Angelicum) for fifty years, from 1909 to 1959. He combined his teaching with working as a consultant or censor for the Holy Office and through these positions he exercised enormous political influence. By many accounts he was an engaging lecturer and one of his claims to fame is that Yves Congar was inspired to join the Dominican Order after hearing him preach a retreat. He is also famous for having supervised the doctoral dissertation of Karol Wojtyła on the topic of the theological virtue of faith in St John of the Cross. Although they had some theological disagreements (Garrigou-Lagrange did not approve of the nascent personalist elements in Wojtyła's thesis, especially Wojtyła's refusal to refer to God as an object), there is no evidence to suggest that Wojtyła was ever unhappy with his doctoral supervisor. A commonly made observation by scholars outside the milieu of Strict Observers is that Garrigou-Lagrange's works on spirituality, such as his *The Three Ages of the Spiritual Life*, published in two volumes in 1938, should not be tarred with the same badly smelling brush as his attitude to theological methodology.

In general however, the name Garrigou-Lagrange is a lightning rod for conflict since he was by disposition opposed to any kind of thinking operating on a different methodological basis from his own. Richard Peddicord, author of a defence of Garrigou's life and teaching, claims that the 'scholastic disputation provided Garrigou-Lagrange with a model and method for arriving at the truth' and indeed, 'the disputation ought to be seen as the heuristic key for understanding Garrigou's fundamental style in philosophy and theology'.[36] This is, of course, quite a different understanding of the theological enterprise from Chenu's notion of the discernment of master-intuitions embodied in historically conditioned conceptual frameworks and from the entire Patristic approach to theology, which was not centred around syllogisms.

Central to the scholastic methodology however is the arrangement of a repertoire of concepts and a rather large amount of syllogistic analysis.

Problems immediately arise whenever anyone comes along who wants to work outside the repertoire or to offer new insights from scholars other than Aquinas and his commentators and/or who have reservations about whether truths about God neatly captured and packaged into tight little maxims arranged in syllogistic patterns have much pastoral value. For example, the point of the young Joseph Ratzinger was not that it is wrong to say that God is the highest good, but rather, after all the dialectical reasoning in the world reaches the conclusion that logically, God must be the highest good, that is cold comfort for the person in the pew who has lost half his or her family in a war or a concentration camp. What they need to know is that this highest good loves them, cares about them, wants to be in a relationship with them, knows their name and their burdens. It was the philosophy of personalism and varieties of Christian and Jewish existentialism as well as Patristic reflections not taken up by Aquinas that could address those matters of the heart in a way that the conclusions of scholastic disputation reliant upon classical Greek philosophical categories did not. The methodology as well as the theological anthropology was too narrow and rigid. It was unlikely to convert the avant-garde intellectuals who regarded the method of disputation as quaint medievalism and it was unlikely to console the shell-shocked faithful who were finding consolation in novels where writers directly addressed their feelings about the credibility of the Christian narrative after Verdun and Auschwitz, that is, after the conflagration that claimed the lives of at least seventy-six million people in two world wars between ostensibly Christian countries. What Peddicord calls 'scholastic disputation', Alexander Dru has disparaged as 'syllogistic brillo'.[37] Brillo is a trade name for a scouring pad, used for cleaning dishes, and made from steel wool impregnated with soap. Dru's point is not that logic is unimportant but that theology should not be reduced to logic-chopping exercises with all the hallmarks of a high-school debate that hinges on fights about conceptual definitions. This kind of argumentation is of limited pastoral value and in fact many find it priggish and repulsive.

The Strict Observers' aversion to thinking within any historical context may be gleaned from the following statement of Peddicord:

> The proper interpretation of St. Thomas is found not through historical erudition but through knowledge of the living tradition of Thomism. Focusing too minutely on what historiography can tell us concerning what the 'historical Thomas' did or did not hold runs the risk of obscuring the fact that it is the truth of the various propositions that matters – not the fact that they can be attributed with certainty to St. Thomas himself.[38]

Peddicord's statement, which is a good summary of the Strict Observer's position, suggests that there are scholars who want to follow the original Aquinas, rather than some subsequent Aquinas, simply because they prefer to have the original. This kind of thinking, were it the case, would be an example of what in other contexts Joseph Ratzinger criticised as 'archeologism' – an intellectual preference for some idea simply because of its historical pedigree. However this misses the point about Stream Three Neo-Thomism's interest in the historical Thomas. The reason for the interest was not intellectual archaeology for the sake of intellectual archaeology. Rather, the interest was motivated by a desire to understand the spiritual trauma of post-sixteenth-century Europe. It was fuelled by the need to understand how the Reformation arose, how the eighteenth-century rationalist philosophies arose and in particular, it was motivated by an interest in the intellectual genealogy of secularism. The reason why Strand Three-type Neo-Thomists were critical of Baroque Thomism was not primarily that it was not Classical Thomism, or that there is something 'fishy' about the Baroque era, but rather the Strand Three criticism is that in breaking with certain understandings of Classical Thomism, the Baroque Thomists opened the door to liberalism and secularism.

In stark contrast to the Stream One/Strict Observer's antidote to the problem of atheism (the twenty-four philosophical theses), in 1969 Joseph Ratzinger wrote:

> The real answer to atheism is the life of the Church, which must manifest the face of God by showing its own face of unity and love. Conversely this includes the admission that the disunity of Christians and their consent to systems of social injustice hide the face of God. It also implies that knowing the face of God is not a question of pure reason alone, that there is an obscuration of God in the world produced by guilt, which can only be removed by penance and conversion.[39]

Transcendental Thomism

Transcendental here is not a reference to truth, beauty, goodness and unity (the transcendental properties of being) but to the influence of Immanuel Kant's transcendental method on this school. The forerunners were the French Jesuits Joseph Maréchal (1878–1944) and Pierre Rousselot (1878–1915), though the key names are Karl Rahner and Bernard Lonergan (also both Jesuits) who, in one of those remarkable coincidences of salvation history, were both born in 1904 and both died in 1984.

The fundamental distinction between the Transcendental Thomists and Thomists such as Garrigou-Lagrange is that instead of beginning their analysis with a consideration of the metaphysical properties of objective being, they begin with epistemological issues. Alan Vincelette explains the project in the following terms:

> The central conclusion of Transcendental Thomism is that the dynamism of a knowing subject toward Infinite and Absolute Being (i.e. God) is ... an a priori condition of knowledge. That is to say, God is in some ways always present as a horizon and necessarily co-affirmed with every act of human knowledge. There are two distinct schools of thought, however, in regard to just how this occurs. According to some proponents of Transcendental Thomism, an a priori *desire* for knowledge of the Absolute Being of God is the transcendental condition of all acts of knowledge (Rousselot, Lonergan); others argue that what allows for knowledge is that to some degree humans have an a priori *apprehension* of God as Absolute Being (by the light of the agent intellect) (Maréchal, Rahner). The world is intelligent then to Transcendental Thomists because we either seek or actually ascend to God (perfectly intelligible being) in every act of knowing.[40]

An accessible summary of Rahner's Transcendental Thomism may be found in two essays by F. J. Michael McDermott in *The Student's Companion to the Theologians*.[41] One essay is directly on the topic of Rahner, the other is on the theology of the Second Vatican Council. The latter includes the following subsection on the Transcendental Thomist critique of 'conceptualism' (associated with Stream One Thomism):

> Transcendental Thomism located truth in a judgment or insight, of which the concept is only a part. The mind therefore goes beyond the concept to reach reality; thus are concepts relativised. Moreover truth is realised not in the passive intellect receiving a concept, but in the activity of the judging intellect. ... Since a judgment synthesises the material object with its spiritual meaning, body and soul, sensation and intellection, are understood as a basic unity, each implying the other. ... The 'in-itself' of conceptualist natures has given way to a whole web of relations.
>
> While concepts ground clear distinctions, transcendental judgements transcend them toward a higher unity: God and man, true and good, intellect and will, body and soul, subject and object, natural and supernatural tend to be amalgamated. Not that the value of concepts is denied; without concepts thought is not possible. The best

transcendental thinkers tried to preserve concepts and all necessary distinctions but did not absolutise them.[42]

Another way to explain this is to say that whereas Stream One-type Thomists are renowned for their interest in discursive reasoning *(ratio)* 'characterised by a primacy of static definitions and deductive reasoning' the Transcendental Thomists give a higher status to the work of *intellectus* (intuition).[43] The Transcendental Thomists, especially Rahner, were also highly conscious of the historical embeddedness of concepts.

Not only did Karl Rahner have a different approach to the faith–reason relationship from Strand One-type Neo-Thomists and a different attitude towards conceptual thought, but he also offered a different account of the grace and nature relationship, which one can find outlined in the first volume of his *Theological Investigations*, in his *Mission and Grace* and in his *Nature and Grace and Other Essays*.

In this context Rahner is famous for coining the concept a 'supernatural existential'. Much ink has been spilt over precisely what Rahner meant by this. For an article that lists all or at least most of Rahner's references to the concept, recourse can be had to David Coffey's 'The Whole Rahner on the Supernatural Existential' wherein he tracks through each of Rahner's publications where the phrase is used.[44] Coffey accounts for some of the opacity of the concept by the fact that Rahner was responding to issues that had arisen in scholastic philosophy using Heideggerian language.

Rahner's account of the grace–nature relationship has been criticised for its tendency to naturalise the supernatural and for its implicit sidelining of the significance of historical Revelation and the role of the Church as a mediator of grace, though scholars debate the issue of whether or not this is a just criticism. The 'naturalising the supernatural' criticism is made by Adam G. Cooper in the following paragraph:

> One gets the continual impression that the deifying experience of grace outlined by Rahner takes place in the individual primarily in the form of a heightened consciousness of what is universally already the case. The concrete bodily and communal events of ecclesial incorporation and sacramental participation seem not so much to be constitutively causative of a new reality as occasions for the conscious experience of an already-existing one. Basically they have as their aim the stimulation of a psychological state of awareness, the elicitation of a primarily gnoseological orientation. Or, to put it another way, they have as their aim the making explicit of what hitherto was already present, given, and real at the level of the 'unthematic'.[45]

This is also Ratzinger's criticism of the general thrust of the mature Rahner's theological projects. In his *Principles of Catholic Theology* Ratzinger wrote:

> Is it true that Christianity adds nothing to the universal but merely makes it known? Is the Christian really just man as he is? Is that what he is supposed to be? Is not man as he is that which is insufficient, that which must be mastered and transcended? Does not the whole dynamism of history stem from the pressure to rise above man as he is? Is not the main point of the faith of both testaments that man is what he ought to be only by conversion, that is, when he ceases to be what he is? Does not Christianity become meaningless when it is reinstated in the universal, whereas what we really want is the new, the other, the saving trans-formation? Does not such a concept, which turns being into history but also history into being, result in a vast stagnation despite the talk of self-transcendence as the content of man's being? A Christianity that is no more than a reflected universality may be innocuous, but is it not also superfluous?[46]

Other scholars distinguish between the real Rahner (a highly sophisticated and loyal son of the Church who was motivated by the desire to make Christianity credible in intellectual circles) and the popularised more Heideggerian-than-Heidegger Rahner. The fact that (according to Küng and Coffey) Rahner had a habit of using classical scholastic vocabulary but injecting the old vocabulary with new meanings is no doubt a contributing factor to what has been described as the difference between the real Rahner and the popularised Rahner. In addition to the ambivalent quality of his prose there is the fact that Karl, unlike his brother Hugo, is notoriously dense in his literary style and this gives a lot of interpretive power to anyone offering a more user-friendly, popularist version. Aidan Nichols has summarised the popular interpretations of Rahner in the following list of propositions:

> In *fundamental theology*, the belief that a transcendental philosophy can anticipate the distinctive content of Christian revelation; in *soteriology*, the idea that the life, death and resurrection of Christ are exemplary rather than efficacious in force; in *theological ethics* the notion that the love of neighbour can be a surrogate for the love of God and Christological confession no longer necessary for Christian existence; in the *theology of religions* the idea that other faiths are ordinary means of salvation alongside the Christian way; in *ecclesiology* the idea that the Church becomes simply the explicit, articulation of what is equally present (though only implicitly so) wherever the world opens itself to the Kingdom; and finally the *theology of history*,

the fact that the universal openness of the human spirit to divine
transcendence in its supernatural offer of salvation is already deemed
to be *Gnadenerfahrung*, 'the experience of grace', even without any
further intervention of the redeeming God in the special history of
revelation.[47]

Such a collection of theoretical propositions (whether they can be justly
attributed to Karl Rahner remains a matter of academic debate) gave Rahner
the reputation for being the Liberal Catholic's theologian of choice in the post-
Conciliar era, especially in the 1970s and 1980s. What is clear, regardless of
how one reads the dense prose and the ambivalent employment of scholastic
language, and how one understands the concept 'supernatural existential', is
that Rahner (unlike Ratzinger, Balthasar or de Lubac) was generally positive
about modernity. This is very clear from an interview given late in his life
and published under the title *Faith in a Wintry Season*. It is clear that Rahner
regarded modernity as something 'here to stay' to which Catholics would
have to adjust themselves, rather than adopting a countercultural stance.
The degree to which Rahner regarded a Catholic accommodation to the
culture of modernity as a necessary pastoral and intellectual project may be
gleaned from reading his *Foundations of Christian Faith*, wherein he takes
the view that 'given that there are different theologies today which cannot
be integrated, it is not to be expected that one and the same basic creed
could prevail for everyone in the church'.[48] In this context Rahner even goes
so far as to formulate his own alternative creeds expressed in the idioms of
Heideggerian philosophy.

Rahner's ideas about transposing Christian beliefs into more
contemporary-sounding 'short formulae' was explicitly criticised by Joseph
Ratzinger in his *Principles of Catholic Theology* and treated with scorn by
Balthasar in *The Moment of Christian Witness* as an exercise in transposing
the mysteries of God into 'modern nursery rhymes'. (Only Balthasar could
equate Heideggerian idioms with nursery rhymes!) The trio Ratzinger, de
Lubac and Balthasar, while agreeing that Catholics should not respond to
modernity by huddling into a medieval ghetto, were nonetheless much more
inclined to critique the culture of modernity from an explicitly Christocentric
Trinitarian perspective and find it wanting, rather than seeking to correlate the
faith to contemporary cultural fashions and idioms. De Lubac and Balthasar's
accounts of the grace–nature relationship and the faith–reason relationship
are therefore often seen as alternatives to the project of Rahner by those who
otherwise share Rahner's judgement about the problems with Stream One-
type Neo-Thomism but not his enthusiasm for the culture of modernity.
Another way to distinguish Rahner from Ratzinger, de Lubac and Balthasar
is to note the comment of Karl-Heinz Weger that 'not the theological drama,

[that is, the Trinity, the Incarnation, the Paschal Mysteries] but the person of today in his own self-understanding, is Rahner's theological starting point'.[49]

Bernard Lonergan shared Rahner's interest in epistemology. With Rahner he belonged to a generation who regarded the Church's intellectual life as woefully backward and he wanted to make Christianity credible to the educated person of the twentieth century. He was well aware of the crisis created by the need to understand the mediation of history in the realm of ontology. In an essay published in 1976 he wrote: 'To put it bluntly, until we move onto the level of historical dynamics, we shall face our secularist and atheistic opponents as the Red Indians, armed with bows and arrows, faced European muskets'.[50] For an extensive analysis of the significance of history for Lonergan students can read Robert M Doran's article 'System and History: The Challenge to Catholic Systematic Theology'.[51]

Lonergan spoke of the need for a 'second Enlightenment', something that sounds almost diabolical to postmodern ears unless it is interpreted as something like a wholesale revisiting of the subject of human cognition in order to fix Cartesian and Kantian mistakes. For those interested in the complex relationship between Lonergan and Kant there is Giovanni B. Sala's work *Lonergan and Kant: Five Essays on Human Knowledge*.[52]

Lonergan's most famous work on the dynamism of human consciousness was *Insight: A Study of Human Understanding*.[53] In this he outlined four levels of consciousness:

1. empirical, which is the level of the sensual;
2. intellectual, which is the level of inquiry, understanding and expression;
3. rational, which is the level of reflection and judgement upon the truth or falsity of a proposition; and
4. responsible, which is the level of applying what we know to ourselves and come to a decision about how we should then act, given what we know.

Lonergan's *Insight* has been hugely influential beyond Catholic circles and is often cited in the fields of pedagogy and the history and philosophy of science. His notion of authenticity linked to the idea of responsible action is also a popular theme among moral theologians. For a user-friendly guide to the significance of *Insight*, that is, for a guide that does not first require one to hold a doctorate in mathematics, students can be directed to +Robert Barron's essay 'Why Bernard Lonergan Matters for Pastoral People', published in his *Exploring Catholic Theology: Essays on God, Liturgy and Evangelisation*. +Barron concludes his essay with this summary:

> Lonergan makes a distinction between the need for certitude and the quest for understanding. The need to be apodictically certain is the mark of many of the philosophies of modernity. Descartes's frantic

sweeping away of received traditions, ideas, and even ordinary sense experience in an attempt to discover an absolutely firm foundation for philosophy is the paradigm. This compulsive desire struck Lonergan as neurotic. To it he contrasted the ... search for understanding guided by the four great epistemological imperatives [listed above]. This rigorous journey of intellectual discovery is conditioned not by the neediness of the ego but rather by that sense of wonder of which Aristotle spoke. It does not involve the gathering of reality around the ego but the dissolving of the ego in rapture at the density and complexity of the real. In both academic and pastoral people, on both the right and the left, I have often sensed the ghost of Descartes. The signs are an intellectuality that is angry, desirous of incontrovertible certitude, and finally afraid.[54]

+Barron thus recommends that attention be given to Lonergan's four levels of human consciousness and their work of cognition as antidotes to the ghost of Descartes.

From the wider perspective of the question of 'how to do Catholic theology', and not merely the narrower question of, 'how to think intelligently', Lonergan's most important work was *Method in Theology*.[55]

Speaking of Lonergan's approach to theological method, and distinguishing it from pre-Conciliar notions of how to do Catholic theology, Kirsten Busch Nielsen wrote:

> He [Lonergan] believes that fundamental theology, the reflection on the foundation and starting point of theology, can no longer be a set of dogmatic propositions about religion, the Church, Scripture and Tradition. It must be 'the horizon within which the meaning of doctrines can be apprehended'. Lonergan is not interested primarily in theological content, but in theology as a process, as something that the theologian does. It is through this process that the content comes into the picture.[56]

Lonergan's eight functional specialisations in theological method are research, interpretation, history, dialectic, foundations, doctrines, systematics and communications. By dialectic Lonergan meant 'a generalised apologetic conducted in an ecumenical spirit, aiming ultimately at a comprehensive viewpoint, and proceeding towards that goal by acknowledging differences, seeking their grounds real and apparent, and eliminating superfluous oppositions'.[57] By foundations Lonergan meant not doctrines, but 'the horizon within which the meaning of doctrines can be apprehended'.[58] Nielsen notes that it is important for Lonergan that 'foundations' come 'not *before*, but *during* the theological work, *after* the investigation of theology's texts and sources from a historical perspective'.[59] According to Lonergan all eight functional specialties are interdependent. The first four he associates with a mediating phase of theology that encounters the past, the second four with a mediating phase that looks forward to the future. He distinguishes his approach to theology as functional specialisation from subject specialisation (ecclesiology, moral theology, sacramental theology, etc.) or field specialisation (Biblical, Patristic, Medieval, Modern, etc.) by the argument that whereas subject specialisation tends to emphasise the mediated phase and field specialisation the mediating phase, his approach works on the basis of a dynamic interdependence of all eight functional specialties.

A short commentary on Lonergan's theological methodology was published by Karl Rahner in the journal *Gregorianum* in 1969.[60] In this commentary Rahner is critical of Lonergan's methodology in a manner that strangely resembles the Balthasar–Ratzinger criticism of Rahner's own theological project. Specifically, Rahner is critical of Lonergan's methodology for disregarding the 'completely peculiar and unique relatedness to the concrete person of Jesus, which is not only distinct to Christian faith and life but also, for that reason, distinct to Christian theology'.[61] Rahner regarded Lonergan's method as an appropriate method for the sciences generally, but he thought that it failed to factor in the specific difference of God who is not 'some arbitrary object within the field of categorical objects', but is rather, 'the incomprehensible mystery which can never be subsumed among the objects of the remaining sciences in a similar method'.[62] Rahner did however praise Lonergan's effort in updating the *Loci theologici* of Melchior Cano (who died in 1560) and for 'attending to the many gaps and omissions in the factual Catholic theology of today'.[63]

From a different (more classically Thomistic perspective) Lonergan's method for doing theology was the subject of an essay by Aidan Nichols. This essay is worth reading in full for anyone with a deep interest in this topic since he relates the epistemology of *Insight* to the methodology of *Method in Theology*. What is particularly interesting about this essay in the light of Rahner's comments is that Nichols (who has never been mistaken for a Rahnerian by anyone) makes a similar criticism to Rahner. Nichols concludes that 'the distinctiveness of the Christian faith on his [Lonergan's] view is not a very interesting distinctiveness. It means in effect that Christianity has the key to what is going on in the other religions, and perhaps outside them too. It does not mean that something different is going on in Christianity'.[64] Nichols also offers several arguments for why he thinks that Lonergan's method cannot properly give an account of the unity to be found within the plurality of Catholic theologies and this, he thinks, is related to Lonergan's epistemology. Nichols believes that Lonergan presupposes that Catholic theologians will be 'orthodox' (i.e. faithful to the Magisterium) but within the method itself he could find nothing to guarantee this.

Existential Thomism

The Existential Thomists are a subset of Strand Three-type Neo-Thomism who focus on the differences between Aristotelian metaphysics and Thomistic metaphysics. In particular they argue that for St Thomas existence (the divine act of communicating being) precedes essence (the whatness of things that limits existence in receiving it). The key scholar here is Étienne Gilson. William Norris Clarke SJ (1915–2008) and David L. Schindler also fit into this category and are leading Anglophone examples. A user-friendly introduction into this area is Clarke's 1993 Marquette University Aquinas Lecture entitled *Person and Being*.[65] Cornelio Fabro (1911–95), Joseph de Finance SJ (1904–2000) and Rudi Te Velde are some of the leading European names in this field.[66]

Frederick Copleston summarised the key ingredient of Existential Thomism in the following statement: 'In *Being and Some Philosophers* Étienne Gilson argues that Suárez, following Avicenna and Scotus but proceeding further in the same direction, lost sight of Aquinas's vision of being as the concrete act of existing and tended to reduce being to essence.'[67] Yet again, Suárez is perceived to be the villain who corrupted Classical Thomism and turned it into a Baroque deviation.

A very comprehensive essay on the influence of Gilsonian Existential Thomism, including internal differences within this category, is Wayne Hankey's 'From Metaphysics to History, from Exodus to Neoplatonism, from Scholasticism to Pluralism: the fate of Gilsonian Thomism in English-speaking North America'.[68] Hankey observes that 'Gilson demolished the common *philosophia perennis* which would embrace the Franciscan doctors, and he sharply distinguished authentic Thomism from that of the great Dominican and Jesuit commentators'.[69] In the United States the 'gospel of existential Thomism' was spread by former students of Gilson at the University of Toronto. For example, A. C. Pegis wrote on nature and grace in Aquinas, confirming de Lubac's claim that the state of pure nature was an invention of the neo-scholastics. Armand Maurer in his 'Cajetan's Notion of Being and Commentary on the "Sentences"' demonstrated that Cajetan and Aquinas differed on the constitution of metaphysics and Joseph Owens 'reconstructed the doctrine of being in Aristotle's *Metaphysics* in order to demonstrate the difference which Gilson asserted between Aristotle and Aquinas'.[70] In the UK, Eric Mascall, a high Church Anglican, spread the idea of an Existential Thomism in his Gifford Lectures of 1970-1 entitled 'The Openness to Being'. Norris Clarke, who was a student of Pegis at Fordham, described his own project as one of integrating personalist philosophy with Thomistic metaphysics. From French and German phenomenologists he learned about the relational aspects of the human person, but the flaw of such phenomenologists is that they had a tendency to reduce the human person to little more than a 'spectrum of relations to others with nobody home inside to ground them in the unity of a single being'.[71] Clarke thought that any adequate understanding of the human person demanded the integration of the disciplines of personalist philosophy with Thomistic metaphysics (what Clarke calls 'the dynamic understanding of existential being in Aquinas') so that each and every unique individual was grounded in a common human nature. This project was endorsed by Joseph Ratzinger who summarised it as the idea that 'relationality and substantiality are equally primordial dimensions of reality'. The most famous proponent of this project was Karol Wojtyła who pursued it under the banner of 'Lublin Thomism'.

Lublin Thomism

Lublin Thomism could be described as the single most important branch of Existential Thomism. Scholars in this school were based at the Katolicki Uniwersytet Lubelski (KUL) and its most illustrious proponent was Karol Wojtyła, now St John Paul II. According to Jarosław Kupczak OP the six Founding Fathers of Lublin Thomism were the historians of philosophy Stefan Swieżawski (1907-2004) and Marian Kurdziałek (1920-97), the logician and philosopher of law Jerzy Kalinowski (1888-1954), the metaphysician Mieczysław Albert Krąpiec OP (1921-2008), the methodologist Stanisław Kamiński (1919-86) and Karol Wojtyła.[72]

Key Lublin Thomism texts are Krąpiec's *I-Man: An Outline of Philosophical Anthropology* and Karol Wojtyła's, *The Acting Person*. In both authors (Wojtyła and Krąpiec) there is a focus on the anthropological dimensions of Thomist thought. These authors sought to develop Thomism with reference to themes in the existentialist and phenomenological movements of mid-century Europe. Wojtyła was interested not merely in universal human nature but also in that dimension of each human being which is totally unique and largely shaped and expressed in relationships with other persons.

He was therefore interested in 'being in time' issues, made famous by Martin Heidegger. In effect he was addressing Jean Daniélou SJ's (1905–74) criticism of scholasticism for 'locating reality in essences rather than in subjects, and by so doing ignoring the dramatic world of persons'.[73] Wojtyła's Thomistic personalism took seriously the impact of history on personal development. Francis Lescoe summarised Wojtyła's project in *The Acting Person* in the following terms:

> Assimilating the classical conception of man as *persona*, Wojtyła does not limit himself to the Boethian definition of man as an individual substance of a rational nature but following such principles as *operari sequitur esse, praxis sequitur theorum* – as found in Aquinas' philosophical anthropology – he attempts to enrich the one-sided aspect of man's rationality by including within the definition of human reality, the entire range of human actions.[74]

An accessible analysis of the relationship of Wojtyła's Lublin Thomism to Thomism in general can be found in Vilma Sliuzaite's dissertation on the notion of experience in Wojtyła's anthropology. She notes that there are some scholars who regard Wojtyła as primarily a Thomist and others who regard him as primarily a phenomenologist, and yet others who consider him as someone providing a synthesis of the two. She summarises the arguments of the proponents of each position and comes down on the side of those who regard his work as a synthesis. Foremost among these is Jerzy W. Gałkowski who argues that Wojtyła regarded a Thomism that can only speak of universal human nature, not particular individual persons, as inadequate and in need of some phenomenological supplements.[75] Sliuzaite concludes that 'for Wojtyła, both metaphysical and phenomenological reflections are necessary to account adequately for the subjective and objective dimensions of human existence' and therefore 'the originality of his philosophical method consists in his attempt to recover the unity between the objective and subjective dimensions in man and to give an adequate response to the modern problem of the subject-object dichotomy'.[76]

A number of scholars have argued that in effecting this synthesis Wojtyła followed the Existential Thomism of Étienne Gilson, Joseph de Finance and Cornelio Fabro. George McLean has emphasised the importance of the influence of Cornelio Fabro, especially Fabro's reading of St Thomas's thought as something encompassing a Platonic notion of participation and Augustinian subjectivity.[77] The influence of de Finance has been noted by both Kupczak and Kenneth L Schmitz.[78] Jarosław Kupczak has also drawn attention to the influence of professor Stefan Swieżawski (a strong supporter of Existential Thomism) on the young Karol Wojtyła at the time when he was writing his *Habilitationsschrift*. Kupczak writes:

> Wojtyła's project of creating a Christian philosophy of the human person became clear in some of his earliest publications. Both poetic and philosophical, they are concerned with the problem of human cognition, both natural and supernatural, of oneself and others. In his poem, 'Song of the Brightness of Water' written in 1950, Wojtyła describes the encounter between Jesus Christ and the Samaritan woman at the well in Sychar. The poem reveals the author's conviction that a natural cognition of man is very difficult, almost impossible. ... Wojtyła writes that the best way to come to know oneself and others is to close one's eyes. Then, one can see everything clearly in the supernatural light of Christ.

Kupczak goes on to conclude that cognition is linked to the transforming power of the grace of Christ and further, 'that it is important to notice that grace is not presented by Wojtyła as something external or merely added to human nature'. Rather,

> in this poem Wojtyła rejects the theory of grace presented in the nineteenth century manuals of Catholic theology, which was based on a strong distinction between the two ends of man: natural and supernatural. Also, it seems that Wojtyła accepts the theory of grace popularised in the twentieth century by Henri de Lubac in his famous *Surnaturel*. Grace is presented there as the fulfilment of all natural human potentialities.[79]

While this literary work was written in 1950, Kupczak argues that the same theology of grace is evident in Wojtyła's *Catechesis on Human Love*, delivered during the early years of his pontificate.

In an essay titled 'The Enduring Relevance of Karol Wojtyła's Philosophy', Richard A. Spinello concluded:

> Karol Wojtyła was a dedicated Thomist, but, unlike his famous teacher at the Angelicum, Pére Garrigou-Lagrange, he was not a Thomist of the 'strict observance'. He did not believe that Aquinas's philosophy always provided comprehensive answers to philosophical questions. Nor did Thomism represent the exclusive way to explore the intricacies of divine Revelation. On the contrary, Wojtyła readily realized some of the shortcomings of Aquinas's metaphysical thought, which did not and perhaps could not give enough attention to human subjectivity.

In addition, Aquinas devoted little attention to the human person. Since antipersonalist perspectives were not a major problem in the thirteenth century, this void was not problematic for Aquinas's broad theological vision. But such was not the case in the twentieth century where these philosophies have exerted a disproportionate influence on the contemporary philosophical scene.[80]

Spinello went on to explain that Wojtyła turned to the philosophy of personalism and the methodology of phenomenology as a 'complement to metaphysical analysis' that sheds light through a thematic investigation of human action.[81] This is clearly evident in Wojtyła's essay 'Thomistic Personalism' wherein he stated:

> We can see here how very objectivistic St. Thomas' view of the human person is. It almost seems as though there is no place in it for an analysis of consciousness and self-consciousness as totally unique manifestations of the person as a subject. Thus St. Thomas gives us an excellent view of the objective existence and activity of the person, but it would be difficult to speak in his view of the lived experiences of the person.[82]

In his preface to Kupczak's *Destined for Liberty*, Michael Novak stated that Wojtyła 'shares with de Lubac the conviction that the concept of pure nature – apart from the fall and grace – is a mere hypothetical, which does not and never did exist'.[83] He added that while it would not be right to say that the views of Wojtyła and de Lubac on these questions are identical, 'Wojtyła's views on them are closer to de Lubac's than to those of any other theologian' and 'he [Wojtyła] reads history and nature sacramentally'.[84] To the extent that this is an accurate reading, and Kupczak and Schmitz would argue that it is, Wojtyła's Thomism is firmly a Strand Three-type Neo-Thomism with debts to the specifically Existential (Strand Three) Thomism of Gilson.

William Norris Clarke has remarked that John Paul II's exploration of the interior life of the person beyond the reach of the traditional method of Thomistic metaphysics was a creative step. However Wojtyła had only proposed complementing the traditional Thomistic metaphysics, interpreted in the manner of the Existential Thomists, with the distinct new phenomenology of Christian Personalism, while leaving the traditional Thomistic metaphysics itself untouched. Clarke described his own work and that of Kenneth L. Schmitz as one of carrying Wojtyła's project further by 'showing how a personalist dimension is actually implicit within the very structure and meaning of being itself in a fully developed Thomistic metaphysics' – hence their interest in human receptivity and relationality. As Clarke expressed the principle, 'To be real is to be related.'[85]

Whig Thomism

Whig Thomism is an expression coined by Michael Novak. It is a project to synthesise elements of the thought of St Thomas with elements of Liberal economic and political theory. Its leading proponents are all Americans keen to argue that that there is no fundamental conflict between the mythos fostered by the Founding Fathers of the United States and the Catholic form of Christianity. Its leading critics are also Americans who believe that at the foundation of the Constitution of the United States there are metaphysical principles loaded against the flourishing of a Catholic culture in America.

Originally the word 'Whig' came from the Scottish word 'Whiggamor' for a cattle driver. It was initially applied to Scottish Presbyterians who opposed the Royal House of Stuart in the wars of the seventeenth century. As a sociological generalisation it can be said that the Whigs were the heirs of the political and economic philosophies of the Scottish Enlightenment fused with a Calvinist form of Protestantism.

In the nineteenth century Lord Acton (1834–1902) popularised the idea that Thomas Aquinas was the first Whig (in the sense of a proponent of Liberal political and economic theory, not, of course, of Calvinism) and this notion was taken up by Michael Novak and others to synthesise ideas from Scottish Enlightenment philosophy with elements of Thomism. The project has not however been popular with historians of political theory. In *Christian Faith and Modern Democracy* Robert P. Kraynak wrote that 'though intriguing, Acton's interpretation is misleading because Thomas defends power sharing and political participation, not as a right of the people to parliamentary consent nor as a means for protecting personal rights and liberties, but as the prudent application of natural law whose ends are best realized in a stable constitutional order dedicated to peace, virtue and Christian piety.'[86] This outlook, he suggested, was a case of 'medieval corporatism applied within the [Augustinian] doctrine of the Two Cities, rather than the first stirring of modern liberty'.[87] A number of scholars are of the view that if one examines both the intellectual and social history of the rise of the modern state and the Liberal political Tradition, the Franciscans Duns Scotus and William of Ockham have a much stronger claim to being the first Whig than the Dominican Thomas Aquinas.

Whatever of the intellectual history side of the debate the theological point in dispute is over how the proponents of a synthesis of liberalism and Thomism treat the relationship between nature and grace. The synthesis works best if one operates from a Stream One-type account of the relationship and does not work well at all if one begins from a Stream Three-type position.

The most comprehensive critique of Whig Thomism is found in David L. Schindler's works *Heart of the World, Soul of the Church* (1996) and *Ordering Love: Liberal Societies and the Memory of God* (2011). Schindler is not opposed to the separation of Church and State and to the recognition of many so-called civil liberties commonly associated with life in a Liberal democracy. Rather, Schindler's criticisms relate to the metaphysical and theological presuppositions underpinning Liberal political theory. In particular he is hostile to Cartesian metaphysics and to the Suárezian account of nature and grace. The latter undergirds the works of John Courtney Murray SJ (1904–67) who might be described as the most significant figure among proponents of this project, although his scholarship anteceded that of Michael Novak. In the following paragraphs Schindler juxtaposes the Murrayite approach to the grace and nature relationship with that of de Lubac:

> According to Murray: faith and grace do not determine the structures and processes of civil society: these are determined by reason, in the light of the lessons of experience. ... [The Church] does not aim to alter the finality of the state, but to enable the state to achieve its own finality as determined by its own nature. Conversely, for de Lubac, the state occupies no special 'secular' space beyond the operation of the law of the relations between nature and grace. It is from within that grace seizes nature. ... It is from within that faith transforms reason, that the Church influences the state.
>
> For Murray, grace's influence on nature takes the form of assisting nature to realise its own finality; the ends proper to grace and nature otherwise remain each in its own sphere. For de Lubac, on the contrary, grace's influence takes the form of directing nature from within to serve the end given in grace; the ends proper to grace and nature remain distinct, even as the natural end is placed within, internally subordinated to, the supernatural end. For Murray then, the result is an insistence on a dualism between citizen and believer, and on the sharpness of the distinction between eternal (ultimate) end and temporal (penultimate) ends. For de Lubac, on the contrary, the call to sanctity 'comprehends' the call to citizenship and all the worldly tasks implied by citizenship. The eternal end 'comprehends' the temporal ends.[88]

In implicit agreement with Schindler, William T. Cavanaugh has argued that the effect of Murray's extrinsicism is that 'Christian symbols must be run through the sausage-grinder of social ethics before coming out on the other end as publicly digestible policy'.[89] This places Catholic public intellectuals in a very difficult position in a time when there is no agreement about the nature of the *humanum*.

Outside of the United States the strongest proponent of the Whig Thomist project is the Australian jurist John Finnis. In his book *Aquinas* Finnis takes up the argument of Lord Acton and presents St Thomas as the first Liberal political theorist. Finnis is also a proponent and leading figure of what is called the New Natural Law school.

New Natural Law

John Finnis, Germain Grisez and Robert P. George are the names most closely associated with the project of offering a theory of natural law that is a fusion of the two-tiered account of nature and grace and faith and reason typical of Strand One-type Neo-Thomism, coupled with some Kantian elements borrowed from Strand Two-type Neo-Thomism (via Lonergan in the case of Grisez) and a novel Humean element not found in any other variety of Thomism. The key texts are Germain Grisez, *The Way of the Lord Jesus*, in three volumes (1983–97), John Finnis, *Natural Law and Natural Rights* (1980), *Human Rights and the Common Good: Collected Essays Volume III* (2011), *Religion and Public Reasons: Collected Essays* Volume V (2011) and Robert P. George, *Natural Law Theory* (1992) and *Natural Law, Liberalism and Morality: Contemporary Essays* (1996).

This group has forced natural law to be taken seriously in departments of law, philosophy and politics in mainstream universities, since Finnis and George are based at Oxford and Princeton respectively and therefore cannot be dismissed as mere religious cranks. However, when the focus is narrowed from the political success of this group in getting the concept of natural law to be taken seriously in elite academies to the issue of the place of the project within Thomist scholarship, the project has been criticised on a number of grounds. The most common criticisms are as follows: (i) it cedes too much ground to the Liberal tradition in its refusal to rank-order what the trio call 'the goods of human flourishing', (religion is one good of human flourishing but not an infrastructural good), and (ii) as a consequence, it offers a moral framework that can potentially be hooked up to any religious tradition, producing different concrete results depending on the foundational tradition, and (iii) it exaggerates the role of the intellect in moral judgement, or at least, is neglectful of the importance of the affective dimensions of the person.

In an article that addresses the tension between the Catholic and Liberal elements in the theory and which begins with lines from a folk song, 'I love Carolina, I love Angelina too, I can't marry them both, So what am I going to do?', Ernest Fortin A.A. ('Augustinians of the Assumption') (1923–2002) wrote:

> While Finnis and Grisez frequently borrow their terminology from the natural law tradition, theirs is anything but the traditional or 'conventional' natural law theory, combining as it does elements native to an assortment of distinct and competing moral systems. The emphasis on pre-moral goods smacks of Hobbes and the utilitarian tradition that grows out of him; the role assigned to practical reason, understood apart from any natural end or ends to which human beings might be ordered, recalls Kant and his present-day descendants; the place reserved for human 'flourishing' reminds us in a roundabout way of classical eudemonism; and the generous sprinkling of such terms as lifestyles, creativity, values authenticity, and commitment bears witness to the pervasive if unacknowledged influence of modern existential thought. ... The basic question is thus whether the final product is a genuine synthesis effected on the basis of a principle that transcends the plane of the original positions, or an eclectic compromise ultimately weaker than any of its individual components[90]

Russell Hittinger has argued that it is the second. Hittinger's critique is focused on Grisez's two-tiered account of human goods and human morals. According to Grisez there is first a theory of human goods, and second, there is a theory of morality proper. Hittinger argues that Grisez and Finnis offer no basis for how to get from one tier to the other; and further, that if there are no proper telic completions to humanity and the goods sought, then there is no compelling reason to opt for Aristotle or Aquinas rather than Nietzsche. As Ian Markham argued: 'You cannot assume a rationality and argue that there is no foundation to that rationality. Either God and rationality go or God and rationality stay: either Nietzsche or Aquinas, that is our choice.'[91] Of all the New Natural Law theorists Grisez has been the most explicit about his preference for an extrinsicist (Strand One Neo-Thomist) account of nature and grace. This is especially evident in his essay on 'The Natural End of Man' published in *The New Catholic Encyclopaedia*.

In addition to these criticisms which all relate in one way or another to the differences between Classical Thomistic natural law and New Natural Law, there are the criticisms that relate to the compatibility of post-Conciliar developments in the area of theological anthropology with presuppositions of the New Natural Law project. The Christocentrism of paragraph twenty-two of *Gaudium et spes*, (the hermeneutical key to *Gaudium et spes* according to St John Paul II) and the implicit rejection of the Suárezian account of Revelation by the Conciliar fathers in *Dei Verbum*, do not sit comfortably with the extrinsicist accounts of the grace and nature and faith and reason relationships at the base of the New Natural Law system. Rufus Black has noted that the New Natural Law theory emerges as a conceptual framework for ethical analysis, the actual character and content of which will be determined by the understanding of reality, that is, the world view, of the person who is using it.[92] Such a system is miles away from Christocentrism. While the New Natural Lawyers would say that there is nothing in their system that opposes approaching it with a Christocentric disposition (indeed, that Christocentrism is one of the possible ways of participating in the good of religion), the problem is that such a Christocentrism is 'tacked on', not infrastructural. In theological parlance it is said to be merely a 'moral Christocentrism', not the 'ontological Christocentrism' of *Gaudium et spes* twenty-two. For analyses of the difference between a mere moral Christocentrism and a deeper ontological Christocentrism, the publications of Livio Melina and David L. Schindler are key texts. Melina argues that the Christocentric principle 'must enter in at the level [of moral reflection] of the formal object: it cannot simply concern a new material content to be juxtaposed to that of the manualistic Tradition, or a project into which all content is resolved. It must rather enter in as a horizon, a point of view from which to illuminate the moral dynamism of Christian life.'[93] Another way to explain this is to say that a mere moral Christocentrism is consistent with a Strand One-type account of the relationship between nature and grace, and faith and reason, while a deeper ontological Christocentrism is consistent with a Strand Three-type account of the relationship between nature and grace, faith and reason.

Speaking generally of Catholic moral theology projects of the 1970s and 1980s Melina observed:

> The heavy emphasis on the rational and universal character of morality, the adoption of a Kantian notion of autonomy, and the prevalent attention granted to the human behavioural sciences led to a bracketing, if not an outright elimination of the specifically Christian element in morality. What occurred was a 'secularisation of morality', which was cut off from the determinative influence of faith: its epistemological character as a specifically theological science was undermined in both its sources and its methods.[94]

Melina is critical of the hyper-rationalism of both Kantian ethics and neo-scholasticism and argues that truth concerns 'not only his [man's] reason, but also his freedom and his affectivity'.[95] Accordingly, 'practical reason is not to be understood as a mere application of speculative knowledge, but as a specific mode of knowing the good, which arises from within the dynamism in which the subject is attracted to the good'.[96]

A final criticism of the New Natural Law project and Whig Thomism in general is Alasdair MacIntyre's argument that the task of transposing the natural law tradition of Classical Thomism into the language of natural right (the idiom of the Liberal tradition), which is one of the central projects of Whig Thomism, is counterproductive. MacIntyre's opposition to the transposition is directly related to his premise that rationality is tradition dependent. He argues that while liberals and Thomists might use the same terminology, they mean radically different things by the same concepts. In particular MacIntyre highlights the fact that the Liberal conception of natural right (i) has a mode of rational justification distinct from a teleological order at once commanded and created by God, (ii) is attached to individuals qua individuals, (iii) is taken to provide standards by which to judge the adequacy of systems of positive law and of a variety of social institutions, from a standpoint external to, and independent of, allegiance to that law or those social institutions, and (iv) is understood to impose constraints upon what goals may legitimately be pursued and how.[97] MacIntyre further argues that it is not merely a problem that such claims to rights must be secular and non-theological; they are also to be constructed so that, if warranted, they outweigh any claims that do appeal to theological considerations.[98] In the absence of a shared conception of the common good, MacIntyre believes that appeals to the rhetoric of rights will be nothing more than ideological shadow-boxing and that the overall effect of the natural right theory of the Liberal tradition is that it dissolves the bonds and undermines the authority of all institutions between the individual and the government, such as families, schools and churches.[99] It also causes a rather large amount of confusion for Catholics who have not studied jurisprudence since they are usually unaware that the Liberal understanding of human rights that dominates the public space is radically different from a Catholic understanding of human rights. When they hear Catholic leaders promoting human rights they assume that they are promoting Liberal human rights.

In the final analysis New Natural Law might be described as the most ambitious attempt of heroic lay scholars in Anglophone countries to try and contend with the Liberal tradition on its own terms. However it runs into internal (intra-ecclesial) criticism for not being consistent with contemporary magisterial teaching in the field of theological anthropology, which is far less rationalist than either Stream One- or Stream Two-type Thomism, and it runs into extra-ecclesial criticism from Liberal scholars for being too 'essentialist' and 'perfectionist'. Liberal and postmodern scholars see it as a Trojan horse for Catholic magisterial teaching and reject it.

At the beginning of the twenty-first century 'perfectionist liberalism' of which New Natural Law could be classified as a subclass, has been largely defeated by the proponents of 'political liberalism' who deny the existence of a universal human nature and therefore any possibility of a list of goods of human flourishing to which all members of the community might reasonably be expected to subscribe. William T. Cavanaugh and others have argued that contemporary political liberalism seeks to parody the Church, assuming to itself the authority to define good and evil.

The Thomism of Jacques Maritain

Significant antecedents to Whig Thomism were the later works of the French philosopher Jacques Maritain (1882–1973). Maritain was a champion of the project, amplified in the New Natural Law scholarship, of transposing the moral teachings of the Church from the language of the natural law to the language of natural rights. In his advice to the drafting committees of the United Nations' *Declaration of Human Rights*, Maritain took the view that it was possible to 'adopt a practical viewpoint and concern ourselves no longer with seeking the basis of philosophic significance of human rights but only their statement and enumeration'.[100] In other words, he was content to reach agreement about the words or lists of rights to be acknowledged by the United Nations even if there was no common understanding among the delegates to the drafting committee of the foundations of the rights so enumerated. Sumner Twiss notes that Maritain's views were explicitly invoked by the French delegate to the Third Committee debate to support the [Maoist] Chinese delegate's position on maintaining metaphysical and justificatory neutrality.[101]

The Maoists signed the *Universal Declaration on Human Rights* but the regime they represented still managed to murder some thirty-five million people between 1949 and 1975. Moreover, since the late 1940s it can no longer be presupposed that Christianity is the foundation of the cultures of the Western world (as they exist today) and thus the territory of rights has become a battle zone between proponents of rights theories based on different theoretical foundations. When there is no agreement about what a human person is, there is no possibility of a shared vision of human rights. John Paul II was aware of this problem. In a speech to the Vatican Diplomatic Corps in 1989 he observed that 'the 1948 Declaration does not contain the anthropological and moral basis for the human rights that it proclaims'.[102]

He then implored his diplomats to work on promoting the Christian understanding of human dignity based on sound anthropological and moral foundations.

In *Jacques Maritain: the Philosopher in Society*, James V. Schall SJ acknowledged that Maritain did not want the word 'rights' to depend on a purely voluntarist conception (i.e. whatever I will is my right) and that he was simply seeking to find a way to bridge the natural law–natural rights relationship so that he could legitimise the usefulness of both natural law and natural right in a consistent understanding.[103] He was not, in other words, trying to adopt a Liberal understanding of natural right and give it a Thomist blessing. As Thaddeus Kozinski explains: 'Maritain strategically attempts to adopt the rhetorical mode of modernity, with its insistence on individual rights, while retaining a traditional Thomistic conceptual foundation.'[104] The contemporary criticisms of Maritain's project relate not to the philosophical substance he tried to give to the concept of rights but to his naïveté about the possibility that people who no longer believe in God might adopt his interpretation of the meaning of human rights. Thus Schall concluded:

> Whether Maritain's tactic to retain the use of the words, while reformulating their meaning, is the best one seems less viable in the years since his death in 1973. Both rights and values are generally understood in a subjective manner that allows no objective component that would examine the meaning or content of the values or rights proposed by comparing them with natural law, the content of which is not solely formulated by the subjective will.[105]

There is therefore a spectrum of positions on the issue of the compatibility of the Liberal and Thomist traditions, from the Whig Thomists at one end, who want to claim St Thomas as the 'first Whig', to, at the other end, scholars such as Alasdair MacIntyre, who take Samuel Johnson's view that 'the devil was the first Whig'. Maritain is situated somewhere in the middle of the spectrum.

Apart from his huge contribution in the field of Catholic social theory Maritain is also known for his epistemological work *Distinguish to Unite*, subtitled *The Degrees of Knowledge*, first published in 1932. Here he went to some trouble to defend the value of the concept, which was later to be subjected to significant critique from the direction of Transcendental Thomism. His idea of a Thomistic Critical Realism expounded in this work was also later subjected to criticism by Étienne Gilson. Gilson's *Thomist Realism and the Critique of Knowledge* (first published in 1939) is generally regarded as offering an alternate Thomist approach to issues in epistemology from that of Maritain, on the one side, and the Transcendental Thomists, on the other. While the Transcendental Thomists have been criticised for kneeling before Kant, Maritain's 'distinguish in order to unite' maxim was for others too much of a nod in the direction of Descartes. The difference between Maritain's epistemology and Gilson's is thus yet another significant fault line in twentieth-century Thomism.

Laval or River Forest Thomism

The expressions 'Laval Thomism' and 'River Forest Thomism' are used interchangeably to refer to those that emphasise the philosophical side of Thomistic thought applied to the natural sciences. The most prominent names are Benedict Ashley OP (1915–2013), William A. Wallace OP (1918–2015), Charles de Koninck (1906–65) and James A. Weisheipl OP (1923–84). Koninck was a professor at the University of Laval in Quebec. River Forest is a suburb of Chicago that was the home of the Albertus Magnus Lyceum for Natural Science, which closed in 1969. A key article by Ashley is 'The River Forest School and the Philosophy of Nature Today'.[106] In this document Ashley lists several principles of the River Forest School, which may be summarised with the statement that River Forest/Laval scholars regard the insights of the natural sciences as epistemologically prior to metaphysics. All of the scholars in this category were in one way or another interested in the relationship between the natural sciences and theology.

Analytical Thomism

The scholars in this field are seeking to bring the ideas of St Thomas into the Tradition of Anglo-American 'analytical philosophy', which concentrates on an analysis of the meaning of concepts in philosophical language. Because of the seminal influence of Wittgenstein on this school, there is an overlap here with the term Wittgensteinian Thomism, which is strongly associated with the works of the Oxbridge philosophers Elizabeth Anscombe (1919–2001) and her husband Peter Geach (1916–2013). The expression 'analytical Thomism' was coined by John Haldane of St Andrew's University, but the methodology is usually traced back to the 'Geachcombes'. One of its achievements has been to foster the study of Thomist thought in prestigious universities such as Cambridge, Oxford, Edinburgh and St Andrews. Eleonore Stump, Bruce Marshall and John Haldane are leading 'Analytical Thomists'. Alasdair MacIntyre also received his early academic training in analytical philosophy, traces of which remain evident in his later explicitly Thomist publications where he is acutely sensitive to the issue that the same concept may mean something completely different in one author from its meaning in another. Today however, MacIntyre is more often described as an Augustinian and/or Romantic Thomist.

Augustinian Thomism

Augustinian Thomism is a label used to refer to the works of individual Thomist scholars who stand opposed to the influence of Kant on the Thomist Tradition, especially Kant's idea of defending Christian ethics without reference to Revelation. More generally Augustinian Thomists oppose the idea of bifurcating the philosophical and theological components of Thomist thought. They prefer the Augustinian idea of faith seeking understanding to the Kantian idea of keeping faith and reason chastely separated. For example, MacIntyre juxtaposes what he calls 'tradition-dependent rationality' to the notion of Enlightenment or Kantian-style rationality. Craig Hovey offers a good description of the mentality of the typical Augustinian Thomist in the following paragraph:

> It is fair to say that the independence of Kant's morality [from revelation] created something other than Christian morality – but this was not its precise goal. Its precise goal was not the creation of an alternative morality but the demonstration that all morality is necessarily independent of religion. It only takes, then, the existence of a rival to blow the enterprise wide open and to expose its pretentious neutrality and universality. This is not the place to detail how this has been done (to do so would in some sense simply be to recount the history of philosophy since the Enlightenment). Nevertheless, this very good point describes a great deal of MacIntyre's lifelong project: arguing that reason cannot be the way out of particular traditions since reason itself is always constituted by traditions, even those traditions against which reason sets itself most doggedly in the attempt to be free of them.[107]

Since Augustinian Thomists wish to keep the theological and philosophical components of the Thomist synthesis together they tend to be interested in issues in theological anthropology, for example, the faith and reason relationship, the nature and grace relationship, and the relationship between God and the human person brought into being through the sacramental economy. They are interested in the God–human relationship as it is in reality, not how it might have been theoretically, had this or that event in salvation history not taken place.

The label Romantic Thomist is often used interchangeably with Augustinian Thomist because Romantics are interested in affectivity, the movements of the human heart as it were, and they are also interested in history, memory and culture and have a strong aversion to rationalism in its various manifestations (which is not to say that they are opposed to reason per se). They believe that the human person was endowed by God with an intellect that is rational. They are not emotivists. They are simply hostile to an anthropology that seeks to place all of its emphasis upon the intellect to the exclusion of other activities of the soul. They oppose the Kleutgen-style reading of the Thomist corpus since it gives priority to epistemology and seeks to distil the philosophical components of Thomism from the theological.

Fribourg Thomism

The two leading names among the Fribourg (Switzerland) Thomists are Charles Journet OP (1891–1975) and Servais Pinckaers OP (1925–2008).

In 1924 Journet became the professor of Dogmatic Theology at the Grand Séminaire in Fribourg, a position he held until 1965 when Paul VI appointed him a Cardinal in time to participate in the last session of the Second Vatican Council. There he contributed to the debates on *Gaudium et spes* and *Dignitatis Humanae*. In 1926 he was the co-founder of the journal *Nova et Vetera*, which is now published in English as well as French and is a leading international journal of Thomist thought.

Journet's major areas of interest were ecclesiology, Mariology, ecumenism, political theology, and the mystery of Israel after the Holocaust. He was a friend of Jacques Maritain and his work is often treated as the theological supplement to Maritain's philosophy. He was especially influenced by Maritain's 'integral humanism' and quest to synthesise Thomism with aspects of Liberal political philosophy. In his most famous work, *The Church of the Word Incarnate*, he drew a distinction between two types of Christendom, one consecrational and one secular. The first was characteristic of medieval Europe; the second, he believed, was a desirable model for the contemporary world. In this he was essentially endorsing Maritain's work in *Man and the State*, though placing it in a more theological context. He was also influenced by the works of Francisco Marin-Sola OP (1873–1932) and Reginald Garrigou-Lagrange. His understanding of the relationship between nature and grace was heavily influenced by Strand One-type Neo-Thomism and accordingly he argued that unbaptised infants will never experience the beatific vision. (The Limbo hypothesis presupposes that there is such a thing as 'pure nature' and thus only works on the basis of a Strand One-type account of the nature and grace relationship.)

Servais Pinckaers, the second 'big name' in Fribourg Thomism, was born to a Dutch-speaking father and a Walloon mother and grew up in a Walloon region of Belgium. He was based at the University of Fribourg from 1975 until his death in 2008. Unlike Journet he was not in the Strand One Neo-Thomist mould. In 1952 he submitted his STL dissertation on de Lubac's *Surnaturel* and he retained in his moral theology a strong sensitivity to Lubacian-style critiques of the dualist tendencies in the Neo-Thomism influenced by Baroque-era commentaries. Against the tendency to mute the theological dimensions of the doctrine of natural law, Pinckaers emphasised that Catholic ethics transforms Aristotle, since 'the advent of divine revelation has occasioned a profound transformation in the doctrine of virtue according to which the first source of moral excellence is ... located in ... God through Christ'.[108] He noted that this transformation is evident in the doctrine of the infused moral virtues, which are not acquired by unaided human effort, but are implanted in the human person by the Holy Spirit. Accordingly, he argued that 'in moral theology, the point is not to observe the commandments of the Decalogue materially, to obey them so as to fulfil one's obligations or through a sense of duty; the point is to observe them out of love, with the heart'.[109]

Pinckaers believed that the lack of attention to the Sermon on the Mount in much of twentieth-century Catholic moral thought can be explained by the fact that it is not easily integrated into a systematisation of moral theology based on obligations. Whereas moral systems of obligation are by nature static, the teaching of the Sermon on the Mount is fundamentally dynamic: 'It is animated by a continuous tendency toward exceeding and surpassing, a tendency toward the progress and perfection of love in imitation of the Father's goodness'.[110] For Pinckaers 'there is no real separation between the moral part of the *Summa* and its two dogmatic parts: the doctrine on the Trinity, in particular on the Word and on the Holy Spirit, found in the *prima pars*, pertains to the morality set forth in the *secunda pars* that we can thus identify as Trinitarian and spiritual'.[111] Pinckaers claimed that in a parallel way, the doctrine of the *tertia pars* on Christ and the mystical Body is intimately linked to Aquinas's moral teaching, which is Christological and ecclesial.[112] Pinckaers' fundamentally Trinitarian framework for moral theology and the treatment of natural law within it thus provides an alternative from within the Dominican Tradition to various currents of Strand One-style Neo-Thomist natural law. His most famous work is *The Sources of Christian Ethics*.

Jean-Pierre Torrell's two volumes on St Thomas Aquinas, the first subtitled 'The Person and his Work' and the second, 'Spiritual Master', are also regarded as classics of the genre of Fribourg Thomism.

Torrell's student, Gilles Emery OP, has become a leading name in Trinitarian theology. In an interview conducted in 2002, Emery stated:

> I do not share the opinion of scholars thinking that the originality of Aquinas lies in the way he contextualized philosophy. I am happy to note today a rediscovery of the leading role of theology in Aquinas: he did theology, and when he did philosophy, he did philosophy without ceasing to be a theologian. Second, I am happy to note not only that the time of neo-scholasticism is over, but also that the time of interpreting Aquinas against neo-scholasticism is over as well. This makes us free to read Aquinas in a renewed way, without depending on problems foreign to him (and foreign to us)![113]

The influence of Servais Pinckaers is also strongly evident in the publications of Matthew Levering, editor of the English language version of the journal *Nova et Vetera,* and through his works 'Fribourg Thomism' enters the currents of contemporary American Catholic theology.

Toulouse Thomism

Since St Thomas is buried in *Le couvent des Jacobins* in Toulouse, it is not surprising that this French city remains a centre for Thomist scholarship. According to Serge-Thomas Bonino the spirit of the *contemporary* Toulousian milieu of Thomist scholars is characterised by four principal traits:

> First, its intention is to pursue zealously the fruitful work of historical-critical exegesis of Thomas's corpus, taking advantage of both the renewal of medieval studies and the shifts in interests connected with current theological developments. Second, it considers St. Thomas above all as a master of Christian wisdom and so puts its stress on the properly theological dimension of Thomism, with respect of the integrated autonomy of the philosophical undertaking and attention to the spiritual climate that should govern the exercise of theology. Third, it wishes to absorb, with discernment, the riches of 'living Thomism', that is to say the Thomistic tradition after St. Thomas, understood within a historical-critical perspective. Fourth, it aims to highlight the resources of the Thomistic tradition for contemporary theology and philosophy.[114]

One of the stars of the Toulouse milieu is Olivier-Thomas Venard OP, author of the trilogy: *Littérature et Théologie, La Langue de l'ineffable* and *Sacra Pagina*. Venard is a professor of New Testament Studies at the École Biblique in Jerusalem. John Milbank has written an extensive essay outlining Venard's appropriation of Aquinas entitled 'On "Thomistic Kabbalah"'. Milbank writes:

> In the first volume of his trilogy, *Littérature et Théologie*, Venard distinguishes four stages in the modern recovery of the exemplary thought of Thomas Aquinas. The first is the nineteenth-century neo-scholastic revival, which reacted against idealism, but failed to separate Aquinas from baroque scholastic recensions which were themselves partly responsible for the 'modernism' which this revival sought to resist. The second is the twentieth-century recovery of a more historically authentic Aquinas by Maritain, Gilson and Chenu, supplemented by the work of later writers who arrived at a better grasp of the neo-platonic element in this thought: Geiger, Fabro, Finance (besides Grabmann earlier, and, more recently, O'Rourke and Te Velde). The third he identifies as a new grasp on an understanding of historicity *internal* to Aquinas's texts, which goes along with a stronger emphasis on Aquinas as theologian and Aquinas as biblical commentator – he mentions O-H Pesch and one could add Serge-Thomas Bonino and others in his own Toulouse school.
>
> The fourth stage in Thomistic studies distinguished by Venard is the appreciation of Aquinas as a *writer* – allied to an understanding of his spirituality. This stage, as Venard acknowledges, has been inaugurated by the work of Jean-Pierre Torrell.
>
> It is this phase which Venard himself is trying further to develop. The discussions of Aquinas's poetry and rhetoric in the first volume are but preparatory to a discussion of Aquinas's explicit and implicit theory of language and theory of sacred scripture as language in the second and third volumes respectively.[115]

Venard's work is still largely unavailable in English translation, though there are at least two significant essays – 'On the Religious Imagination and Poetic Audacity of Thomas Aquinas' – and 'Under what conditions could there be a Literary Thomism'?[116] In the latter of these Venard sets out the methodological framework for his 'Literary Thomism'. In this he argues that science in the Middle Ages was primarily a matter of discourse and, as a consequence, for St Thomas, science was 'less a matter of discursive logic deployed from propositional principles than it is the self-disclosure of an actually existing object'.[117] The works of St Thomas, he suggests, need to be studied as an architecture of words as much as an architecture of ideas.[118] In an age dominated by the hermeneutics of suspicion, Venard responds that Literary Thomism is 'not content to merely restate, in a reactionary manner, the obvious contradictions of relativism, nor simply to endorse the Aristotelian semantic triangle'.[119] Rather, 'faithful to the intra-textual hermeneutics of *sacra doctrina* and the attentiveness of St Thomas to language, it perceives the *theological* dimension of the objections to metaphysics (and every speculative theology) raised by linguistic deconstruction, and, from its own linguistic meditation, opens up the way towards a renewed (non-"foundational") trust in language'.[120]

Christocentric Thomism

The label 'Christocentric Thomist' is often given to contemporary moral theologians who are following in the trajectory of the third stream of Neo-Thomism and resetting moral theology on firm Christological foundations with specific reference to the Christology of Aquinas. Leading examples include Cardinal Carlo Caffarra, as expressed in his *Living in Christ*; Livio Melina, as found in his *Sharing in the Virtues of Christ*; Olivier Bonnewijn, as presented in his *La béatitude et les béatitudes dans la Prima Secundae de la Somme Théologique de saint Thomas. Élements pour une théologie morale de l'agir excellent*; Oana Gotia, exemplified in her *L'amore e il suo fascino: Bellezza e castità nella prospettiva di san Tommaso de'Aquino;* and Joel Wallace, as found in his *Charity, the Source of Christ's Action according to Thomas Aquinas*. José Noriega, Antonio Prieto-Lucena, José Manuel Horcajo-Lucas and Juan-José Pérez-Soba are leading Spanish Christocentric Thomists interested in integrating Christology with an understanding of human action. Each of these authors has a strong interest in the theological anthropology of Karol Wojtyła/John Paul II, especially as it is presented in his suite of Trinitarian encyclicals, beginning with *Redemptor Hominis*, and in his moral theology encyclicals, especially *Veritatis splendor*. The Christocentric Thomists are each seeking to address issues in contemporary moral theology by reference to insights to be found in St Thomas's Christology. At the foundation of much of their work is what Joseph Ratzinger called 'the daring new theological anthropology' to be found in *Gaudium et spes*, especially paragraphs twenty-two to twenty-four. They regard Thomistic Trinitarian theology as a valuable resource in need of retrieval with reference to contemporary moral problems. These types tend to follow Wojtyła and Ratzinger's preference for Strand Three-type Thomism, and then valorise dimensions of Thomistic Christology and apply them to contemporary pastoral problems.

Postmodern Thomism or Thomas after Heidegger

Within the broader realm of postmodern theology a major issue for the post-Conciliar generations has been dealing with the Heideggerian charge that Aquinas committed the error of 'onto-theology' (the attempt to make the mysteries of Divine Revelation fit within an already existing philosophical world view). In *Aquinas: an Interpretation* John Milbank and Catherine Pickstock sought to defend Aquinas against this charge. John D. Caputo also mounted at least a partial defence of Aquinas by amplifying the more mystical dimensions of Thomist thought and thereby drawing attention to the importance he gave to *intellectus* and mystical intuition. The mystical dimensions of the works of St Thomas were also highlighted by Graham McAleer in his *Ecstatic Morality and Sexual Politics,* which seeks to construct a bridge between Thomist metaphysics and the Nuptial Mystery theology found in John Paul II's *Catechesis on Human Love.* The subject of the relationship of Aquinas to onto-theology has also been a recurring motif in the work of Jean-Luc Marion, who initially read Aquinas as an exponent of onto-theology but has in later works reached the alternative verdict. None of these authors normally carry the label of 'Thomist', but they have made substantial contributions to the field of theology through their engagements with Aquinas with reference to issues in contemporary theology.

In his essay 'American Catholic Theology at Century's End: Postconciliar, Postmodern and Post-Thomistic' Di Noia noted that postmodern theology, in the sense of theology that seeks to think outside of modernity's boundaries, (i) rejects the modern quest for a foundation for all knowledge, modelled on mathematical or scientific paradigms of rationality, (ii) insists on the centrality of Tradition and authority in legitimating and supporting truth and rationality, and (iii) seeks to secure the objectivity and realism of knowledge with reference to a shared world of meaning and truth embodied in the linguistic practices of a community. Di Noia concluded that 'read straightforwardly – rather than in the modernizing construal given him by transcendental Thomism – Aquinas supports precisely this displacement of the Cartesian separation of mind and matter, of spirit and body, of subject and object, and of moral self and moral agent'.[121] 'Postmodern Thomism' can therefore be construed as a label to cover the interest in the appropriation of Thomist ideas to overcome the above dualisms. It is not 'postmodern' in the popular sense of an affirmation of relativism.

Conclusion

Some five decades after the Second Vatican Council, a key issue for Catholic theologians is what to make of St Thomas's legacy. Included in that question are subsidiary issues – for example, are you for or against Suárez and are you for or against Kant? Another highly important question is this: 'How do you appropriate Heidegger?' In other words, do you want to convict or acquit Aquinas on the charge of onto-theology? This in turn raises the baseline issue of how one understands the relationship between philosophy and theology in the work of Aquinas, and in particular how one reads the Aristotelian contribution. As Mark Jordan argued: 'How one describes Aristotle in Thomas reveals how one situates Thomas's thought with regard to philosophy and how one narrates the historical life of philosophy or justifies the usefulness of pagan science after the preaching of the Gospel.'[122] Further, there is the question, if you are for Aquinas, do you want to take him neat or do you want to add other ingredients? And if you do want to add other ingredients, which ones do you want to add? Do you want to synthesise Thomist thought with intellectual ingredients from another tradition of another century and if so, which ones?

Quite a number of the many appropriations summarised in this chapter are compatible with each other and simply focus on different facets of the works of St Thomas. Aspiring young millennial generation scholars who seek to work within this Tradition would be well advised to learn French since much of the really creative work in this field is coming from Francophone scholars in Toulouse and Fribourg.

The *Communio* Approach

The event of the Second Vatican Council had the effect of doing away with the idea that Catholic theology was a monolithic intellectual system. The luminaries among the Conciliar *Periti* all agreed on this but as the decade of the 1960s wore on it became apparent that the leading theologians of the Church could agree only on their opposition to the pre-Conciliar 'monolithic system', not on alternative ways forward. The tensions became stretched to their limits at the *Concilium* World Congress in Brussels in 1970. Many of the European *Periti* were members of the editorial board of the journal *Concilium* founded in 1965 by Anton van den Boogaard, Paul Brand, Yves Congar, Hans Küng, Johann Baptist Metz, Karl Rahner and Edward Schillebeeckx. Just prior to the Congress in September 1970, Hans Küng published his book *Infallibility?* Karl Rahner did not like it, and Küng's proposal to have an edition of *Concilium* dedicated to the issue of papal infallibility was rejected. During the Congress Rahner communicated his negative appraisal of Küng's work to Walter Kasper and Kasper carted Rahner's comments back to Küng.[1] Later, in November 1970, Rahner published his criticisms of Küng's ideas in the journal *Stimmen der Zeit* and in this article he claimed that he was no longer able to relate to Hans Küng as a fellow Catholic scholar but had to relate to him as if he were a liberal Protestant or mere sceptical philosopher.[2] Cracks were beginning to widen between the theological trajectories of the Conciliar generation of theologians.

One of the Congress participants, Cornelius Ernst OP (1924–77), published an account of his experience of the event in *New Blackfriars*. Ernst complained that the organisers had conceived of the Congress as a political event, an exercise to put pressure on Church authorities; that they had drawn up resolutions prior to the meeting which they then attempted to ram through the Congress amidst much opposition and rancor; that there was no daily Mass; that the Sunday Mass was delayed for the benefit of the media and taken over by a 'choir of Belgian school-children singing bouncy tunes'; and that undergirding this whole unedifying spectacle was a theory about the nature of theology itself. According to Ernst the idea was that the essential function of theology is to act as a critique of society, including the society of the Church. It was a view of theology as a critical *praxis*, a theological analogue to the work of the Frankfurt School of sociology.[3]

At the Brussels Congress it was also rumoured that Hans Urs von Balthasar, Joseph Ratzinger and Marie-Joseph Le Guillou OP (1920–90) were planning to start an alternative journal. That journal came into being in 1972 with Balthasar, Ratzinger and Henri de Lubac as the key foundation members. In Italy they received logistical assistance from members of the new ecclesial movement *Communione e Liberazione* (known colloquially as 'CL') founded by Luigi Giussani (1922–2005). Joseph Ratzinger recalls that the name *Communio* was of CL provenance.

In his *Meine Schriften im Rückblick* (My Works in Retrospect) de Lubac spoke of these times in the following, almost apocalyptic manner:

> Destructive machinations discover a dual complicity that fosters yet further the devastation they cause. On the one hand this complicity consists in a false conception of 'openness to the world', which brazenly proclaims itself as the concern of the Council, thereby stripping the faithful people of precisely that which has ever been the strength of Christians most engaged in the world: the knowledge of their obligation to be the life-conveying soul of this world, in order to make Christians of the destitute, faceless beings in their wake. On the other hand, it consists in a shocking state of crisis regarding intelligence and culture – particularly prevalent in numberless clerics – which delivers them up, defenceless, to the most contradictory speculations; to the most presumptuous fantasies, often as flashy as cheap trumpery. This is abundantly confirmed by visits to Catholic bookstores and the delivery of countless reproductions of private or even official provenance. Attempts to ward off this latter aspect of the crisis are being undertaken by – among others – two of my friends: the philosophers Etienne Borne and Claude Bruaire (†1985). One is also acquainted – I need not emphasise it here – with the principal role played by Father, later Cardinal, Daniélou. He gave one of his final books the title: *La culture trahie par les siens*. The self-same volition – to begin anew – also stands at the origin of the 'International Catholic Journal *Communio*', which has been founded by a group of German theologians, first and foremost Joseph Ratzinger and Hans Urs von Balthasar (†1988).[4]

Communio in contrast to *Concilium*

Reference has already been made to Philip Trower's observation that since the 1970s the journals *Concilium* and *Communio* have become the two poles towards which theologians tend to gravitate, and through which they undertake a theological star wars over the heads of the faithful.[5] As a generalisation, the star wars metaphor is appropriate. For some two decades after the Council, from its closure in 1965 until the Synod assessing its reception in 1985 and beyond, lay Catholics were presented with different and often conflicting accounts of what the Council was all about, depending on the clerical and parochial circles in which they moved, and the theological circles in which the leaders of these circles were formed. In so many situations a particular interpretation could be tracked back to articles in either *Concilium* or *Communio*.

In shorthand terms *Concilium* stood for the 'spirit of the Council' – a general openness to new ideas of every kind – and for what Ratzinger was to label a 'hermeneutic of rupture' – an interpretation of the Council as a radical irruption in Church history for which, according to Karl Rahner, the only precedent was the Council of Jerusalem in 49 AD. *Communio* on the other hand stood for what Ratzinger called 'the hermeneutic of reform' (rather than revolution or rupture). In some places Ratzinger/Benedict used the alternative expression 'hermeneutic of continuity'. Both expressions refer to an interpretation of the Conciliar documents that views them as merely reforming certain aspects of the intellectual presentation of the faith to overcome a lopsided emphasis on one or other teaching, or to overcome a dualistic mode of thinking, or to place Church teachings on stronger scriptural and Christological foundations but in no sense overturning centuries of settled dogmatic teaching. Where *Concilium* authors tended to discuss Church teaching with reference to the 'spirit of the times', usually the *zeitgeist* of the 1960s, *Communio* authors tended to reflect upon theological questions with reference to the whole intellectual history of a doctrine or practice from Patristic times to the present, and to approach such studies with a disposition of respect for the received teaching. In some cases *Communio* authors would regard the teaching as having been derailed or unnecessarily ossified at some point and would suggest reforms or a deepening of the Tradition by reference to new scholarship, but their approach was never one of regarding the 'spirit of the times' as ipso facto something to which Church teaching should be adapted as a matter of principle blessed by the Second Vatican Council.

Two different interpretations of the 'signs of the times'

Authors associated with each of the journals had fundamentally different interpretations of the meaning of the passage in the Gospels of St Matthew and St Luke where Christ exhorts his disciples to read the signs of the times.

According to Ratzinger and his *Communio* colleagues, the best exegesis of these passages is that Christ was telling his disciples to be aware that he, Christ, was the sign of their time. In an article published in 1969 Ratzinger noted that article two of the Zurich text of the Conciliar document *Gaudium et spes* had attempted to justify the whole notion of the Church's dialogue with 'the world' by means of the scriptural reference to reading the signs of the times (Mt. 16.3; Lk. 12.56). However, this earlier draft was rejected by the Council Fathers as bad exegesis. Nonetheless, the idea became a *leitmotiv* of many of the scholars associated with the *Concilium* journal. Although this might seem like a small issue, in fact one could say that it is the most fundamental issue dividing the typical *Communio* scholar from the typical *Concilium* scholar. The typical *Communio* scholar wants to read the Second Vatican Council as an event that emphasised the importance of Christocentrism and therefore the renewal of theological anthropology and Trinitarian theology. The typical *Concilium* scholar wants to read the Second Vatican Council as an event that exhorted Catholics to be aware of the signs of the times and to enter into dialogue with the world on the world's terms.

Writing in a 2005 edition of *Concilium* José Comblin noted that the Council's references to the signs of the times are found in *Gaudium et spes* 4a; 11a and 44b; in *Presbyterorum ordinis* 9b; in *Unitatis redintegratio* 4a; and in *Apostolicam actuositatem* 14c, and he acutely observed that these references are very ambiguous. He suggested that '"the signs of the times" were understood by John XXIII and the Council in two different senses which are not always clearly distinguished' and that 'the relationship between the two is still somewhat indistinct.'[6] Comblin distinguished the two senses as, first, the idea of signs as indications of movements in contemporary Western society, and secondly, the idea of signs in the eschatological meaning of biblical passages like Matthew 16.4. Comblin concluded that in the Conciliar documents and papal speeches of the early 1960s the two senses were often conflated and the problem of how an acceptance of and adaption to the trends of the modern world would fall within the framework of Christian eschatology was not generally considered.[7] Ratzinger and his *Communio* colleagues were the exceptions to the general trend of conflating the two meanings. For Ratzinger, there was only one viable exegesis and that was an eschatological one, and Balthasar was equally contemptuous of the non-eschatological reading. As early as 1965 he was aware of the issue and wrote:

> The Church, they say, to appear credible, must be in tune with the times. If taken seriously, that would mean that Christ was in tune with the times when he carried out his mission and died on the Cross, a scandal to the Jews and folly to the Gentiles. Of course, the scandal took

place in tune with the times – at the favourable times of the Father, in the fullness of time, just when Israel was ripe, like fruit ready to burst, and the Gentiles were ready to receive it on their own soil. Modern is something Christ never was, and God willing, never will be.[8]

Underlying this emphatic 'No!' to the project of making contemporary social movements a lodestar to which theologians should correlate Church teaching are theological precepts that one can find set out in the *Catechism of the Catholic Church* under the heading 'there will be no further revelation' in paragraphs sixty-six to sixty-eight. These principles include the statements that the Christian economy is 'the new and definitive covenant' and that 'no new public revelation is to be expected before the glorious manifestation of our Lord Jesus Christ'. This idea that the Revelation of Christ brought to completion a 'definitive covenant' meant for Balthasar that the covenant did not require additives or supplements from contemporary social theory and should not be correlated to it.

The genealogy of secularism

The scholars who provided the intellectual leadership for the establishment of *Communio* did not offer some alternative systematic theology badged '*Communio* theology'. They were not offering a new grand synthesis. Ratzinger, for example, described his own work in the following terms:

I have never tried to create a system of my own, an individual theology. What is specific, if you want to call it that, is that I simply want to think in communion with the faith of the Church, and that means above all to think in communion with the great thinkers of faith. The aim is not an isolated theology that I draw out of myself but one that opens as widely as possible into the common intellectual pathway of the faith. For this reason exegesis was always very important. I couldn't imagine a purely philosophical theology. The point of departure is first of all the word. That we believe the word of God, that we try really to get to know and understand it, and then, as I said, to think it together with the great masters of the faith.[9]

This approach to 'doing theology' is typical of *Communio* scholars. Often they begin with a contemporary pastoral problem and then comb through the relevant scriptural exegesis and Patristic, medieval and more contemporary writing on the topic or ancillary topics to get a bird's eye perspective on the issue, and then they zero in on what they perceive to be the key issues in need of reflection and refinement. In doing so they either implicitly or explicitly follow Newman's criteria or something similar to it, in discerning whether or not an idea could represent a legitimate development of a doctrine rather than a disintegrative solvent of the doctrine.

Nonetheless, while not offering a specific step-by-step methodology, implicit within much *Communio* scholarship is a common understanding of the causes of the current 'crisis of the West'. There is, in other words, a particular set of judgements about how secularism arose and the intellectual foundations of the contemporary culture wars in the countries of the developed Western world. This common reading of the causes of the crisis was well summarised in the following passage by +Javier Martinez who was in his youth a protégé of Luigi Guissani, the founder of *Communio e Liberazione*:

> Once the analogy of being and the idea of being as participation in being was rejected by Duns Scotus in the thirteenth century and was substituted by the idea of the univocity of being, God had necessarily to be 'separated' from the world, and at the same time, he had to be reduced to 'a being' among others. ... This move was accompanied by other intellectual changes needed or provoked by it, all of which were loaded with consequences: human beings began to understand themselves and their relationship with the world as a 'copy' of this infinitely intelligent, powerful and capricious being that usurped the name of the Christian God.[10]

Similarly, Kevin J. Vanhoozer has summarised Balthasar's criticism of Scotus's univocity of being doctrine in the following words:

> Epistemologically, it provides a *magna carta* for reason to undertake an independent study of all that has being without having recourse to revelation; the metaphysical project – the attempt to gain knowledge of being, including God, through reason – here achieves legitimacy. The 'God' thus known, however, is only a conceptual idol manufactured by human reason; and the 'God' proclaimed dead or unbelievable by Nietzsche is, likewise, only the construction of modern 'ontotheology'. On this account, then, the deconstructive or nihilist versions of postmodernity are actually the logical culmination of basically modern tendencies.[11]

+Martinez went on to explain that one significant consequence of this move towards the univocity of being is that one's own ego becomes the absolute and the relationship between one ego and another becomes dominated by 'instrumental reason'. Another consequence is that nature becomes 'a mere artefact, first of God, and finally, a commodity for human consumption'. Nature can no longer be a sign of anything else and this in turn sets up a barrier to a sacramental reading of nature.

This pathology is in turn fostered by movements in Baroque theology that brought about a radical separation between 'nature' and the 'supernatural'. This particular part of the genealogy of secularism comes straight from the works of de Lubac in which Francisco Suárez features as the chief villain, aided and abetted by a platoon of Dominicans promoting a *natura pura*. The most significant work here is de Lubac's publication, *Surnaturel: Études historiques,* written during the final stages of the Second World War while de Lubac was in hiding from the Gestapo. The work offers an intellectual history of the use of the concept of the 'supernatural' in Catholic theology, along with the concept of 'pure nature'. Themes in this work were later amplified and clarified in *Le mystère du surnaturel* (1965) and *Petite catéchèse sur Nature et Grâce* (1980). Specifically de Lubac argued that neither the early Church Fathers nor Thomas Aquinas ever maintained that human persons have a purely natural end attainable by their own powers of intellect and will. These ideas he traced back to Denys the Carthusian (1402–71) and the Dominican Cajetan (1469–1534). In a review of *Surnaturel* Joseph Huby (1878–1948) summarised the thesis in the following paragraph:

> By supporting the possibility of a substantial natural order, giving satisfaction to the needs and desires of nature, by presenting the latter as a well-closed whole, having the power to achieve its own balance, it made the supernatural order something superfluous, which man was tempted to do without, since this supernatural found no anticipation, no desire, no aspiration in him. This conception of the supernatural as a superstructure coming to rest from outside on an edifice that stands on its own opened the way to a philosophy and a morality that were separate, constituted in complete independence not only of any positive revelation but of any fundamental orientation of the soul to the beatific vision.[12]

The politically explosive nature of *Surnaturel* lay not merely in its deviation from the neo-scholastic 'two-tiered' construction of the orders of nature and grace but also in its conclusion that this construction was a contributing factor in the emergence of secularism.

In short, although the *Communio* scholars are not offering an alternative step-by-step method for doing theology, they do share, in their intellectual

DNA, a rather negative attitude towards the influence of Duns Scotus, especially his doctrine of the univocity of being; towards Francisco Suárez, especially his understanding of the end(s) of human nature and the nature of Revelation; towards any version, whether of Jesuit or Dominican provenance of the *natura pura* concept; and towards Immanuel Kant, especially his ideas about 'religion within the limits of reason alone', that is, his project to sever any intrinsic relationship between faith and reason.

This point is significant because not all theologians who describe themselves as Catholics would accept this 'pathology report' on contemporary Western culture. Some would want to defend Scotus, or Suárez and Baroque scholasticism in general and/or Kant. Others would say that de Lubac was right to go to war against the two-tiered system but that he mistakenly conflated Cajetan with Garrigou-Lagrange, failing to detect the subtle differences between them. Yet others would say that they accept the genealogical analysis but differ from the *Communio* theologians in the value they place on the developments. Whereas the *Communio* scholars read the intellectual history as a downward spiral into the abyss of nihilism and as such nothing less than an epic theo-dramatic tragedy, other theologians take the view that this process of secularisation has been a positive development. As +Martinez explains, there is the view that 'this process was not only an unavoidable process but also a desirable one, one that was in the last resort inscribed in the very nucleus of the Christian faith, and that it finally permitted the autonomy of the created world to shine and the world to be simply as it is'.[13] This was the view taken by the Conciliar *Peritus* Bernard Lambert OP (1921–2004) who was associated with the drafting of *Gaudium et spes*. Lambert argued that the sociological phenomenon of secularisation 'carries through the logical development of creation'.[14] He defined secularisation as 'the process by which a society frees itself from religious notions, beliefs or institutions which used to order its existence', adding that 'society now is constituted as an autonomous society and finds in its own consistency, methods, structures and laws for its own organisation'.[15] This second view, which draws on *Gaudium et spes* (paragraph thirty-six) for its legitimacy, is more typical of scholars associated with the *Concilium* journal. The idea is particularly strong in the publications of Karl Rahner. Writing in *Thought*, a journal of the Jesuits' Fordham University, Patrick J. Lynch SJ observed:

> Although this process [secularisation] has caused anxiety within the Christian religious tradition, one of the most respected Roman Catholic theologians of the twentieth century, Karl Rahner, has found this process a source of hope – a way for manifesting more fully the power and glory of God in the world. Instead of viewing secularization as a threat to God's activity in the world, he sees it as a change in the

way in which people discover God's action within both themselves and the world.[16]

While *Concilium* scholars tend to follow in the line of Lambert and Rahner on this issue of secularisation, Thomists (of almost every species except the small number following Rahner) agree with the *Communio* scholars that secularisation is a bad development. However Stream One-type Thomists reject that part of the *Communio* metanarrative that holds the intellectual moves in Baroque-era scholasticism to be partly responsible for the secularisation of Western culture. Stream One-type Thomists do not have an alternative metanarrative or explanation of how Western civilisation became so militantly anti-Christian apart from the fact that some key social players had bad wills and poor intellects. They do argue however that secularism got inside the tent of the Church because the barriers set up against it by the Leonine Thomists, building on the work of the Baroque scholastics, got torn down by de Lubac and his *Communio* colleagues. Once the neo-patristic camel got his nose under the flap of the tent, the result could only be chaos. The *Communio* theologians respond to this argument by saying that the strategy of building Baroque barricades was about as effective as sending in the Polish cavalry against Nazi tanks, that is, well meaning and heroic, but ultimately not successful. To change the animal metaphors, the *Communio* theologians think that the Stream One-type Thomists have their heads in the sand ostrich-style if they believe they can defend the faith without addressing the issue of the mediation of history in the realm of ontology.

Both groups accept that intellectual wars can only be won intellectually. Stream One-type Thomists tried to answer the militant rationalists on the rationalist's own terms, that is, according to the rationalist's own canons of rationality, while the *Communio* theologians believed that this strategy was inherently flawed because it required Catholics to begin from presuppositions at odds with Christian anthropology and which carried within them a secularist or a-theistic logic. Moreover, *Communio* theologians tend to regard the postmodern turn against rationalism (which is especially strong in Europe, though not as strong in the United States) as rendering the kinds of pragmatic apologetic arguments marshalled by the Stream One-type Thomists obsolete. The very last way that anyone might convert a postmodern is through a rationalist apologetics.

Reason linked to a higher eros or Kant as villain

A hallmark of postmodernism is its acceptance of Theodor Adorno and Max Horkheimer's thesis in *The Dialectic of Enlightenment*. The thesis may be summed up in the proposition that 'Kant led to the Somme and Auschwitz' or 'eighteenth-century rationalism has a propensity for violence'. Quite a number of Catholic scholars have since agreed with this judgement and do not wish to defend the faith at the Bar of Kantian rationality. This is especially true of the *Communio* scholars for whom the aversion to Kant is very strong. While Stream One-type Thomists are not Kantians, they have bought into the Kantian strict separation of faith and reason and this means that they differ from the *Communio* theologians in their understanding of how faith and reason are related.

The Anglican theologian, John Milbank, has described the difference between what he calls the 'neo-scholastics' and *Communio* theologians as a difference between a classical and a romantic orthodoxy:

> The 'romantics' think that the collapse of a reason linked to the higher *eros* led to the debasement of scholasticism and then to secular modernity. Resistance to the latter had therefore to oppose rationalism and even to insist more upon the role of the 'erotic' – the passions, the imagination, art, *ethos* etc. than had been the case up till and including Aquinas. ... The exponents of 'classicism' on the other hand (largely located in the United States) trace secularity simply to a poor use of reason and regard the scholastic legacy, mainly in its 'Thomistic' form, as sustaining a true use of reason to this very day. ... The conflict between these two parties is therefore one between opposed metanarratives.[17]

Specifically, the romantically orthodox *Communio* scholars trace the current theological crises to dualisms that had their origins in fourteenth-century scholasticism (as +Martinez argued), and which came to the fore in the post-Tridentine era, and to issues that were the unfinished business of the Councils of Trent (1545–63) and Vatican I (1869–70). The neo-scholastics want to defend Baroque-era scholasticism and blame de Lubac and his *Communio* colleagues for the current theological crises because they undermined the stable pre-Conciliar edifice. What one group reads as 'stable' and 'certain' and 'rational', the other group reads as 'ossified', 'pastorally ineffectual' and based on an anthropology that gives a lopsided emphasis to discursive reasoning in human decision-making.

Milbank has suggested that a reason why contemporary proponents of scholasticism are found mostly in the United States may be that 'the United States never had a nineteenth century'. By this he means that the intellectual, political and economic culture of the United States is very much a product of the rationalism of the eighteenth century rather than a product of the romanticism of the nineteenth century. The latter had a seminal influence on twentieth and now twenty-first century European culture but failed to make the Atlantic crossing. The difference in sensibility may also have something to do with the different reactions to the First and the Second World Wars. After his experience of the First World War the German theologian Paul Tillich wrote:

> All that horrible, long night I walked along the rows of dying men, and much of my German classical education philosophy broke down that night – the belief that man could master cognitively the essence of his being, the belief in the identity of essence and existence.[18]

Although the American experience of the wars would have been no less traumatic, the reaction was not one of disillusionment with the Enlightenment project. America did not cause either world war. Americans were dragged into a European catastrophe to bring it to an end.

In stark contrast, European intellectuals often trace the belief in the 'rationality' of the violence of the First and Second World Wars back to Kant. The claim was made as early as 1914 by Vladimir Ern in his famous 'From Kant to Krupp' lecture.[19] Artur Mrówczyński-Van Allen has observed that the conclusions of Ern were later echoed in an essay by the Polish philosopher Leszek Kołakowski (1927–2009). Kołakowski described the 'recurrent German philosophical desire as one which consists in the attempt to discover God without God, to find secular and transcendental foundation for moral and epistemological security apart from God'.[20] Balthasar was of the view that at a certain moment in the eighteenth century the German intelligentsia had a choice between following Goethe and following Kant, and the predominant choice of Kant over Goethe was a decisive event in the narrative of the secularisation of German culture.

There is therefore in the world of German letters a convergence of anti-Kantian criticism from anti-liberal Catholics on the one side and Frankfurt School-style Marxists on the other. Both identify a link between Kantian rationality and social violence.

The reading of the relationship between philosophy and theology

Far from wanting to keep philosophy and theology separated *Communio* theologians often draw faith and reason together into a symbiotic or intrinsic relationship. This is strongly evident in the scholarship of Joseph Ratzinger. In this context it is said that his approach accords more with the Thomism of Josef Pieper and Étienne Gilson than with the so-called Aristotelian (Stream

One) Thomism. Pieper never accepted a sharp dichotomy between theology and philosophy.

In his *Theology of Karl Barth*, Balthasar drew attention to Pieper's following introductory remarks in *The End of Time*:

> It is a peculiarity of philosophical inquiry, inherent in the matter itself, that it stands from the outset in a fully-fledged 'contrapuntal' relationship to theology; there is no philosophical question which, if it really wants to strike the ground intended by itself and in itself, does not come upon the primeval rock of theological pronouncements.[21]

Similarly, in his 1969 essay on *Gaudium et spes,* Ratzinger explicitly rejected the notion of 'pure reason'. He stated that reason can be either impure or purified but never pure in the sense of theologically neutral. He commended Augustine for his recognition that the 'necessary purification of sight takes place through faith (Acts 15.9) and through love, at all events not as a result of reflection alone and not at all by man's own power'.[22] In 1996 he reiterated this judgement in a speech delivered to the bishops of Mexico at a time when he was the Prefect of the Congregation for the Doctrine of the Faith:

> It is my view that the neo-scholastic rationalism that was trying to reconstruct the *praeambula fidei*, with pure rational certainty, by means of rational argument that was strictly independent of any faith, has failed; and it cannot be otherwise for any such attempts to do that kind of thing.[23]

In this context there are also strong resonances between Ratzinger and Rousselot. In the following passage Alan Vincelette explains that for Rousselot the so-called preambles of the faith can certainly point to the truth, but to arrive safely at the truth one needs more than these preambles; one needs 'the eyes of faith' and hence supernatural grace:

> Rousselot argues that faith is rational, i.e., that there are good reasons for believing (the preambles of the faith) and so that grace perfects nature, but that these reasons are only discernible (or at least discernible with a certainty and not a mere probability) through supernatural grace. ... In Rousselot's own words, 'the infused gift of faith, by elevating intelligence, allows it to discern supernaturally the signs of the supernatural world in sensible things'. ... So while the credibility of faith is rationally demonstrable, this cannot be perceived with certainty without a supernatural light. ... Rousselot also links his theory of connatural knowledge with his theory of faith. He argues

that grace gives us new eyes to see by providing us with a love or an appetite (a connatural or sympathetic intelligence) that imparts its own coloration to perceived objects.[24]

Ratzinger's pre-papal position, expressed in the speech to the bishops of Mexico, is further elaborated in paragraph thirty of his encyclical *Caritas in Veritate* (2009). As Pope Benedict, Ratzinger makes the claim that 'knowledge is never purely the work of the intellect'. While 'it can certainly be reduced to calculation and experiment', if it 'aspires to be wisdom capable of directing man in the light of his first beginnings and his final ends, it must be "seasoned" with the "salt" of charity'. Moreover, he emphasises that charity is not an added extra, like an appendix to work already concluded in each of the various disciplines: it engages them in dialogue from the very beginning. In effect 'this means that moral evaluation and scientific research must go hand in hand, and that charity must animate them in a harmonious interdisciplinary whole, marked by unity and distinction'.

The work of the intellect is thus assisted by faith and love, and also by the theological virtue of hope. In paragraph thirty-four of *Caritas in Veritate*, Ratzinger/Benedict wrote that hope encourages reason and gives it the strength to direct the will: 'In every cognitive process, truth is not something that we produce, it is always found, or better, received. Truth, like love, is neither planned nor willed, but somehow imposes itself upon human beings.'

Ratzinger's strongly Augustinian epistemology is also evident in the encyclical *Lumen Fidei*, which was drafted by him but settled and promulgated by Pope Francis. It completed his triptych of encyclicals on the theological virtues. In *Lumen Fidei* the sacraments are said to communicate 'an incarnate memory, linked to the times and places of our lives, linked to all our senses'. In them the whole person is engaged as part of a network of communitarian relationships, including, of course, the relationships with the Persons of the Trinity.

Lumen Fidei also emphasised the inseparability of truth and love. In paragraph twenty-seven we find the statements that 'love and truth are inseparable', that 'love is an experience of truth', and we also find an endorsement of St Gregory the Great's maxim, '*amor ipse notitia est*' – love is itself a kind of knowledge possessed of its own logic.

The model of rationality received from the eighteenth century, especially from Kant, is radically different from this anthropology. This difference was a central theme in the work *Augustine and Modernity*, written by the American *Communio* scholar, Michael Hanby.[25] Hanby argues that this modern detachment of the two sources of human motivation from one another (i.e. the separation of love and reason) represents the undoing of the unity of knowledge and love in creatures created in the image of the Trinity. In Hanby's narrative, Pelagianism is blamed for creating possibilities for human nature outside the Trinity and the mediation of Christ, and Hanby noted that the Pelagian error was in turn related to the influence of the Stoic account of volition on Pelagius. Comparing the Augustinian and Pelagian accounts of the will, Hanby observed:

> In the one, *voluntas* is the site of our erotic participation in an anterior gift, and it is at once self-moved and moved by the beauty of that gift. Here will, whether human or divine, is constituted in a relation of love for the beloved and its freedom is established as dispossession. In the other, will names an inviolable power, and freedom consists in demonstrating this inviolability, through the double negation both of itself and of created beauty.[26]

The baseline difference is therefore between theological research built on the premise that reason ought to be dispassionate, and theological research built on the premise that reason normally is and ought to be linked to a higher *eros*.

An alternative interpretation of *Dei Filius*

In taking a stance in favour of reason linked to a higher *eros*, the romantically orthodox place themselves at odds with the typically Stream One Thomist interpretation of *Dei Filius* as promoted by Joseph Kleutgen.[27] As explained in Chapter 2, Kleutgen's interpretation was the subject of extensive critique by Alasdair MacIntyre in his *Three Rival Versions of Moral Enquiry* published in 1990. More recently MacIntyre's criticisms have been echoed by Fergus Kerr in his Gonzaga Lecture delivered in Glasgow in 2010. In this lecture Kerr offered an extensive analysis of *Dei Filius* based on a study of the debates of Vatican I. His conclusion was that chapter II of *Dei Filius* has been the subject of many popularist constructions that are not really consistent with what the Council Fathers had in mind.[28] In particular he argued that the Council Fathers were not trying to assert the proposition that the existence of God can be proven by rational argumentation. The belief that it can be is something of a cornerstone for Stream One Thomists but it is rejected by those who prefer to read the Thomistic corpus in the light of a neoplatonist metaphysics of participation.

The much-quoted 'anathema' sentence of *Dei Filius* reads: 'If anyone says that the one, true God, our creator and lord, cannot be known with certainty from the things that have been made, by the natural light of human reason, let him be anathema.' Precisely what this statement means – how it should be construed within the context of theological anthropology and the history and ontology relationship – is the key theoretical point dividing the classically and romantically orthodox. The classically orthodox tend to read this passage through the lens of Kleutgen, the romantically orthodox read it backwards through the lens of *Dei Verbum*. Kerr's argument is that the historical documentation favours an interpretation that is more sympathetic to a post-*Dei Verbum* perspective. He concluded that 'it remained unsettled at Vatican I whether the natural light by which reason can attain knowledge of God should be equated with the prelapsarian light enjoyed by Adam in the Garden of Eden or the light in which someone in a state of grace might exercise his reasoning powers, or the light which someone might supposedly have independently of the effects of sin and grace.'[29]

In his commentary on *Gaudium et spes* published in 1969, Ratzinger wrote that the aim of the document's paragraph twenty-one was to 'limit the neo-scholastic rationalism contained in the formula of 1870 and to place its over-static idea of "*ratio naturalis*" in a more historical perspective.'[30] Specifically, the text indicates that 'the possibilities of reason in regard to knowledge of God should be thought of less in the form of a non-historical syllogism of the *philosophia perennis* than simply as the concrete fact that man throughout his whole history has known himself confronted with God and consequently in virtue of his own history finds himself in relation with God as an inescapable feature of his own existence.'[31]

Ratzinger's interpretation of *Gaudium et spes* paragraph twenty-one is in complete accord with Kerr's reading of what the Fathers of the First Vatican Council really intended in chapter II of *Dei Filius*. In his summary, Kerr claimed that the Vatican I dogma does not say that knowledge of God's existence is a conclusion to be reached by a chain of inferences, let alone that the certainty depends on a 'syllogism'.

In another of his works, *After Aquinas: Versions of Thomism*, Kerr drew attention to the fact that St. Thomas's famous 'five ways' of proving God's existence had a different reception in twentieth-century Europe from their common reception in the Anglophone world.[32] Whereas in the Anglophone world they were often taken as 'proofs' in the strict sense, in Europe this was not the case.[33]

A few decades after Vatican II Ratzinger helped to draft the *Catechism of the Catholic Church*, in which paragraph thirty-one states:

> Created in God's image and called to know and love him, the person who seeks God discovers certain ways of coming to know him. These are also called proofs for the existence of God, not in the sense of proofs in the natural sciences, but rather in the sense of converging and convincing arguments, which allow us to attain certainty about the truth.

In arriving at these converging and convincing arguments paragraph thirty-three refers not to discursive reasoning, not to *ratio*, but to the human person's openness to truth and beauty, his sense of moral goodness, his freedom, the voice of his conscience and his longing for the infinite and happiness. *Ratio* no doubt has some place in all of this, but it is not specifically mentioned. Paragraph thirty-five of the *Catechism* further states:

> Man's faculties make him capable of coming to a knowledge of the existence of a personal God. But for man to be able to enter into real intimacy with him, God willed both to reveal himself to man, and to give him the grace of being able to welcome this revelation in faith. The proofs of God's existence, however, can predispose one to faith and help one to see that faith is not opposed to reason.

The point of this rather long analysis has been to explain the fault lines between the classically and romantically orthodox understanding of the relationship between faith and reason. Some Thomist scholars and all *Communio* scholars reject the Kantian sharp separation of faith and reason in favour of what Milbank calls a more erotic or romantic conception. Students seeking to understand the works of any particular theologian can therefore scan the 'pedigree papers' by asking questions such as, where does this particular theologian stand on Scotus, on Suárez, on Kant? Included within the question of where he or she stands on Kant is the subsidiary question of whether his or her understanding of reason is Kant's 'pure reason' or Augustine's 'purified reason' or some other alternative. A belief that Scotus, Suárez and Kant are in part responsible for the rise of secularism and that this has been a negative development for Christianity is a common *Communio* hallmark, along with a preference for reading the philosophy and theology relationship in the manner of Pieper (and Gilson) rather than in the manner of Kleutgen. For an extensive account of how Leonine era Thomism fell into the Kantian stance of defending the independence of philosophy, recourse can be had to Wayne Hankey's essay 'Making Theology Practical: Thomas Aquinas and the Nineteenth Century Religious Revival'.[34]

The methodology of de Lubac and Balthasar

While it is true that the *Communio* journal publishes material from theologians with expertise in a diverse array of theological subjects and that the objective of the journal is not one of the construction of a new system, it is nonetheless the case that common to many scholars who publish in the journal is an interest in the theological *oeuvre* of de Lubac and Balthasar. As Antonio Sicari, an editor of the Italian edition of the journal, expressed the idea: 'Theological work conducted from the point of view of *communio* has its authoritative practical models in the great theology of Henri de Lubac and Hans Urs von Balthasar.'[35] Accordingly, it is helpful to understand how these two went about doing theology.

Balthasar described de Lubac as a young David contending against 'the Goliath of modern rationalisation and the reduction of the Christian mystery to logic'.[36] In *La révélation divine*, de Lubac wrote:

> To reflect on Christ or, as they say, to 'do theology', then, does not mean simply to 'organize truths' and to reduce them to a system or to draw new inferences from the revealed 'premises'; it is much rather to demonstrate the 'explanatory power' of the truths of faith with respect even to the constantly changing context of the world. To do theology means to attempt to understand the world and man, his being, destiny and history, in the most diverse situations, precisely in light of those truths. To do theology means to endeavour to see all things in the mystery of Christ. For the mystery of Christ is an *illuminating mystery*, and by considering it thus, we grasp its true depth, without for all that robbing it of any of its mysteriousness. It follows that the enterprise of a 'theology of history' must not be looked upon as a merely marginal phenomenon; every theologian must be more or less a 'theologian of history'. None of this means, however, that history as such is the medium of revelation or salvation. On the contrary. Whether we are talking about profane or ecclesiastical history: by themselves, historical events bring us no increase in supernatural revelation. They remain always 'ambiguous' and in a kind of state of 'expectation', and it is they that must be enlightened for us by the light that comes from the Gospel.[37]

This is about as far away as one can go from Comblin's Sense One-type interpretation of the 'signs of the times'. Like Ratzinger and Balthasar, de Lubac's reading of the 'signs of the times' scriptural passages was thoroughly Christocentric and eschatological.

Another significant source for understanding de Lubac's approach to doing theology is the tenth chapter of his *Corpus Mysticum* titled 'From Symbolism to Dialectic' in which he is critical of the medieval move towards a focus on dialectical rationality and a corresponding devaluation of symbols. De Lubac concluded this chapter with an observation that St Bonaventure, whom he described as a 'conservative by instinct' did not go down the path of giving priority to dialectical rationality, and instead 'retained all that [he] could of ancient symbolic thought'.[38] Others however so exalted the role of dialectical rationality that the Patristic sacramental ontology, reliant as it was on a mystical dimension, was undermined. As Jens Zimmermann has noted, for Patristic humanists the rational image of God in man is 'geared not primarily toward logical analysis but toward relation and communion with the divine'.[39] In the post-Scotist scholastic world, the 'rich language of God's love for and indwelling in human beings changed to a more instrumental view of grace, according to which God, instead of 'revivifying the human being to its very depths' now merely restored [the human] ability to keep the divine law', with the result that 'colder, juridical categories replaced the older relational ones'.[40]

De Lubac wanted to fight secularism, relativism, liberalism and modern ideologies in general with Patristic humanism, its anthropology, its passion, its union of love and reason, not with syllogisms, not with hair-splitting logic and concepts arranged into systems for rote learning.

Paradox and conceptual clarity

A contemporary critic of de Lubac from a classically orthodox perspective is Lawrence Feingold.[41] Feingold acknowledges that Aquinas was not clear on the issues about the relationship between nature and grace that came to be in dispute in the twentieth century, but he prefers the reading of Cajetan to that of de Lubac. Nicholas J. Healy has succinctly identified the difference between the two in his statement that whereas de Lubac interprets St Thomas 'as an authoritative witness to a tradition that preceded him, Feingold begins with Aquinas and then microscopically traces the tradition of commentary on Aquinas's writings'.[42] In other words, one scholar (de Lubac) reads Aquinas forward through the lens of his Patristic antecedents, the other (Feingold) reads Aquinas backward through the lens of his scholastic commentators.

A major reason why de Lubac 'read Aquinas forward' was explained by Joseph Fessio SJ. Fessio has noted that because de Lubac was wounded at Verdun (indeed shot in the head) his health was too fragile for him to attend the regular classes in philosophy and theology that were the standard fare for Jesuit seminarians of his era, and instead he privately read the entire *Patrologia Graeca et Latina*. This meant that he came to the Thomist sources with a comprehensive knowledge of the Patristic antecedents to Aquinas. He could therefore see how Aquinas had appropriated the Patristic heritage. To draw a musical analogy it is as if Aquinas occupies a similar place in theology to that of Beethoven in music. While Beethoven is a figure poised between the classical and romantic sensibilities, St Thomas is a figure poised between the Patristics and the neo-scholastics. De Lubac was a master at identifying the Patristic threads in the tapestry of Classical Thomism and did not like what he regarded as neo-scholastic occlusions or distortions of these Patristic elements.

More significant however than this genealogical difference is what Aaron Riches has identified as two distinct approaches to theological perplexity. Riches argues that 'whereas de Lubac sees theological perplexity as essentially internal to the paradox of the hypostatic union and the mystery of Christology – the very core of Christian thought and practice – Feingold sees perplexity as a problematic failure of reason to understand faith, and thus an aspect of theology in need of resolution in the quest for systematic clarity'.[43] For de Lubac a paradox in theology is not in itself a problem since the Incarnation is itself a paradox. Again to quote Riches:

> For de Lubac, the Christological paradox entails that the Church's doctrine will be constituted by 'a comprehensive assembly of opposing aspects', and that these 'opposing aspects' are raised to signify the full depth of the mystery of truth in direct relation to the degree that 'they are mutually supported like flying buttresses (*arc-boutant*), each one braced against the other in the most extreme degrees of tension'. The tensive image of the *arc-boutant* as the soul of orthodoxy, suggests the polyphony of the synthesis of theology at the service of the one objective truth.[44]

A further contrast between the classically and romantically orthodox approaches to theology has been highlighted by +Rudolf Voderholzer. He notes that one of de Lubac's chief concerns is to reunite things that belong together and to expose false alternatives.[45] In other words, de Lubac's intellectual orientation was towards synthesis. His motivation was to sew pieces of the Christian tapestry back together after they had fallen apart in successive intellectual crises beginning with the rise of nominalism in the fourteenth century. In contrast, the scholastic orientation is towards conceptual clarification and thus the making of finer and finer distinctions. From the perspective of de Lubac's anthropology, the neo-scholastic accent upon conceptual clarification places rather too many eggs into the basket of one particular type of rationality – in scholastic terms, into the basket of *ratio*. For de Lubac a pastoral crisis could just as easily be caused by what Paul Claudel (1868–1955) called 'the poverty of a starved imagination' (the malady common to the business manager style of religious leader) as much as by a breakdown in dialectical rationality.

Hans Urs von Balthasar

While Balthasar paid de Lubac the compliment of describing him as a 'young David' going to war against the Goliath of rationalism, de Lubac famously described Balthasar as 'perhaps the most cultured man of our time'. Neither was lacking in creativity and each appreciated this quality in the other. Both came from patrician families. Balthasar was from his childhood classically educated, multilingual, musically literate, and surrounded by friends and family who were socially important people. Within his family circle he had an uncle who was a bishop, a sister who grew up to become a superior-general of a Franciscan Order of nuns, a little brother who became a Swiss Guard, a cousin who became a Jesuit and a bishop. The uncle, Bishop Vilmos Apor, was martyred during the Second World War and beatified in 1997.

Coming from such a family it is no surprise that Balthasar grew up intellectually precocious. He checked himself out of secondary school and chose to be matriculated at university rather than be bored at school. In 1929 he entered the South German Province of the Society of Jesus. Compared to the intellectual life he enjoyed within his own family, life as a Jesuit student was dull. He was later to write: 'My entire period of study in the Society was a grim struggle with the dreariness of theology, with what men had made out of the glory of revelation.'[46] Like fellow *Communio* founder, Joseph Ratzinger, scholasticism just 'wasn't his beer'. Balthasar was of the same mind as Maurice Blondel who spoke negatively of those who had sought 'to deprive the philosophy of St. Thomas of the inspiration it drew from Augustine himself, to separate the intellect from the other faculties of the soul, to turn wisdom into a purely theoretical science'.[47] Blondel complained that 'a strict, dry, rational process ends in such static concepts, in a dialectic so firmly riveted in concatenations of immovable ideas or mere verbal formulas that minds, grown callous in such an ideological casing, reject any suggestion of a less rigid attitude, and, self-confident and infatuated, oppose their dense mass of abstractions even to the living authority of the Church or the teaching of real life'.[48]

Since Balthasar's childhood was spent happily immersed in a Catholic culture that was much richer and more vibrant than what he found in the seminary, and in particular that was one in which the true, the beautiful and the good were all significant, he felt as though he could do a better job of making the faith credible to people who live and work outside of a neo-scholastic mental universe. Erich Przywara SJ (1889–1972) counselled Balthasar to endure the lectures on scholasticism, to 'offer it up' as it were, but Balthasar still defiantly attended classes wearing earplugs and carrying works of Patristic authors that he proceeded to read through the lectures. De

Lubac introduced him to the works of Origen and St Maximus the Confessor and the novels of the French Catholic literati, including François Mauriac and Georges Berñanos, which he read during the time otherwise allotted to seminarians for playing football. De Lubac once remarked to Joseph Fessio that Balthasar would sit at the back of the classroom during lectures on scholasticism reading Origen in Greek. While doing so, he marked passages he thought were likely from Evagrius Ponticus rather than Origen. A later critical edition of Origen confirmed Balthasar's intuitions. Fessio believes that Balthasar also used his classroom time to translate at least a part of Paul Claudel's *Soulier de Satin*.

The influence of Guardini

Behind Balthasar (and Ratzinger) there also stands the influence of Romano Guardini (1885–1968). Guardini was one of Balthasar's lecturers at the University of Berlin and one of Ratzinger's at the University of Munich. Ratzinger later wrote that he was taught by Guardini that 'the essence of Christianity is not an idea, not a system of thought, not a plan of action. The essence of Christianity is a Person: Jesus Christ himself.'[49] This principle became enshrined in the Conciliar document *Dei Verbum* (1965) and it formed the central theme of Ratzinger/Benedict's first encyclical, *Deus Caritas Est* (2007). Ratzinger also gave credit to Guardini for giving him an approach to the spiritual interpretation of Scripture:

> Guardini recognized that the liturgy is the true, living environment for the Bible and that the Bible can be properly understood only in this living context from which it first emerged. The texts of the Bible, this great book of Christ, are not to be seen as the literary products of some scribes at their desks, but rather as the words of Christ himself delivered in the celebration of the holy Mass.[50]

In Ratzinger's Erasmus Lecture of 1989, which was titled 'Biblical Interpretation in Crisis', he emphasised that scriptural analysis should take place within the horizons of faith itself, and not, as contemporary neo-Kantians might have it, from a perspective of complete indifference or alleged neutrality.

On another occasion Ratzinger said that 'Guardini was convinced that only thinking in harmony with the Church leads to freedom, and, above all, makes theology possible'. He added that 'this approach is of new relevance, and should be taken into consideration in the deepest way possible, as a requirement of modern theology'.[51] These remarks are amplified in the following paragraph:

> For Guardini there can be no constructive theological understanding as long as the Church and dogma appear only as 'limitation and restriction.' This led to his provocative motto, from the theological point of view: 'we were definitely not liberals', a motto that alludes to the fact that for him, divine Revelation presented itself as the ultimate criterion, the 'originating element' of theological understanding, and the Church was 'its bearer'.[52]

The motto 'we are definitely not liberals' holds true for all the scholars in the *Communio* world. Fundamentally, whatever their specific academic interests, they all begin from the same baseline, which accepts Revelation as a gift received from membership within a transnational, supernatural Church. While they accept that the human understanding of Revelation may deepen in various ways throughout salvation history and that a development of doctrine is possible and may even be given impetus by changing historical conditions insofar as the new conditions raise questions never before imagined, they do not believe that theologians should treat the Catholic Tradition as something like a work of art to which they may legitimately add their own embellishments or new panels, drawing inspiration from sources outside the original deposit of the faith.

Balthasar was to compose his own work of tribute to Guardini, which was published in English with the title *Romano Guardini: Reform from the Source*. In this he wrote that Guardini believed that the realm of creation is investigated by philosophy and that the realm of biblical Revelation is investigated by theologians, but what really interested Guardini as a scholar was 'what happened when the realm of creation is illuminated by the light of knowledge given in Christian faith'.[53] In other words, Guardini was intellectually excited about the union of philosophy and theology, and precisely for this reason his Chair at the University of Berlin was described neither as a Chair in philosophy nor as a Chair in some subdiscipline of theology, but rather as a Chair in the philosophy of Religion and the Catholic *Weltanschauung* (world view).

In his 2013 McGivney Lectures delivered in Washington DC, Stanisław Grygiel presented the outlook of John Paul II in similar terms. He said:

> Bishop Karol Wojtyła and Bishop Jan Pietraszko, who spiritually influenced him, helped me to understand an intuition that had been present in me for a long while: that excessively distinguishing theological thought from philosophical thought, as well as from the thought proper

to the exact sciences, would cause all of these – theology, philosophy and the exact sciences – to lose their way. It would warp their *praxis*, which then devastates the human person, society and the whole world.[54]

An opposition to the concept of 'pure nature' is also strong in Guardini's theological anthropology. In *Freedom, Grace and Destiny* he wrote:

> God did not design man as a 'natural' being to fulfil his purpose, as do animals, within his natural environment. There is no such thing as the 'natural' man. This is an abstraction which the theologian needs to draw certain distinctions and establish relationships. The only real man that exists is the man called to the order of grace. Either he obeys and is then raised above the merely natural level or he refuses obedience and falls below the level of nature into a debasing dependence on evil. 'Pure Nature' when applied to man is an imaginary yardstick by which he cannot measure himself. Modern Naturalism attempts to construct a purely natural man with a self-contained reality and significance. His only function is that of developing his natural capacities and his association with the world. Should he so please, he may enter also into a religious association but this is of no primary importance for his evolution because his manhood is wholly realised in the interplay of his own nature and that of the world. A little attention will show this theory to be false and that man's whole being is in a state of confusion that would be impossible if there existed a 'natural man'.[55]

Guardini, like de Lubac, was fighting against secularism with the weapons of Patristic humanism and like de Lubac he regarded the concept of a 'pure nature' capable of fulfilment without grace as a trapdoor that opens the way for a secularisation of Christian culture.

Finally, Guardini insisted on the principle of the priority of *logos* over *ethos*, about which more will be said in Chapter 5.

Mystical experience as a *Locus Theologicus*

Another significant intellectual collaborator in Balthasar's life was Adrienne von Speyr (1902–67). She was a doctor, writer and mystic from a Swiss Protestant aristocratic family. She converted at the age of thirty-eight and together with Balthasar established the scholarly and spiritual Community of St John (*Johannesgemeinschaft*) in Einsiedeln. Balthasar was both her intellectual colleague and spiritual director. He left the Society of Jesus in 1950 in order to focus on the work of this Community, but remained a priest in the Diocese of Chur. In 1965 he wrote that Speyr's work and his 'cannot be separated from one another either psychologically or philologically. They are two halves of one whole, with a single foundation at the center.'[56] The part of his work most obviously in debt to Speyr is the one dealing with the Paschal Mysteries. Her mystical experiences included intense suffering from Fridays through to Sundays and her body was marked by the stigmata. She also claimed to have had a mystical encounter with St Ignatius of Loyola in her childhood. She dictated her experiences to Balthasar, and his theological work embodies the theological insights acquired through these mystical events. Those who oppose substantive elements of Balthasar's theological vision are usually quick to argue that this way of doing theology – becoming a spiritual director to a person who claims to have visions of the events narrated in the Book of Revelation, conversations with deceased saints, insights into Christ's descent into hell on Holy Saturday and even visions of evil events taking place in the corridors of the Vatican, and then applying this knowledge acquired mystically to one's theological studies – is a very offbeat way of doing theology.

Nonetheless, one of Balthasar's foundational principles was that there exists an intimate connection between one's spiritual and intellectual life. In his essays 'Theology and Sanctity' and 'Spirituality' in the first volume of *Explorations in Theology: The Word Made Flesh* he was critical of the separation of spirituality from academic theology in the collapse of the medieval theological syntheses. One of his many criticisms of neo-scholasticism was precisely that it fostered a separation between theoretical and affective theology: 'While the theoretical theology of the Baroque era proceeded from a fixed "teaching of the Church" as object and therefore missed the spiritual, existential dimension which runs through everything biblical; the affective theology of the Baroque missed the biblical center and proceeded "mystically" instead of eschatologically.'[57]

In the essay on 'Theology and Sanctity' Balthasar quoted the following passage from Matthias Scheeben's *The Mysteries of Christianity*, which draws attention to the significance of the Holy Spirit in theological study:

> The Holy Spirit anoints with his light the spiritual eye, and so imparts a moral receptivity enabling us to attain a fuller and purer comprehension of the content of faith; and so our knowledge only comes to full strength and life through the realizing of the supernatural life flowing out within us from the Spirit.[58]

Balthasar went on to assert that theology 'proceeds always as a continuous dialogue between Bridegroom and Bride. The Bridegroom gives and the

Bride receives, and only in this acceptance of faith can the miracle of the pouring forth of the Word, which is both sower and seed, be accomplished.'[59] In a full frontal assault on Kantian epistemology, Balthasar concluded that there is 'no neutral standpoint outside the encounter between Bride and Bridegroom'. As a consequence,

> it is of the utmost importance to see that what is lacking [in the relationship between spirituality and theology] is not just a piece of material that can be easily incorporated into the existing structure, or else a sort of stylistic quality to be reproduced anew. ... The fact is that the spiritual dimension can only be recovered through the soul of man being profoundly moved as the result of his direct encounter with revealed truth, so that it is borne in upon him, once and for all, how the theologian should think and speak, and how he should not. This holds good for both the estranged disciplines, dogmatic theology and spirituality.[60]

Speaking directly of dogmatic theology, Balthasar asserted that it is 'no mere connecting link between revelation and something else, such as human nature or reason or philosophy'. Rather,

> human nature and its mental faculties are given their true center when in Christ; in him they attain their final truth, for such was the will of God, the Creator of nature, from eternity. Man, therefore, in investigating the relationship between nature and supernature, has no need to abandon the standpoint of faith, to set himself up as the mediator between God and the world, between revelation and reason, or to cast himself in the role of judge over that relationship. All that is necessary is for him to understand 'the one mediator between God and man, the man Christ Jesus (1 Tim. 2.5), and to believe him in whom "were all things created in heaven and on earth ... all by him and in him" (Col. 1.16). Christ did not leave the Father when he became man to bring all creation to fulfilment; and neither does the Christian need to leave his centre in Christ in order to mediate him to the world, to understand his relation to the world, to build a bridge between revelation and nature, philosophy and theology.[61]

There is, in other words, no neutral space in which any scholar may stand. The desire for such neutrality is a kind of infidelity, if not outright idolatry. It is a case of kneeling before the altar of an eighteenth-century god. As Ratzinger put the idea, there is no such thing as 'pure reason', there is only 'impure reason' or 'purified reason'.

One of the most eloquent expositions of Balthasar's intensely Christocentric–Trinitarian methodology can be found in Marc Ouellet's essay 'The message of Balthasar's theology to modern theology', which begins with the heading 'either theology is holy in its aim and its method, or it is nothing at all'.[62] Ouellet explains that fundamental to Balthasar's whole approach to theology is his insistence on the priority of Trinitarian mediations:

> Hans Urs von Balthasar conceives theology, like St. Thomas Aquinas, as a participation in the knowledge God has of himself. The Father communicates this knowledge adequately in his incarnate Word, his Exegete, who is himself interpreted by the Holy Spirit, poured into our hearts. The 'theology of God' becomes theology in the Church through a strict Trinitarian mediation which involves the whole man Jesus, with his personal and ecclesial body. It becomes anthropological only in its subordination to God's descending movement which invites an adequate response from his creature, a response to adoration and obedience, within the context of the covenant. Here, in a few words, is the global perspective of Balthasar's theology. Within the panorama of contemporary theologies, it distinguishes itself as a theology 'from above' in opposition to the theologies 'from below' which attempt to interpret revelation from the perspective of man as transcendental and historical subjectivity. While these theologies are anthropological with respect to method and content, Balthasar's is first of all Christological, and discloses its anthropological implications only in relation to Christology.[63]

Ouellet suggests that the deliberately unsystematic nature of Balthasar's theological publications is a symptom of this critique of modern rationalism, his steadfast opposition to Kantian philosophy. Balthasar is not embarrassed to acknowledge that faith participates intrinsically in the scientific character of exegesis and theology. In this sense he is making a classic Gadamerian and MacIntyrean claim that all thinking takes place within the horizon of a tradition, be it a scientific tradition, a metaphysical tradition, or in Balthasar's case, the Tradition of Christianity founded in the Revelation of a Trinitarian God.

The nuptial structure of Revelation

A further hallmark of Balthasar's approach to theology is his emphasis on the Gospel of St John, which he reads through the lens of the theology of Origen and St Maximus the Confessor with the key concepts *Sacrum Connubium* (sacred marriage) and *Admirabile Commercium* (marvellous exchange). Ouellet observes that this 'nuptial structure of revelation entails certain consequences for theology'.[64] Specifically it means that 'theology has meaning only in faith because the existential attitude of faith alone grants access to the intimacy of the relation between the Bride and Bridegroom which is the locus of revelation and theology'.[65] Ouellet further argues that 'the implications of this contemplative priority emerge in the format of Balthasar's trilogy which holds the aesthetic is first'.[66] This is a reference to Balthasar's fifteen-volume series, which is divided into three parts: *The Glory of the Lord* – which offers a theological aesthetics in seven volumes – that is, an account of Revelation as the appearance of divine glory or the transcendental of beauty; *Theo-Drama*, which analyses the relationship between God and the human person in five volumes from the perspective of the transcendental of goodness, and this includes Balthasar's very creative account of the events of Holy Saturday; and *Theo-Logic*, which addresses the relationship between Christology and ontology in three volumes from the perspective of the transcendental of truth. Ouellet is making the point that when offering a presentation of Christian theology from the perspective of the transcendental properties of being (truth, beauty and goodness), it is very significant that Balthasar gives epistemic priority to beauty over truth. This is in sharp contrast to much modern theology, which starts with questions about truth and then moves on to the ethical consequences of what can be rationally argued, and either leaves beauty out altogether as something associated with subjective human taste (as Kant would have it), or treats beauty or divine glory as a mere frosting or, one might say, 'strawberry', on the intellectual cake. Edward T. Oakes described Balthasar's reasons for giving priority to beauty in the following terms:

> According to Balthasar this approach [truth first, beauty last] has proved in the long run to be sterile, and he saw today's rampant secularization as due, at least in part, to modernity's habit of looking at things through the wrong end of the telescope. Rather, he said, one must first *perceive* Christian revelation as beautiful (arguments just get in the way of the contemplative gaze); only then would the soul be prompted to assent to follow Christ in a *dramatic* life of Christian discipleship; and finally, once inside that life of obedience to Christ, one comes to see how and why Christianity is *true*.[67]

Oakes goes on to give a concrete scriptural example of this principle in operation. St. Paul was first 'enraptured by his encounter with Christ (Acts 9. 1-19) and taken up into the third heaven (2 Cor. 12. 2-4), he [then] launches on a life of evangelization, proclaiming the resurrection of Christ

(Rom. 1. 1-6), at which point those who subscribe to other philosophies and worldviews debate with him: "A group of Epicurean and Stoic philosophers began to dispute with him'" (Acts 17. 18).[68] Contrary to the approach of the pre-Conciliar and many contemporary Thomists, for Balthasar apologetics comes 'after one has gazed on revelation and responded by saying Yes to a mission of kerygmatic proclamation'.[69]

The *analogia entis*

Notwithstanding his academic practice of looking at Revelation from the 'reverse end of the telescope' from most Thomists, Balthasar nonetheless emphasised the importance of the concept of 'esse' in the work of St Thomas, as filtered through the Stream Three Existential Thomists, as well as the doctrine of the analogy of being (*analogia entis*), also interpreted existentially with reference to works of Erich Przywara SJ (1889–1972) and Gustave Siewerth (1903–63). For those seeking to understand the significance of these concepts in the work of Balthasar, a helpful guide is *The Analogy of Being: Invention of the Antichrist or the Wisdom of God?* edited by Thomas Joseph White OP. This collection of papers takes its title from Karl Barth's statement that the doctrine of the analogy of being (broadly understood as knowing God through an analogy with his creation) is the invention of the Antichrist and Barth's reason for remaining a Protestant. St Bonaventure explained the *analogia entis* in the following terms:

> All created things of the sensible world lead the mind of the contemplator and wise man to eternal God. ... They are the shades, the resonances, the pictures of that efficient, exemplifying, and ordering art; they are the tracks, simulacra, and spectacles; they are divinely given signs set before us for the purpose of seeing God. They are exemplifications set before our still unrefined and sense-oriented minds, so that by the sensible things which they see they might be transferred to the intelligible which they cannot see, as if by signs to the signified. (*Itinerarium mentis ad Deum*, 2.11)

The essay by John R. Betz in the work edited by White contains valuable material on the intellectual history of the *analogia entis* concept, and on the influence of Erich Przywara on Karl Rahner, Balthasar and Edith Stein (1891–1942), among others. Peter Casarella narrows the focus to Balthasar's engagement with the *analogia entis* concept in the thought of Przywara and Barth, and Martin Bieler argues that the manner in which Ferdinand Ulrich unfolds the philosophical *analogia entis* of Aquinas is of great help in explaining the treatment of the *analogia entis* in Balthasar. Bieler also notes that for Balthasar the metaphysics of being is an integral part of God's Revelation in the world:

> For Balthasar, Christ himself is the concrete *analogia entis*, because he measures all dimensions between God and human beings through his own person in the unity of his divine and human nature. The philosophical *analogia entis* has the same relation to Christ as world history has to the history of Christ: It is like promise to fulfilment, and like provisional to final.[70]

Ouellet remarks that 'the heritage of Thomistic metaphysics, exhumed from the ruins of rationalism and phenomenologically deepened in the service of a theological aesthetics, represents for Balthasar a precious mediation for countering the predominant tendency in our day to incline toward the formless'.[71] Here the significant point to note is that while Balthasar was not enthusiastic about scholasticism he was highly supportive of Thomist metaphysics as filtered through the Stream Three Existential Thomists, especially the ideas of Gustave Siewerth (1903–63).

Andrzej Wierciński is a leading international authority on Siewerth's reading of Thomist metaphysics and has published a bilingual (English and German) edition of the Balthasar–Siewerth correspondence. This collection includes Balthasar's obituary for Siewerth, titled 'A Farewell to Gustave Siewerth'. In this he praises Siewerth for his hostility to Suárezian metaphysics. For Siewerth, 'being is not a concept belonging to reason, which can be defined and objectivized in relation to a being'.[72] Balthasar also praised Siewerth for his lack of interest in a philosophy separated from theology. He wrote that for Siewerth, as for Aquinas, 'Aristotle was "the last philosopher", since all that followed always-already thinks well or ill, with approval or censure, to its salvation or damnation, within the space of the Revelation that has already taken place'. He concluded: 'After Greek philosophy, all great philosophy is theology'.[73]

In short Balthasar regarded Siewerth's metaphysics as a necessary corrective to the errors of Suárez that had led to what Heidegger criticised as 'onto-theology'.

The place of philosophy

The standard Stream One-type Thomist response to Balthasar is to shout out 'fideism' and start quoting passages from Vatican I's *Dei Filius* and various papal encyclicals on the perennial value of philosophy. The standard

Communio theologian's response is to say that Balthasar was not opposed to philosophy *per se*, but only to the varieties of philosophy, especially epistemology, that emerged from the collapse of the medieval syntheses.

Two leading Anglophone *Communio* scholars, Adrian J. Walker and David C. Schindler, have published numerous articles defending Balthasar against the charge of fideism. Walker points to Balthasar's own statement that 'without philosophy there is no theology' and he argues that 'precisely because of his radical Christocentrism', Balthasar is 'before anything else, a theologian of the so-called "Catholic and": of the unity-without-confusion of the "from above" *and* the "from below"; of grace *and* of nature; of philosophy *and* of theology; of the radical following of Christ *and* of passionate love for the world; of tradition *and* of the development of doctrine'.[74] Anyone wanting to understand a *Communio* account of philosophy can have recourse to David C. Schindler's two major works – *Hans Urs von Balthasar and the Dramatic Structure of Truth: A Philosophical Investigation* and *The Catholicity of Reason* – and to Adrian Walker's essay 'Christ and Cosmology: Methodological Considerations for Catholic Educators'.[75] In this paper Walker wrote:

> There exists an intimate relation between human knowing and Christ such that the decision for or against Christ that *in concreto* occurs in all knowing because of the universality of the offer of grace does not determine only one's openness or closure to Christ himself, but also the openness or closure of reason itself to reality as a whole (which, indeed, holds together in Christ) – and therefore, affects, either positively or negatively, but, in any case, from top to bottom, the quality of one's every explicit cognitive engagement with particulars within that reality.[76]

Such a position, of course, presupposes that de Lubac was correct when he rejected the notion of a *natura pura*. Here both concepts, *natura pura* and *ratio pura*, are equally rejected, but it does not follow that rationality is rejected or that philosophy is rejected, merely that *Communio* theologians have a different understanding of the relationship of philosophy and theology from those who believe in a *natura pura* and a *ratio pura*. They read the faith and reason relationship very much as Pieper and Gilson did. This is apparent from the following statement of Balthasar about the significance of St Thomas Aquinas:

> Thomas is … a *Kairos* as a historically passing moment between an old world that thought in monistic terms, inasmuch as it saw philosophy and theology (both in their Greek and their Christian forms) as a

whole, and an approaching dualistic world that attempted to posit a separation (both in Christian and post-Christian ways) between philosophy and the theology of revelation and turn each of them into a totality. However, the historically transitional form can still hold them together, provided it is conceived and shaped with sufficient comprehensiveness.[77]

The Pieper-Gilsonian reading of Aquinas represented such an attempt to hold together the transitional form.

Ratzinger's spirituality of a pure heart

While Balthasar eschews any temptation to defend the faith at the Bar of Kantian rationality and makes Christ the one and only 'concrete universal', Ratzinger follows in the same trajectory but offers as his own specific contribution to a *Communio* approach to the discipline of theology, an emphasis on the importance of the theological virtues (faith, hope and love) for a sound spirituality ancillary to theological work. Ratzinger's reflections on the significance of the theological virtues can be tracked back to Josef Pieper's analysis of the theological virtues in the thought of St Thomas Aquinas and they find his (Ratzinger's) mature expression in the trilogy of encyclicals written during his pontificate: *Deus Caritas Est* (on love), *Spe Salvi* (on hope) and *Lumen Fidei* (on faith). Paragraph thirty-six of *Lumen Fidei* draws out the link between the theological virtue of faith and theological work:

Theology is more than simply an effort of human reason to analyse and understand, along the lines of the experimental sciences. God cannot be reduced to an object. He is a subject who makes himself known and perceived in an interpersonal relationship. Right faith orients reason to open itself to the light which comes from God, so that reason, guided by love of the truth, can come to a deeper knowledge of God. The great medieval theologians and teachers rightly held that theology, as a science of faith, is a participation in God's own knowledge of himself. It is not just our discourse about God, but first and foremost the acceptance and the pursuit of a deeper understanding of the word which God speaks to us, the word which God speaks about himself, for he is an eternal dialogue of communion, and he allows us to enter into this dialogue. Theology thus demands the humility to be 'touched' by God, admitting its own limitations before the mystery, while striving to investigate, with the discipline proper to reason, the inexhaustible riches of this mystery.[78]

In *Porta Fidei*, the Apostolic Letter announcing the Year of Faith in 2011, Benedict XVI wrote: 'Knowing the content [of the faith] to be believed is not sufficient unless the heart, the authentic sacred space within the person, is opened by grace that allows the eyes to see below the surface and to understand that what has been proclaimed is the word of God.'[79] Balthasar made a similar point in his essay, 'Theology and Sanctity' and in the following passage taken from his book *Prayer*:

> If I am to hear properly ... I must not come before the word with specially selected acts of reason and will: I must encounter the word with my whole conscience, or rather, with my whole person. For faith, the organ of hearing has to do with the whole person, not [with] the [individual] faculties of the soul.[80]

The primary importance of a pure heart was also emphasised by John Henry Newman who was one of Ratzinger's heroes when he was a seminarian. In his famous 'Sermon 12', Newman wrote:

> What, then, is the safeguard [of faith], if Reason is not? I shall give an answer, which may seem at once common-place and paradoxical, yet I believe it is the true one. The safeguard of Faith is a right state of [the] heart. This it is that gives it birth; it also disciplines it. This is what protects it from bigotry, credulity, and fanaticism. It is holiness, or dutifulness, or the new creation, or the spiritual mind, however we word it, which is the quickening and illuminating principle of true faith, giving it eyes, hands, and feet. It is Love which forms it out of the rude chaos into an image of Christ; or, in scholastic language, justifying Faith, whether in Pagan, Jew, or Christian, is *fides formata charitate*.[81]

Peter McGregor has argued that for Ratzinger the heart is the 'place' of integration for the intellect, will, passions, and senses of the body and the soul and that this is consistent with the treatment of the heart in the thought of both Newman and Guardini.[82] Michael Paul Gallagher SJ has also observed that 'Newman always proposed the integration of rationality, heart and imagination, seeing the whole self as an instrument of truth'. He offered an 'epistemology of the imagination' as a 'key mediator between theology and spirituality'; 'his pedagogy of faith does not begin with arguments but with paying attention to preconceived spiritual attitudes'.[83]

The moment one begins to treat faith as an indispensable element of any hermeneutical framework, one runs into the territory of Trinitarian theology, and above all, into Christology. It is for this reason that Ratzinger emphasised that the Beatitude, 'Blessed are the pure of heart', is 'profoundly Christological'.[84] We will see God when we enter into the 'same attitude ... in Christ Jesus' (Phil. 2.5). The spiritual and academic enterprises thus become one of 'entering into the mind of Christ'.[85]

Literature as a *Locus Theologicus*

The interest in the interrelationship of all the activities of the soul, the imagination and the memory, the will and the intellect, drawn together by the heart, gives rise to yet another trait of the *Communio* approach to the discipline of theology. This is the interest in mythopoesis, commonly understood as a narrative genre in modern literature and film where a fictional mythology is created by the writer, such as C. S. Lewis's *Chronicles of Narnia* or J. R. R. Tolkien's *Lord of the Rings*. Classical Greek mythology is also relevant in this context. In his collection of letters published under the title *Illustrissimi*, Pope John Paul I remarked that 'where Rahner doesn't succeed with his great tomes of theology, Tolstoy may creep in with his fables'.[86] John Paul I was making the point that theological ideas are often more persuasively expressed in poetry and literary works than in systematic theology texts precisely because of their appeal to the human imagination. Balthasar's doctoral dissertation on eschatological themes in German literature is prototypical of this *Communio* trait of reflecting on theological topics by reference to their appearance in literary work. So, too, were some of the publications of Erich Pryzwara, especially his *Humanitas*, wherein he trawled through centuries of literary classics for theological reflections on human nature. The many publications of Stratford Caldecott, including *The Power of the Ring: the Spiritual Vision behind the Lord of the Rings,* also evince an aptitude for this kind of analysis.

While *Communio* theology is sometimes disparaged as 'mere poetry' precisely because of its treatment of literature as a *locus theologicus*, Michael Paul Gallagher SJ has argued that St Thomas Aquinas would actually applaud the project of offering a more symbolic approach to theology as a supplement to dogmatic theology. Gallagher refers to two specific Thomist texts – St. Thomas's prologue to his *Commentary on the Sentences of Peter Lombard* and his *Quaestiones quodlibetales*. Gallagher observes that in the first of these texts Aquinas suggests that 'insofar as theology invites us toward the "contemplation of truth", we need to develop not just a rational, but also a symbolic theology'. Moreover, 'Aquinas argues that because the Christian faith is grounded in a "narrative of signs", reflection on faith will require "metaphorical, symbolical and parabolical" approaches'. In the second text 'Aquinas accepts that – where the challenge is to clarify the content of faith – an appeal to biblical or ecclesial authority is correct and appropriate'. However, 'Aquinas indicates a deeper task for the student of theology than finding certitude about doctrines' and this deeper task is one of going to the 'root of the truth'. Gallagher concluded: 'Without this more ambitious wavelength, says Aquinas, students may arrive at some "certitude" about truths, but if they acquire no knowledge or understanding, they will go away empty (*nihil intellectus acquiret et vacuus abscedet*).'[87] De Lubac made the same point when he wrote that to do theology 'does not mean simply to "organise truths" and to reduce them to a system or to draw new inferences from the revealed "premises"; it is rather to demonstrate the "explanatory power" of the truths of the faith'.[88]

The *Communio*–Radical Orthodoxy convergence

The *Communio* style of 'doing theology' is often discussed in common with the scholarship of the Radical Orthodoxy ('RO') circle of scholars. There are strong convergences between *Communio* and Radical Orthodoxy scholarship on a number of fronts. First, there is a shared interest in the genealogy of secularism and in this context a shared 'rogues gallery' (especially Scotus, Suárez and Kant). Here one can read Milbank's 2011 Stanton lectures delivered in Cambridge for a detailed account of the RO explanation of how the world became hostile to Christianity. As he explained in his first Stanton Lecture: 'Philosophy had become autonomous, not because pipe-smoking men in tweed had rebelled against men in clerical gowns, but because the men in clerical gowns had opened up that space for their own peculiar religious reasons.'[89]

Secondly, associated with the anti-Scotistic and anti-Suárezian trajectory there is a shared antipathy to the metaphysical presumptions of Liberal political theory. This antipathy is strong in the works of David L. Schindler from the *Communio* camp and John Milbank, the leader of the Radical Orthodoxy camp. Thirdly, there is a shared opposition to Kantian conceptions of the relationship between faith and reason and a shared respect for the philosophy of Blondel. Fourthly, following Blondel, there is a mutual affirmation of de Lubac's opposition to extrinsicist accounts of the relationship between nature and grace. There is, moreover, a common negative judgement on many elements of the culture of modernity and therefore a common opposition to pastoral strategies that seek to correlate the faith to the culture of modernity. As William L. Portier has put the matter, both *Communio* types and Radical Orthodoxy types want to dialogue with culture, but they 'refuse to dialogue with culture on non-theological terms'.[90] This puts both groups at odds with the *Concilium* types.

Radical Orthodoxy is not however the name of a collection of theological doctrines. It has been described as more of an intellectual sensibility. It grew up in Cambridge in the early 1990s after John Milbank published his seminal work *Theology and Social Theory: Beyond Secular Reason*. The driving idea of this work is that there is no such thing as theologically neutral social theory. At around this time a new generation of doctoral students appeared on the scene. Many in this generation had grown up as the guinea pigs in the pastoral experiments of the 1960s generation. This younger generation stood opposed to the idea that the task of theologians should be one of correlating Christian truths to sit comfortably with modern intellectual fashions.

The leading lights of the RO circle, John Milbank, Graham Ward and Catherine Pickstock, are all High Church Anglicans, but those who have published under the RO banner include Catholics, Calvinists and Anabaptists, and a significant number of scholars have converted to the Catholic faith while studying in the RO circle. They include Michael Hanby, Conor Cunningham, Eric Lee, Aaron Riches and Christopher Hackett.

Graham Ward has described Radical Orthodoxy as a project of Christian cultural criticism whose chief concern is 'unmasking the cultural idols, providing genealogical accounts of the assumptions, politics and hidden metaphysics of specific secular varieties of knowledge – with respect to the constructive, therapeutic project of disseminating the Gospel'.[91] Students of Milbank, Ward and Pickstock often joke that this trio is running a 'witness protection service' for graduate students who want to do theology without first genuflecting before a statue of Kant.

While *Communio* scholars are all Catholics and have as the focus of their work the pastoral needs of Catholics and contemporary magisterial 'hot topics', the Radical Orthodoxy scholars tend to have as their focus an engagement with the intellectual fashions in humanities departments in the world's elite universities. It is common therefore for the two groups to have different interlocutors. Radical Orthodoxy scholars are frequently engaged in debates with leading postmodern philosophers. Often the engagement will take the form of acknowledging that some postmodern critique of modernity is valuable but then going further to argue that the real solution to the problem identified by x or y postmodern philosopher may be found in some work of Augustine or Aquinas or other great Christian theologian. A typical complaint of faithful and educated Catholics who try to read books that have come out of the Radical Orthodoxy stable is that they cannot make head nor tail of the ideas because they lack sufficient grounding in postmodern philosophy and French literary theory. A caricature of Radical

Orthodoxy is that, instead of defending Christianity at the Bar of Kantian rationality, it is a case of defending Christianity in the bars around the Latin quarter of Paris. The *Communio* scholars tend to regard this work as highly valuable, but they themselves are usually occupied on more intra-ecclesial fronts. While the *Communio* scholars are often employed in specifically Catholic academies, offering a theological education to those who are already faithful Catholics, the two groups are nonetheless self-consciously aware of common goals and very similar approaches to the study of theology. Close bonds of friendship and what might be called genuine Christian fellowship exist between scholars across the *Communio* and RO circles. For a work comparing Milbank and Ratzinger, recourse can be had to Peter Samuel Kucer's *Truth and Politics: A Theological Comparison of Joseph Ratzinger and John Milbank.*[92] While acknowledging the many points of convergence between Milbank and Ratzinger, Kucer nonetheless argues that a significant difference is to be found in their respective approaches to the ideas of the Italian political philosopher Giovan Battista (Giambattista) Vico (1668–1744).

The most significant difference, however, between the two groups is that some (not all) Radical Orthodoxy members take a different stance on the theological significance of gender differences from that of card-carrying *Communio* authors. The typical concrete issues here are the ordination of women and the moral status of homosexual practices. The Anglicans who publish under the RO banner have no opposition to the ordination of women, and some, not all, regard homosexual practices as morally unproblematic, whereas the Catholics tend to follow the magisterial teaching of the Catholic Church on all issues, including those pertaining to gender distinctions and sexual morality. As a generalisation, there is a tendency for RO scholars who concur with the Catholic understanding of the significance of sexual difference to 'swim the Tiber', something that was psychologically easier during the pontificate of Benedict XVI who was not only a world-class scholar to whom Oxbridge types could relate, but also someone who shared many of the intellectual presuppositions of the RO circle. There was also a noted intellectual affinity between Rowan Williams, the former archbishop of Canterbury and mentor for some in the RO circle, and Pope Benedict, by virtue of their common interest in the works of St Augustine. Even in the context of sexual ethics, it is interesting to note that in his famous 'The Body's Grace' lecture, Rowan Williams acknowledged that once the Church of England accepted contraception, it opened the gate to homosexuality. Ratzinger would probably agree with William's logic but would suggest that the Anglicans made a mistake in opening this particular gate.

A Christocentric moral theology

Consistent with the eschewal of a purely secular rationality, the *Communio* scholars are also inclined to approach moral theology from the perspective of a specifically Trinitarian anthropology. As Gil Bailie explains:

> Cardinal Joseph Ratzinger insisted that the communion of Persons in the Trinity constitutes man's 'basic anthropological shape'. In assessing this basic anthropological shape, the *Genesis* story contains treasures galore, if we but take the time to extract them. Of course, a truly Trinitarian understanding of the God in whose image and likeness man is made comes into focus only with the Incarnation of the second Person of the Trinity. A Trinitarian theology necessitates a Christological anthropology, for the self-donation within the Trinity illuminates the overflowing of the Trinity in the Incarnation of the one who, 'though he was in the form of God, did not count equality with God a thing to be grasped, but emptied himself' (Phil. 2.6-7). Creatures made in the image and likeness of such a God will have an ordination to self-gift written into their spiritual DNA. 'The Trinitarian love is the only ultimate form of all love', writes Balthasar, 'both the love between God and men, and that between human persons'.[93]

A good introduction to this territory is *Principles of Christian Morality* by Ratzinger, Schürmann and Balthasar. In his contribution to this work Ratzinger responds to the statement of B. Schüller that 'in view of the fact that all ethical demands are in principle accessible to rational insight, the ethical message of the New Testament must be seen as a communication of ethical insight in a Socratic manner'.[94] Ratzinger remarks that while he agrees with St Paul's idea that the Gentiles who know not the law, nonetheless have it written on their hearts, what is 'gravely lacking' in Schüller's statement is 'the realistic context of experience by which Paul explicates and qualifies it'.[95] Ratzinger states emphatically that 'the fact that the Bible's moral pronouncements can be traced to other cultures or to philosophical thought in no way implies that morality is a function of mere reason'.[96]

Balthasar treats a supposed 'pure reason' approach to moral issues as a return to pre-biblical ethics. A pre-biblical ethics takes its bearings by *physis*. It enquires into the good of human beings by drawing analogies with the good(s) of natural things. Any such human good so discerned will 'retain a worldly and finite dimension and to that extent hinders human freedom of decision from attaining its full stature'.[97] However once the biblical vision is allowed entrance to the discernment process, 'man is raised to a freedom that can no longer take its pattern of behaviour from subhuman nature'.[98] Further if this freedom 'will not render thanks to the God of grace in the Christian understanding, it will logically seek its source in itself. It will understand ethical action as self-legislation, initially, perhaps, recapitulating earlier patterns of cosmology (cf. Spinzoa, Goethe, Hegel) and ultimately jettisoning this preliminary state (cf. Feuerbach, Nietzsche).'[99] Note that it is significant here that Balthasar offers his own alternative genealogy of morals to that of Nietzsche. For Nietzsche all biblical-based moralities are rooted in resentment. For Balthasar all pre-biblical-based moralities are limited in their intellectual horizons, and the post-biblically based moralities of Feuerbach and Nietzsche and their descendants are themselves based on a form of resentment – specifically a resentment of the fact that human freedom cannot be realised without grace. Balthasar concludes that it is impossible to achieve a synthesis between the fulfilment of the individual and that of the community on the basis of a post-Christian social agreement to recognise reciprocal limits on the actions of free subjects who are per se unlimited. The logic of Balthasar's position is that social decay and barbarism are the most likely outcomes of attempts to ground morality on something other than the God of Revelation.

Livio Melina has summarised Balthasar's approach in the following propositions:

> We have here a powerful theological synthesis of moral theology anchored in the following elements: (1) the main axis is a Christocentric theological anthropology of a filial nature: in Christ we are predestined to be 'sons in the Son'; (2) the moral bond is placed within the personal relationship of sons in the Son with regard to the Father; (3) the Law of the Old Testament is summed up in the link of obedience of the Son to the Father; and thus the natural law too becomes a fragment of the Christological whole; (4) the exterior aspect is retained, but it becomes polarized in the Spirit with interiority.[100]

Melina concludes that for Balthasar the idea of constructing an ethics with reference to reason alone is 'the extreme consequence of the pharisaical temptation of an autonomous justification of man before the law'.[101] He adds that Balthasar is also reserved about attempts to link ethics to ideas about human happiness, which he regards as selfish, and prefers the Ignatian principle '*ad maiorem Dei gloriam*' (all for the glory of God), which alone makes sense of martyrdom and is consistent with the disinterested purity of love.[102]

Central to the moral theology of the *Communio* theologians is an understanding of the nature and grace relationship, which is both non-extrinsicist and non-Rahnerian. Stratford Caldecott explained Balthasar's position on the nature and grace relationship in the following terms:

> Balthasar does not accept Rahner's argument that the a priori conditions for our acts of knowing and willing include a supernatural existential towards the Triune God. ... His own way of understanding the gratuity of grace is less in terms of a metaphysics of knowledge than of a metaphysics of freedom. ... In Balthasar's understanding, grace is a participation in God's nature, and thus precisely in God's freedom. Grace cannot after all be inbuilt at the creation (i.e. within the pre-conscious structure of human subjectivity). A personal 'call' addressed from without is necessary to open us to grace, a call ultimately from the Cross – a call to which grace itself gives us the ever-greater capacity to respond. The 'first gift' of existence and receptivity, including the desire for a gift that would exceed our nature, must be clearly distinguished from the 'second gift' that is sanctifying grace. Balthasar writes that God 'offers to provide a home in the realm of the infinite (that is, of God) for finite freedom's essential self-transcendence; he offers it the right of citizenship there. This is something to which finite freedom cannot itself lay claim, on the basis of its own transcendental structure [Rahner's supernatural existential] ...; any such 'claim' would conflict inwardly with the act of thanksgiving for the gift itself.[103]

For a more extensive account of these topics, recourse can be had to Volume III of Balthasar's *Theo-Drama,* especially the section on Infinite and Finite Freedom.

The nuptial mystery

The leading proponent of the *Communio* approach to theology in contemporary times is Cardinal Angelo Scola, the Archbishop of Milan and alleged runner-up in the last papal conclave, described by *The Tablet* as the Crown Prince under the papacies of John Paul II and Benedict XVI. Prior to his elevation as Patriarch of Venice and then Archbishop of Milan, Scola was the Rector of the Pontifical Lateran University and a President of the John Paul II Institute for Marriage and Family. In this academic post he developed John Paul II's ideas contained in his *Catechesis on Human*

Love in conjunction with Balthasar's ideas on Trinitarian theology, and the combination of the two produced his proposal for a Nuptial Mystery perspective for systematic theology. His outline of this methodology was presented in his farewell address to the scholars of the Lateran in 2002 and has been published as an appendix to his book *The Nuptial Mystery*.[104] In this address he distinguished between 'spousal vocabulary', 'nuptial language' and the 'nuptial mystery'. By 'spousal vocabulary' he meant concrete images such as bride–bridegroom, the wedding feast and adultery. By 'nuptial language' he meant the 'hermeneutical elaboration of spousal categories, the most outstanding of which occurs in Ephesians 5: 21-33', while by 'nuptial mystery' he meant a 'critical and organic elaboration of nuptial language for the sake of the *intellectus fidei*'.[105]

Scola's Nuptial Mystery approach to systematic theology has been taken up by younger scholars associated with the international network of John Paul II Institutes. These scholars are careful to avoid what Scola called a 'maximalist' interpretation of the nuptial mystery – one that is too literalist or univocal and does not heed the principle that in the use of analogical language in theology, the difference between God and the human person, or some divine attribute and human attribute, is always greater than the similarity. Specifically, Scola warned that a failure to heed this principle could lead to an 'anthropomorphic deformation of our understanding of God' and even the introduction of sexuality into God himself. He stated that 'nuptial language must remain analogical, limiting itself to uncovering yet another point of view that can enrich the great tradition of Christian thought. If we take our cue from the spousal vocabulary of the Bible, we can opportunely integrate the language of being, substance, causality, the transcendentals, and gift with the nuptial mystery'.[106] Scola wanted to avoid the situation where spousal intimacy became a kind of one-size fits all hermeneutical lens through which to process every element of the kerygma. He did not want the nuptial mystery to serve the same function in Catholic theology that the class war serves in Marxist philosophy and varieties of Liberation Theology.

Some interpretations of John Paul II's *Catechesis on Human Love* have fallen over the cliff in a maximalist direction, leading to the criticism, from intelligent Thomists with a good sense of humour, that the difference between Thomists and *Communio* scholars is that Thomists think that human beings are most like God in their intellectual attributes, while *Communio* scholars think that human beings are most like God in their reproductive capacities. In part this is a contemporary revival of the old Dominican and Franciscan debates about the relationship between love and reason. Nonetheless (all caveats notwithstanding) Scola was proposing that where the hot-button issues of the day are about freedom and self-development and sexual identity, the Nuptial Mystery theology has much to contribute and is not dangerous, provided one keeps in mind that where analogies are used of God and the human person, the differences are always greater.

The nuptial mystery was a core theme of Pope Benedict's Apostolic Exhortation *Sacramentum Caritatis*. In paragraph twenty-seven he offered an extensive presentation of the links between Eucharistic theology and the nuptial mystery in the following terms:

> The Eucharist, as the sacrament of charity, has a particular relationship with the love of man and woman united in marriage. ... 'The entire Christian life bears the mark of the spousal love of Christ and the Church. Already Baptism, the entry into the People of God, is a nuptial mystery; it is so to speak the nuptial bath which precedes the wedding feast, the Eucharist.' ... By the power of the sacrament, the marriage bond is intrinsically linked to the eucharistic unity of Christ the Bridegroom and his Bride, the Church (cf. Eph. 5.31-32). The mutual consent that husband and wife exchange in Christ, which establishes them as a community of life and love, also has a eucharistic dimension. Indeed, in the theology of Saint Paul, conjugal love is a sacramental sign of Christ's love for his Church, a love culminating in the Cross, the expression of his 'marriage' with humanity and at the same time the origin and heart of the Eucharist.

These themes have been amplified in the theology of Cardinal Ouellet who understands the sacrament of marriage, including the exchange of love between husband and wife, as the couple's participation in the exchange of 'gifts' between the Divine Persons:

> God's covenant with Israel and humanity is the story of a wedding. The symbol par excellence of the biblical revelation is conjugal love. A couple stands at the beginning of salvation history and another at its conclusion: Adam and Eve set the history of humanity in motion, while the Lamb and his Bride, who descends from God in heaven, concludes the adventure of historical time. In the span of time between the initial couple and the eschatological couple, the Holy Spirit implores and summons; he prays for the final fulfilment together with the Bride whom he has called.[107]

In the context of the theology of marriage, Ouellet argues that 'the task of theology today is to rethink the "goods" (St Augustine) and "ends" (St Thomas) of marriage from the Christocentric perspective of "gifts" (Mattheeuws) and "fruitfulness" (Balthasar), in order to integrate all the dimensions of marriage and conjugal life within love'.[108] He believes that such 'a deeper understanding of nuptial sacramentality is certainly one of the most necessary and pressing tasks of contemporary theology' and, further, that 'we need to deploy a nuptial Christology in order to explore further the foundations of the Church's sacramentality'.[109] Scholars currently working within this field include Angelo Scola, Alain Mattheeuws, Piero Coda, Giorgio Mazzanti, Adam G. Cooper and Conor Sweeney. Piero Coda is based at the Sophia University in Loppiano, outside of Florence, where, consistent with the emphasis on the nuptial mystery, there is not a separate department of theology and philosophy but one department of Trinitarian Ontology.

Ouellet concludes that the 'overcoming of modern rationalism, and of the separation it has introduced between nature and grace, faith and reason, opens space for such a new "Trinitarian ontology" and for the symbolic realism it naturally engenders'.[110] Such an ontology 'builds organically upon the heritage of St. Thomas Aquinas, whose conception of *esse* as *actus essendi* is open to new developments that take their starting point from the absolute a priori of all human knowledge: love'.[111] Ouellet is prepared to concede that Heidegger was correct about Western philosophy being marked by a 'forgetfulness of being' that descended into onto-theology. However Ouellet believes that Aquinas was not guilty of this error because his *actus essendi* is not an idea but a gift.[112]

Against the 'hinduisation' of the Catholic faith

Although this may sound odd, in the sense of being so obvious as to be unremarkable, the *Communio* scholars are all united in the judgement that so-called 'pastoral theology', now in the pontificate of Francis commonly called 'field hospital theology', must be predicated upon or nested within, the entire intellectual treasury of the Church, and not treated as itself a kind of 'master discipline' that takes epistemic priority over Scripture and Tradition. This principle (of the *Communio* scholars) is often summarised in the phrase 'the priority of *theoria* over *praxis*', or 'the priority of *logos* over *ethos*'. It is presupposed in all *Communio* theology, but especially strong in the works of Ratzinger. In relation to the *Dutch Catechism* (1966) and the so-called 'new catechesis' of the 1970s with its emphasis on the social acceptibility of the faith, Ratzinger wrote:

> It was necessary [according to the proponents of the *Dutch Catechism*] to limit oneself to questions for beginners instead of looking for ways

to go beyond to things not yet understood. Yet this latter is the only method which positively modifies man and the world. Thus, the faith's potential for change was paralyzed. From that point, practical theology was no longer understood as a concrete development of dogmatic or systematic theology but as having a value in itself. This corresponds perfectly with the new tendency to subordinate theory to praxis, which, in the context of Neo-Marxist and positivist philosophies, was making headway even in theology. All these things have the effect of a restricting anthropology: the priority of method over content means the domination of anthropology over theology, in the sense that theology has to find a place for itself in a radical anthropocentrism. The decline of anthropology in its turn causes new centers of gravity to appear: the reign of sociology, again with the primacy of experience as new criteria for the understanding of the traditional faith. ... The fact that one no longer has the courage to present the faith as an organic whole in itself, but only as selected reflections of partial anthropological experiences, is founded in a certain distrust of totality. It is to be explained by a crisis of faith, or more exactly, of the common faith of the Church of all times.[113]

Ratzinger was never likely to go along with the Dutch trend given Guardini's influence on his intellectual formation. Before the priority of *praxis* revolution of the Leuven–Nijmegen theologians in the 1960s and the Liberation Theologians in the 1970s, Guardini had already traced the trend to give priority to *praxis* or *ethos* back to Kant and condemned it as a quintessentially Protestant mental habit. In *The Spirit of the Liturgy* Guardini wrote:

The Church forgives everything more readily than an attack on truth. She knows that if a man falls, but leaves truth unimpaired, he will find his way back again. But if he attacks the vital principle, then the sacred order of life is demolished. Moreover, the Church has constantly viewed with the deepest distrust every ethical conception of truth and of dogma. Any attempt to base the truth of a dogma merely on its practical value is essentially un-Catholic. The Church represents truth – dogma – as an absolute fact, based upon itself, independent of all confirmation from the moral or even from the practical sphere. Truth is truth because it is truth. ... The will has to admit that it is blind and needs the light, the leadership, and the organizing formative power of truth. It must admit as a fundamental principle the primacy of knowledge over the will, of the Logos over the Ethos.[114]

In his book *The Nature and Mission of Theology: Essays to Orient Theology in Today's Debates*, Ratzinger adopted Albert Görres' expression 'the Hinduization of the faith' to refer to the mentality that wants to give priority to *ethos* over *logos*.[115] Whether the mentality is of Protestant or Hindu provenance, or both, the *Communio* thoelogians stand opposed to any lowest common denominator presentation of the faith in the interests of pastoral pragmatism.

Communio ecclesiology

The key works in the ecclesiology of the *Communio* scholars are de Lubac's *Catholicism* (1947), *The Splendor of the Church* (1953), *The Motherhood of the Church* (1971) and Balthasar's *The Office of Peter and the Structure of the Church*, first published in German in 1974 as *Der anti-römische Affekt*.

The *Communio* ecclesiology follows upon that of Pope Pius XII in the 1943 encyclical *Mystici Corporis Christi*. According to this encyclical, there does not exist within the Church a dichotomy between an active and a passive element, for example, the clerical as the active element, the laity as the passive element, but rather all members of the Church are called to work on the perfection of the Body of Christ.

In order to explore this idea of the Church as the Mystical Body of Christ, both de Lubac and Balthasar focused on developing a deeper understanding of the spiritual relationships within this Body. Here the relations with the Trinity are of primary importance, along with the typological relationships found in the Scriptures, the sacramental relationships, the historical relationships between the Old and New Testaments, and the social relationships both within the Church and between members of the Church and those outside her governance.

With reference to the Trinitarian relationships the important point is that the Divine Persons are not in a hierarchy. God the Father is not superior to God the Son or God the Holy Spirit. There is an equality within a difference, with the individual Persons taking their identity from their own spiritual missions. With reference to the notion of sacramental relations, de Lubac emphasised that the sacramental form of relationality is one that ties together the Church as the Mystical Body of Christ with the Church as the historical people of God. He argued that 'if Christ is the sacrament of God, the Church is for us the sacrament of Christ: she represents him, in the full and ancient meaning of the term, she really makes Him present'. Moreover, the Church not only links the visible with the invisible, time with eternity, but also the universal and the particular, the Old and New Covenants. This link between the invisible and visible elements of ecclesial communion constitutes the Church as the Sacrament of Salvation.

In *The Motherhood of the Church* de Lubac held that the 'particular Church is always universalist and centripetal'. The particular or local Church is not merely an administrative division of the total Church, like a province or state in a federal union. Rather, 'at the heart of each particular Church, all the universal Church is present in principle' and between the two there is a mutual interiority.

A hallmark of *Communio* ecclesiology is therefore the idea that the Mystical Body of Christ is a Communion or symphony of different spiritual missions, all reliant on each other. Specifically, Balthasar argued that when one reads the Gospels one can see that Christ's friends and disciples form what he called a 'Christological constellation' of typological characters, each representing a different spiritual mission in the life of the Church. For example, the Johannine mission, (i.e. the mission of St John the beloved disciple) was one of self-sacrificial love and contemplation; the mission of St James was one of preserving the Tradition; the mission of St Peter was one of Church governance; the mission of St Paul was one of prophetic movement and utterance. Each mission is dependent on the others and operates in a symphonic harmony.

In both Balthasar's theology and the theology of Vatican II's *Lumen Gentium*, the Petrine mission is linked to the ministerial priesthood, which is stated to be different in essence from the priesthood of all believers. According to *Lumen Gentium* paragraph eleven, the two priesthoods – the ministerial priesthood and the royal priesthood of all believers – are different in kind, and not just different in degree. The difference is based on sacramental ordination. This is an important distinction and one that of course differentiates the Catholic form of Christianity from most versions of Protestantism.

Balthasar also emphasised that all the individual missions participate in the whole. Speaking specifically of the missions of the 'apostolic foursome' (Peter, Paul, James and John), Balthasar wrote:

> James will not put forward any other law but the perfect law of liberty (James 1.25), nor will he be any less firm than Paul in opposing contentiousness (James 4.1). Paul cannot proclaim any freedom that does not express itself in the 'law of Christ' (Gal. 6.2; cf. Rom. 8.2). He expects the Gentiles to accept the faith of Abraham and to be acquainted with the Old Testament prototypes (1 Cor. 10.11) and exercises a veritably 'Petrine' control in the communities, while constantly holding up to them the ideal of Johannine love. As we know

Peter was only permitted to take office on the basis of his (Johannine) love, and the letters attributed to him clearly show a process of osmosis between his understanding of the gospel and that of the other three. John, finally, is also an apostle, and even in later years can sound a 'Petrine' note when it is a question of guarding or restoring order in a local church. All their missions are clearly defined, but, as we have seen, they are not hermetically sealed off from each other.[116]

Thus, a further most significant hallmark of the *Communio* ecclesiology is the respect it confers upon the Petrine Office and the ministerial priesthood. There is, one might say, a 'high theology' of both. Priests are not mere pastoral workers but an '*alter Christus*'. The Petrine Office is something more than a clearing house for new ideas and pastoral projects. Since *Communio* scholars have a Christological reading of the priesthood and since they view the relationship between priests and the Church as spousal, they affirm the practice of the reservation of the priesthood to men. The Church is feminine, the priesthood masculine. It is for this reason that battles over the issue of the ordination of women are often fought on the territory of Balthasar's Trinitarian anthropology and his understanding of the theological significance of gender distinctions.

The importance of friendship and scholar-saints

A final point to be made about the *Communio* approach to doing theology is that there are strong bonds of friendship among many of the scholars in the *Communio* circles and that this is consistent with an epistemic principle of respecting the witness of scholar-saints. In *Fides et Ratio*, John Paul II argued that 'truth is attained not only by way of reason but also through trusting acquiescence to other persons who can guarantee the authenticity and certainty of the truth itself', adding that 'the ancient philosophers proposed friendship as one of the most appropriate contexts for sound theological enquiry'.[117] Similarly, in his book *On the Way to Jesus Christ*, Ratzinger remarked that 'evangelisation is never merely intellectual communication; it is a process of experience, the purification and transformation of our lives, and for this to happen, company along the way is needed'.[118] Antonio Sicari has suggested that 'the value of communion and communication among the greatest possible number of reflective believers, as if all were simultaneously in the circle, co-present today to form the gathering and assembly of today, stands at the foundation of this new conception of theology and of its method'.[119]

Conclusion

The *Communio* method of doing theology is based on a particular genealogy of secularism, a particular reading of what has gone wrong in the history of Catholic theology and the social embodiment of successive waves of understanding the relationship between God and creation, nature and grace, faith and reason, the Church and the world. Included in this is the idea that Christ's exhortation to his disciples to read the signs of their times was a plea for them to understand the significance of his Incarnation, of the effect of his Incarnation on human nature and the meaning of human life. It was not a call for them to become competent sociologists who can analyse social trends and then in the manner of professional spin-doctors, correlate Christian ideas to the top trending issues. It was not a point about marketing or the way to do theology. It was a point about Christ being the Lord of time and history. It was a point about eschatology. Further, the fact that Christ is the Second Person of the Trinity, the 'Word made Flesh', and that human persons were made in the image of God to grow into the likeness of Christ, means that there is no neutral intellectual space. There is no 'pure reason' and no 'pure nature' and no 'purely secular social space'. As Abraham Kuyper put the proposition: 'There is not one square inch in the whole domain of our human existence over which Christ, who is Sovereign over all, does not cry, Mine!' Kuyper was a Calvinist, like Karl Barth whom Balthasar dearly wanted to convert. While the understanding of sacramentality of a Calvinist and that of a *Communio* scholar are worlds apart – and hence the sticky problem of the *analogia entis* – there is nonetheless common ground on the assessment that secularism is a Christian heresy that arises when people try to offer the world a rationality without God, a morality without Christ, and truth separated from beauty and goodness. As Aidan Nichols wrote in one of the earliest Anglophone assessments of the theology of Balthasar: 'Balthasar aims at nothing less than a Christocentric revolution in Catholic theology'.[120] Since impiety is rooted in the heart and the heart is the place of integration of all the activities of the soul, any analysis of the correct way to do theology requires an acknowledgement of the need to have all the faculties of the soul in good operational order. This includes their nourishment by the theological virtues and the 'help along the way' given in friendship through the mediation of saints both living and in eternity.

The *Concilium* Alternative

Since its foundation in 1965 the *Concilium* journal has been the flagship for Catholic theologians interested in correlating the faith to contemporary political movements or recontextualising the faith with reference to the 'critical consciousness' of a given era. Included in its mission statement is the following paragraph:

> Since 1965, with a critical and constructive discourse, Concilium has contributed to new ways of doing theology. We want to reach our readers between the faithful and all persons of good will, leaders and members of churches and of social movements, and persons in institutions dedicated to or interested in theology. We seek to respond to the signs of our times, to the longing for a new humanity and for the integrity of creation. We are in solidarity with the irruption of the poor and with theological insights of women and men throughout the world and especially of marginalized peoples.[1]

What de Lubac, Balthasar and Ratzinger are to the *Communio* approach to theology, Karl Rahner, Edward Schillebeeckx and Johann Baptist Metz are to the *Concilium* approach to theology. In the early years of the journal's foundation Rahner was a central figure, though Schillebeeckx is the most influential among the foundation trio for the contemporary generation of *Concilium*-style theologians who are most prominent in the Low Countries. The expression '*Concilium* alternative' should not however be narrowly construed to refer solely to those theologians who regularly publish in *Concilium* but should also refer to those theologians throughout the world whose approach to doing Catholic theology exhibits the hallmarks of the methodology of the founding fathers of the *Concilium* project.

Karl Rahner's project list for post-conciliar theology

In volume nine of Karl Rahner's *Theological Investigations* one finds several essays that outline his vision of the theological enterprise after the Second

Vatican Council. In the first essay 'The Second Vatican Council's Challenge to Theology' Rahner observed that the Council's endorsement of a project of 'dialogue with the world' does not entail 'merely a new, additional and partial region of study for theology – although it does mean that as well'; in addition to this, it entails engagement with every dimension of theology.[2] In Rahner's parlance the 'world' refers to non-Catholic scholars and other persons who control the switch points of cultural power, the 'Commentariat' as it were.

Rahner specifically recommended an extension and further development of historical theology, including the history of doctrine, Patristic literature and canon law. In biblical theology he stated that the most immediate task is to 'show that there is a profound difference between the historical Jesus and the Christ of Faith', though he acknowledged that 'there is a real connection between them'.[3] In this essay Rahner was particularly critical of the propensity within systematic theology to drive biblical scholarship in search of scriptural proof texts for theological arguments. He argued that, in contrast, 'biblical theology is commissioned to determine, as a result of its own studies, what are to be the themes of systematic theology, i.e. not merely to insert the appropriate biblical material into a given scholastic framework'.[4] Moreover, 'as opposed to the previous analytic and scholastic method (whereby a thesis is propounded, analysed according to its concepts and then proved from "sources"), there can be no doubt that an a posteriori and synthetic method will facilitate a considerable enrichment and change of perspective of the compass of dogmatic theology. Themes such as a Theology of History, a Theology of the Word, the Hermeneutics of Theological Statements, will then automatically find a place in systematic theology'.[5] For Rahner, biblical theology must be the 'mistress, not the handmaid' of dogmatic theology. *Communio* scholars would strongly agree with this last statement and with the call for a more synthetic approach to theological scholarship.

Rahner also observed that the documents of the Second Vatican Council have 'moved many themes in ecclesiology to the forefront of our theological awareness', themes that will require much deeper study.[6] Specifically Rahner offered the following list of topics in need of theological reflection: the more precise relation of papal primacy to the whole episcopate, the nature of the Magisterium, the relationship of Scripture and Tradition; the place of law in the Church as the sacramental gift of the Holy Spirit; charismatic roles in the Church; the non-Christian's possibility of salvation; the ecclesiological aspect of Penance (and of all the sacraments); the nature of Revelation and salvation history; the general application of the synodical principle in the Church's constitution; the ecclesiological significance of the Evangelical Counsels and of the Religious Orders in the Church; the meaning and importance of what is called the hierarchy of revealed truth; the theology of mission; the possibility of a communication *in sacris* among separated Christians; the theology of the function of the non-Christian religions in collective and individual salvation history; the pope's obligation to avail himself of the Church's collegial organs (even if this obligation cannot juridically be standardised any further); the theology of the local community and altar-congregation as the Church; the possibility of a historical development of the *jus divinum* in apostolic times; the theology of the Word and theological hermeneutics; the Church as *sacramentum salutis mundi*; the theology of sin in the Church; the theology of the Church's historically determined knowledge of truth; and of the equally possible fallibility of this knowledge.[7]

To this list of issues in ecclesiology Rahner added that the Conciliar *Decree on Priestly Formation* called for a reform of the territory of moral theology so that it too would be placed on biblical foundations and connected to the subject of love. Rahner then listed a whole array of projects in the field of theological anthropology and Christology that he believed were thrown open by the Council but not resolved. He asserted that 'modern-man's' experience of God requires a new perspective uniting the metaphysical with the theology of the Revelation of God'; that Christology requires a presentation of Christ 'within an evolutionist world-view and within the perspective of a salvation-history which embraces the whole of humanity from the very outset, understanding Christ really as the apex of this general history of salvation and Revelation'; that 'there is the question of a framework of Christological concepts avoiding any undertones likely to seem mythological to the ears of modern man, and the search for a method of retracing the progress of the earliest pre-Pauline Christology from the Historical Jesus to the Christ of Faith'.[8] With respect to theological anthropology, theologians need to 'interpret modern man to himself as he actually experiences himself in an existence embracing more than the "animal rationale" of an abstract metaphysics'; they need to develop 'a Christian anthropology which grasps the original unity of nature and grace and does not banish what we in Christian terms call "grace" to some region beyond concrete existence, an anthropology which does not simply abandon facts like inter-communication, love, the experience of the absurd, of death, to moral theology or the realm of pious literature'.[9]

In the territory of dogmatic theology, Rahner called for a 'real hermeneutics of eschatological statements' that addresses the issue of the relationship between individual and collective eschatology, as well as a theology of hope that goes beyond 'text-book' treatments of the theological virtue of hope.[10]

Finally, Rahner argued for the necessity of the development of a pastoral theology that would address issues such as the following: 'how the Church as a whole is to live and act, how the central authorities in Rome should be constructed, how we should have a strategy of mission and not merely "tactics", how a diocese should be administered, and how we should be influencing the "politics" of learning and culture with its wide sphere of penetration'.[11]

This list is very extensive and highlights the fact that the documents of Vatican II raise many more questions than they answered and arguably some of the issues enumerated above were not raised by the Council at all, but are projects close to the heart of Rahner and which he can easily defend with reference to the Conciliar call for dialogue with the world. It is a point of historical interest that the topic of the general application of the synodical principle in the Church's constitution began to be studied by the International Theological Commission in 2014 when it became clear that this is a hot issue during the papacy of Francis, which has been described as one in which the Church exists in a state of constant synodical reflection. The list of topics for pastoral theology, namely, 'how the Church as a whole is to live and act, how the central authorities in Rome should be constructed, how we should have a strategy of mission and not merely "tactics", how a diocese should be administered, and how we should be influencing the "politics" of learning and culture with its wide sphere of penetration' also sound quite prescient in the second decade of the twenty-first century. The problem of clerical pragmatism and the practice of giving priority to tactics over mission, the problem of dioceses being run like miniature corporations with all the alienation of the lay faithful and rank and file of the parish clergy that such practices entail (including the problem of delegating episcopal pastoral responsibilities to lawyers and accountants), the problem of financial corruption within the curia, the problem of the intellectual marginalisation of the Catholic academy and of the usurpation of authority over the development of curricula in Catholic educational institutions by national and provincial governments are all serious issues in the current era.

It was Rahner's contention that 'the subject-matter which the Council has delivered to tomorrow's theology is not the same subject-matter as discussed explicitly by the Council itself', and he was critical of the idea that 'the main task of systematic theology in the next few decades [is that] of writing commentaries on the Council's documents, and justifying historically and deepening systematically the themes explicitly discussed by the Council'.[12] For Rahner the event of the Council became a springboard for a kind of systematic house-cleaning and renovation exercise in the different fields of theological study. In a footnote on the final page of his essay on the Council's challenge to theology he wrote that the first fruits of the kind of international cooperation of theologians he envisaged in this essay were the establishment of the theological journal *Concilium* and the publication of the lexicon *Sacramentum Mundi*.

Another significant element in Rahner's long list of theological projects is what he acknowledged to be the state of flux in which the discipline of philosophy finds itself. He observed that theologians are confronted with numerous philosophies that cannot be synthesised with each other, and as a consequence 'theology today is experiencing perforce what we may be permitted to call its "gnoseological concupiscence"'.[13] Concretely, for Rahner this meant that 'every theologian will bring to his theology the particular form, the historical and fragmentary nature of his own given understanding of existence'.[14] Different theologians will be influenced by different philosophical schools. Rahner added to this his prediction that in the future theology's chief partner-in-dialogue will not be philosophy in a traditional sense at all, 'but the "unphilosophical" pluralistic sciences and the kind of understanding of existence which they promote either directly or indirectly'.[15] It is precisely here that one begins to identify the lines of fissure between the former Conciliar *Periti*. The *Communio* types, who would have little difficulty agreeing with quite a number of Rahner's proposals above, were not tempted by this 'gnoseological concupiscence'. In part this was due to their strongly Patristic anthropology, which made them hostile to modern conceptions of rationality.

Modern canons of rationality and gnoseological concupiscence

Arguably it is the openness or closure to modern conceptions of rationality that is the most important marker for distinguishing liberal from non-liberal theology. Underlying these differences is a different stance towards magisterial teaching and the authority of the Congregation for the Doctrine of the Faith. In a 2012 article for *Concilium* Agenor Brighenti noted that 'a particular point of tension within theology itself has to do with the type of reason that underpins it, pre-modern rationality or modern rationality. If theology wants to be a science, in the sense of an academic discipline, it must start from the basis of modern rationality'.[16] He added that 'since science is carried out in the academy, it must be an anomaly for a theologian to require the *nihil obstat* of the magisterium to do theology in the Church's academies'.[17]

While the idea of obtaining the *nihil obstat* for something that is supposed to be defended by reference to 'modern conceptions of rationality' is indeed somewhat comical, even farcical, the presumption that theologians 'must start from the basis of modern rationality' is however far from universally accepted. Almost all Thomists and *Communio* theologians and even many Liberation Theologians have a different opinion and refuse to approach the work of theology by acceding to the demands of modern conceptions of rationality. The American *Communio* scholar Larry Chapp summarised the trajectory of what he classified as 'liberal theology', or one might say 'theology that is undertaken with reference to modern canons of rationality', in the following paragraph:

> [Gotthold Ephraim] Lessing [1729–1781] held that historical-contingent events were inadequate vessels for the timeless and universal truths of reason. In the wake of this critique, critical philosophy will question the validity of a historical revelation that claims immunity from the historicists' insight that all knowledge – including religious knowledge – is culturally conditioned. Therefore, the so-called 'hermeneutics of suspicion' engages in the deconstruction of the once-normative tradition in order to reconstruct it along the lines of modernity's canons of rationality. Liberal theology is, therefore, characterized by a deep distrust of the historical particularity of revelation and an even deeper distrust of the particularities of the ecclesial mediation of that revelation. The result is the liberal quest to distil the essence of revelation by boiling away the various 'media' of revelation (Scripture, Church) in the heat of critical abstraction in order finally to discover the residue of truth left behind.[18]

From the mid-1960s onwards, wave after wave of scholarly articles appeared subjecting the content of Revelation to the heat of critical abstraction, with the effect of deconstructing one or other element of Catholic doctrine or practice. After 1989, when modernity and its canons of rationality ceased to be fashionable, the projects of deconstruction continued unabated with reference to a plethora of postmodern philosophies. The cumulative effect was that it became hard to distinguish Catholic theologians and their projects from New Left and post-modern philosophers and their projects.

In his essay 'What Does a Non-Christian Expect of the Church?' published in *Concilium* in 1968, Roger Garaudy (1913–2012), then a French communist philosopher and later a convert to Islam, stated that non-Christians expect the Catholic Church to do the following:

1. Recognize the autonomy of human values in the fields of knowledge and action;
2. Embrace man's Promethean ambition for a continuous creation of the world of man and by man;
3. Enfranchise socialism as the condition for the unbounded development of all men and the whole of man.[19]

Many Catholic intellectuals of the generation of 1968 found it easy to accede to these three expectations. In his *The Spirit of Vatican II: Western European*

Progressive Catholicism in the Long Sixties, Gerd-Rainer Horn made a study of the Christian, predominately Catholic, backgrounds of many of the New Left intellectuals. In a chapter titled 'From Seminarians to Radical Student Activists', subtitled 'The Hidden Christianity of Leading Student Radicals', Horn observed that the most significant radical leaders of the generation of 1968 were not merely nominally Catholic or Calvinist, as one might expect in the countries of Western Europe, but time and again they were people who had studied for the priesthood or Protestant ministry and abandoned Christianity for varieties of Marxism. Moreover, in Belgium and Holland it was the Catholic (not Protestant or secular) institutions of higher education that were the centres of New Left radicalism. Although the student picketing of the lecture theatres of the Sorbonne in May 1968 is regarded as the iconic moment in New Left student radicalism, such radicalism actually began its life in Europe at the Catholic University of Leuven in May 1966, some two years earlier than the irruption of the drama in Paris.

Horn diagnosed this social phenomenon (former Catholic seminarians and other seriously committed Catholics leaving the Church for radical political movements) as the consequence of a utopian, messianic dimension of Catholicism overlapping with secular ideals. As he wrote: 'Marxist and/ or anarchist dreams of classless societies were then common currency in many countries across Europe and the wider world, precisely at the same time that his apocalyptic eschatology propelled Johann Baptist Metz to front-line status in the galaxy of European radical Catholicism.'[20] In the theology of this particular *Concilium* editorial board member, there could be found an intoxicating fusion of New Left and Catholic eschatology.

Johann Baptist Metz

Metz (a former student of Karl Rahner) was influenced by the Marxist philosopher Ernst Bloch (1885–1977). Bloch's most important ideas are presented in his *Geist der Utopie,* first published in 1918 and revised in 1923, his *Das Prinzip Hoffnung,* published in three volumes in the 1950s and his *Atheismus im Christentum* published in 1968. In the third volume of *Das Prinzip Hoffnung,* Bloch argued that Christian ideas about the immortality of the soul are pure fantasy but nonetheless they are not without value as they are manifestations of a human need for utopia. Instead of working towards a utopian eternal life, he recommended that attention be given to building utopia on earth.

In an article on Bloch's influence on Metz's approach to theology, Murray Hofmeyr (the theologian, not the rugby player) argued that it was Bloch's

Jewish Messianism more so than his Marxism that Metz found attractive. According to Hofmeyr, 'Bloch taught Metz to appropriate eschatology as belonging to the centre of Christianity, to relate transcendence and future, and to clarify the relationship between human praxis and [the] future as transcendence.'[21] In his appropriation of Jewish eschatological themes Metz moved away from a theological interest in dogma to a theological interest in *praxis* and in this way he became the intellectual bridge between the *Concilium*-style theologians and the Liberation Theologians. Metz's most significant publications include *Theology of the World* (1968), *Faith in History and Society: Toward a Foundational Political Theology* (1979), *The Emergent Church: The Future of Christianity in a Post-bourgeois World* (1981) and *Faith and the Future*, co-authored with Jürgen Moltmann (1995).

A shortcut into these works can be found in John Marsden's essay 'The Political Theology of Johannes Baptist Metz'.[22] Marsden begins by explaining that Metz welcomed the 'anthropological shift' in Kant's critical reason and its democratic aspirations, and he felt impelled by the Marxist critique of religion to steer Catholic theology in the direction of social and political analysis. As Marsden expressed the idea: 'Too often Christianity had been domesticated to serve conservative interests and acted as opium to dull the pain of the oppressed, whereas if it bore witness to true liberty of the Gospel, it would be more of a menace to the status quo.'[23] Marsden concluded that 'it was this markedly political dimension to his theology, later deepened through his interest in the work of the Frankfurt School, which set Metz on a different course from his gratefully acknowledged mentor Karl Rahner'.[24] Taken as a whole, Metz's work can be read as a fusion of Jewish eschatological interests and the New Left's critiques of hierarchical structures and so-called bourgeois Christianity.

Feminist hermeneutics

Running alongside the interest of *Concilium*-inspired Catholic scholars in the New Left currents of Marxism was a parallel interest in Feminism, including, though not exclusively, Marxist varieties of Feminism. Writing in *Theological Studies* in 2001 Gloria L Schaab offered the following account of the methodology of feminist theologians:

> Critique in the feminist theological process begins with a 'hermeneutics of suspicion' that is wary of underlying prejudices and presuppositions that exclude women's perspectives. During this stage of the process, oppressive texts are demythologised, exclusive male

symbolism for the divine is exposed, dualisms of body and spirit are rejected, and hierarchical understandings of power are destabilised. Having thus exposed the insufficiency of the biblical and theological tradition at face value, the process moves below the surface of texts and beyond traditional sources to a retrieval of women's experiences found between the lines, in the silence, and from alternative sources. In the movement to (re) construction, feminist theology enters in to the task of reshaping key religious symbols, especially those that are problematic from the Christian feminist perspective, through strategies elaborated from the critiques outlines above. Among such concepts are Christology and soteriology, particularly as regards the maleness of Jesus. Posing particular difficulty is the doctrine of the Cross, with its conflicting symbolism of victimization and violence, as well as empowerment and solidarity. Ultimately the mystery of God articulated in predominately male imagery and Trinitarian symbolism based upon hierarchical gender models is fundamentally challenged as subversive to the reality of woman as *imago Dei* and *imago Christi*.[25]

While there are different strands in Feminist Theology, for example, liberal, Marxist, structuralist, poststructuralist, first-wave, second-wave, third-wave, radical and others, Schaab's description above does identify the typical hallmarks of the genre. Feminist hermeneutics has been a powerful component of what Rahner identified as the post-Conciliar 'gnoseological concupiscence'.

The Frankfurt School's 'Critical Theory'

Of all the philosophies on the intellectual smorgasbord, the most influential among the *Concilium* network of theologians has been the Critical Theory of the Frankfurt School of Social Research. The fundamental principles of 'Critical Theory' were set out by Max Horkheimer (1895–1973) in the *Zeitschrift für Sozialforschung* (Journal for Social Research), most of which were republished in 1968 under the title *Kritische Theorie* (Critical Theory). The historian of Marxist theory, Leszek Kołakowski, has described Horkheimer's thought as 'permeated by the Marxist principle that philosophical, religious, and sociological ideas can only be understood in relation to the interests of different social groups (but not that everything "in the last resort" comes down to class-interest), so that theory is a function of social life'.[26] Accordingly, there are no such things as 'facts' – 'perception cannot be isolated from its social genesis; both it and its objects are a social and historical product' – and 'the facts ascertained are in part determined by the collective praxis of human beings who have devised the conceptual instruments used by the investigator.'[27] Finally, 'objects as we know them are partly the product of concepts and of collective praxis, which philosophers, unaware of its origin, mistakenly petrify into a pre-individual transcendental consciousness.'[28] In short, as William L Portier concluded: 'Critical Theory attempts to exploit one of the fundamental insights of the Marxist tradition ... that the interpretation of any tradition likely involves systematic distortions of communication in the interests of those who have power and privilege.'[29]

Other luminaries of the Frankfurt School include Theodor Adorno (1903–69), Herbert Marcuse (1898–1979) and Jürgen Habermas. Habermas began his studies with Adorno and Horkheimer and then completed his *Habilitationsschrift* under the Marxist political theorist Wolfgang Abendroth (1906–85) at the University of Marburg. Adorno attacked existentialist philosophy as 'bourgeois' and together with Horkheimer in 1944 he published *Dialektik der Aufklärung* (*The Dialectic of Enlightenment*), which represented a full frontal assault on the ideal of reason as a tool of human emancipation. They regarded the universality of ideas as developed by discursive logic and the general practice of deductive reasoning and system building to be particularly oppressive. They also took a dim view of the commercialisation of art. Herbert Marcuse became famous for his 1964 publication *One Dimensional Man*, which offered an extensive critique of capitalist culture, especially 'modern man's' captivity to the dynamics of the market and Jürgen Habermas is best known for his *Theory of Communicative Action* (1981) where he tries to salvage some of the eighteenth century's faith in reason from the negative judgement of Horkheimer and Adorno, while nonetheless agreeing with them that conceptions of rationality as they developed in the post-Kantian environment did not in fact deliver the promised human emancipation from oppressive social forces, but merely got themselves entangled in systems of oppression.

Without getting too bogged down in the intricacies of 'Critical Theory' and the specific contributions of each of its proponents and their internal debates, it is sufficient to say that when 'dialogue with the world' was the top item on the theological agenda of the 1960s and 1970s, and when Catholic scholars looked around to find 'the world', the philosophers of the Frankfurt School of Social Research were the hottest team in Europe with whom they might engage in play.

In his article 'Theology and Praxis' published in 1973 Charles Davis described the attraction of the Frankfurt School's Critical Theory to contemporary Belgian and Dutch theologians in the following terms:

> Fundamental for them as a consequence of their acceptance of the
> Marxist unity of theory and *praxis* is a conviction that the permanent

self-identity of the Christian faith cannot be presupposed. ... They reject a theoretical system of identity. There is no purely theoretical centre of reference, which can serve in an abstract, speculative way as a norm of identity. Truth does not yet exist; it cannot be reached by interpretation, but it has to be produced by change. For these theologians therefore, faith is in a strong sense mediated in history through *praxis*. *Praxis* is not the application of already known truth or the carrying out of a transhistorical ideal; it is that process in and through which one comes to know present reality and future possibilities. If faith is mediated in *praxis*, it must renounce an a priori claim to self-identity and universality.

However, if the mediation of faith through *praxis* is consistently accepted, that means the destruction of theology in the current sense of the articulation of the immanent self-understanding of faith. Theology loses its boundaries as an independent discipline, because the only appropriate context for the conscious articulation of *praxis* is a theory of the development of society in its total reality. Included within such a comprehensive theory would be a critique of theological consciousness, replacing theology as a separate science.[30]

In the final paragraph of his article Davis pointed to the significance of this appropriation of Critical Theory with the rhetorical question: 'Is theology, as Schillebeeckx says, the critical self-consciousness of Christian *praxis*, or is [Leszek] Kołakowski right when he says: "For theology begins with the belief that truth has already been given to us, and its intellectual effort consists not of attrition against reality but of assimilation of something which is ready in its entirety?"'[31]

This could be described as the 'billion dollar' question of post-Conciliar Catholic theology. All Thomists and *Communio* scholars would agree with Kołakowski. The great majority, if not almost all *Concilium* and Liberation Theologians, would agree with Schillebeeckx.

Edward Schillebeeckx

As a Dominican, Schillebeeckx began his scholarly life as a Thomist but he became an enthusiast for the Enlightenment project. As he wrote:

One of the most important consequences of this movement of emancipation, which began with the Enlightenment and has continued unabated ever since, has been that authority together with all traditions, institutions and norms can no longer be justified simply by the fact that these already exist in society. They can only be justified in the light of human reason. Enlightened reason has become the principle of non-violent, free communication, which rejects everything that is repressive or oppressive in society and provides the means of solving all human conflicts and contradictions. ... What is more, the Christian critical faculty was developed not directly from the Bible or theology, but indirectly, via human reasoning.[32]

Speaking of the Frankfurt School authors, Schillebeeckx stated:

> It cannot be denied that Christians who are attempting to adapt the Church to a modern society which they have not yet subjected to critical scrutiny have much to learn from these critical theories, which have brought to light so many new forms of inhumanity caused by the present social system. The Church should above all pay attention to the just criticism that these un-critical attempts are in fact a legitimation of the status quo in society.[33]

According to Habermas, the basis of the Enlightenment is 'that science is bound to the principle that all discussion must be free from established power structures and to no other principle'.[34] Schillebeeckx concurred with Habermas and this of course impacted upon his understanding of the value to be placed on official magisterial teaching and the Congregation for the Doctrine of the Faith. In this context he wrote:

> Whereas the Church has, until quite recently, been judged only according to evangelical or theological criteria, it has now come to be regarded as one part of the whole complex establishment of society and as such subject to the same criticism as such institutions as parliament, the legal system, state education, and so on, all of which share in the evils of society. ... It is above all this situation which has made many Christian communities critical not only of society as a whole, but of the institutional Church in particular. To regard this as an infiltration of un-Christian, even demonic elements into the Church is to be blind to the 'signs of the times' and is attributable to a false ideology or to wrong information.[35]

Schillebeeckx went on to assert that 'the specifically Christian aspect of this criticism of the Church and society comes from a new understanding of Jesus of Nazareth and the Kingdom of God, often stimulated by study at various levels' and further, that 'it is impossible to believe in a Christianity that is not at one with the movement to emancipate mankind'.[36] At the conclusion of his article Schillebeeckx did offer the caveat that 'the Christian critical community must always be conscious of the limits to man's critical reason', but he did not analyse how such limits are to be ascertained in circumstances where reference to the authority of Tradition or, in the strong ecclesial sense, the authority of the Magisterium, would be contrary to the whole 'Enlightened Reason' project he is otherwise seeking to endorse.

Schillebeexkian tests for orthodoxy

In *The Understanding of Faith* (1974) Schillebeeckx offered three criteria as a test of orthodoxy: the criterion of the proportional norm, the criterion of orthopraxis and the criterion of the reception by the whole people of God. Schillebeeckx defined the first criterion as 'a certain proportion in which subsequent expressions (in their different contexts) find themselves with regard to the intentionality of the faith as inwardly determined by the mystery of Christ'.[37] This definition is particularly opaque. Schillebeeck's former student Erik Borgman has decoded the statement to mean that 'what is normative, from the perspective of faith, are not Jesus' words and actions but the relationship between the words and the deeds of Jesus on the one hand and their context on the other. Believers here and now are not asked to imitate what Jesus said or did, rather they are to relate to their context as Jesus related to his.'[38] According to Borgman, Schillebeeckx took this idea from the liberation theologian Clodovis Boff.[39] With regard to orthopraxis he says that it 'is not a consequence of a previously given, communal unity of faith, but the manner in which such a communal unity and conviction is realised'.[40] With regard to the reception 'of the whole people of God' Schillebeeckx does not say what percentage of Catholics have to agree about something for it to be classified as having received the approval of the 'whole people of God'; he merely states that one part of the Church, one region, might be a *locus theologicus* for the rest of the Church. In this list of criteria the teaching office of the Church, including the Petrine Office as it is sometimes called, is not mentioned. When Schillebeeckx does address the question of the 'teaching office' he suggests that it can act as a means of communication within the Catholic community, as a 'regulator' of the use of theological language and as a decision-making authority in circumstances where 'someone expresses certain views concerning faith in a particular situation with its own special historical conditions'.[41] Construed this way the pope becomes a kind of 'game show host' whose responsibility it is to moderate debates.

Erik Borgman underscored this tendency of the *Concilium* scholars to let go of the anchor of strong magisterial authority. According to Borgman:

> Theologians need to abandon the fiction that the truth of the tradition and the authority of the church form a firm foundation on which they can build further, up to and including the last remnants and traces. Theology has no other foundation than the God of salvation, whose mystery it may and must constantly decipher and clarify. If it takes that completely seriously, it will inevitably change fundamentally, time and again.[42]

In a statement that is unequivocally hostile to what Charles Davis described as the position of Kołakowski, though he could equally have written the names of Ratzinger and Balthasar and a very long list of former Doctors of the Church, Borgman stated that for Schillebeeckx 'theology has no reference to a reality which lies behind things and to which access is to be had only through the Catholic Tradition'.[43]

Schillebeeckxian moral theology

Such a position of course has significant consequences in the field of moral theology. In this context Bradford E Hinze has observed that for Schillebeeckx, 'it is no longer possible to find a secure ethical foundation in any objectivistic construal of human nature or natural law. ... Schillebeeckx concludes that the New Testament has no specific ethical principle, no ethic of the categorical imperative, no commandments or prohibitions, no virtues or values that are not socially and historically conditioned'.[44] Moreover, Schillebeeckx 'differs from the tradition by insisting that there is no decisive disclosure of what the I is, either in creation or historical revelation'.[45] In *Christ the Sacrament of the Encounter with God* (1987) Schillebeeckx wrote: 'We do not have a pre-existing definition of humanity – indeed for Christians it is not only a future, but an eschatological reality'.[46] Hinze concluded that 'since [for Schillebeeckx] there are no transhistorical material norms given in the Bible or in human nature, we need to remain open to insights from philosophical ethics, the natural sciences and above all the social sciences'.[47] The opportunities for indulging in the temptations of the gnoseological concupiscence are highly evident here.

Listening to foreign prophets

Schillebeeckx followed through the logic of the above principles with his promotion of a particular conception of 'dialogue', according to which the

Church had things to learn from the 'world'. According to Schillebeeckx, 'The Church cannot fulfil her prophetic task with regard to the worldly problems of man and society simply by appealing to revelation, but only by listening very carefully to that "foreign prophecy" (*Fremdprophetie*) which appeals to her from the situation of the world and in which she recognises the familiar voice of her Lord.'[48] As he put it: 'The relationship between the Church and the world is no longer the relationship of a "teaching Church" to a "learning world".'[49]

Adam G Cooper has suggested that the provenance of Schillebeeckx's *Fremdprophetie* idea may well be St. Paul's appropriation of a line from Isaiah in his First *Letter to the Corinthians*:

> I suspect the word *Fremdprophetie* derives from Paul's use of Isaiah 28:11 ('Very well then, with foreign lips and strange tongues God will speak to this people') to explain the public liturgical use of speaking in tongues. More broadly, however, it denotes an idea in Isaiah's prophetic theology that God will use foreign nations and aliens to the covenants to correct Israel and lead them back to true worship of God (see, e.g. Isa. 66.19-21). Paul draws on this teaching in explaining the relationship between Israel and the Gentiles in judgement and salvation (see, e.g. Rom. 10.16-21). The key theme present in all these passages, as Colin Patterson says, is that the foreign nations only call God's people back to what they have already received through his explicit word but have departed from. We perhaps see a contemporary example in the child abuse scandal: God has been using secular courts and powers to humble the Church, expose its sin, and lead it back to repentance and moral uprightness. But the legitimate moral teaching and authority which these powers invoke to do this do not derive from them, nor does the (legitimate) moral standard they refer to amount to something new, but has already been given by God to the Church (and more besides).[50]

Cooper's comments highlight the difference between a Thomist and/or *Communio*-style reading of the *Fremdprophetie* idea from that of Schillebeeckx. In the one case the foreign prophets operate as a kind of conscience for the Church, reminding her of what she is supposed to be, how she is supposed to act; in the other case (the perspective of Schillebeeckx) while the foreign prophets may certainly play the role of the Church's 'conscience', they have a more extensive brief and purpose, they have knowledge that supplements that of Revelation.

In their memoriam for Schillebeeckx, Lieven Boeve (from Leuven) and Ben Vedder (from Radboud University in Nijmegen) noted that Schillebeeckx was open to other religions because, as he put it, 'God has such an abundance of truth that he cannot be fully interpreted by just one religion', and further that 'our knowledge of God cannot be grasped in the best of all religions combined'.[51] They also recalled that in a Pastoral Letter Schillebeeckx drafted for the Dutch bishops in 1960 with a view to explaining the idea of a Church Council, Schillebeeckx took the view that 'the pope's task is to express the life of the faithful, rather than the other way around'.[52]

In addressing the question of what it is that the Church might learn from the world which she has not received from Revelation, Schillebeeckx referred to the concept of 'contrast-experiences' and offered as examples the experiences of two world wars, concentration camps, the colour bar, the developing countries, the hungry, the underprivileged and the homeless. Schillebeeckx acknowledged that in the past such 'contrast-experiences' had led people like St Vincent de Paul to 'recognise the ethical imperative of charitable deeds in the private sphere'. Today however, he asserted, the dialogue with the world has helped people to understand that society as a whole needs to be reformed.[53] Implied here is the idea that in the past people have assumed that social hierarchies are 'natural', that social inequality is inevitable, and that all one can do is to ameliorate the more extreme cases with personal acts of charity. Schillebeeckx believed that these 'contrast-experiences' serve as stimuli for social protest movements based on other presuppositions.

Schillebeeckx did not officially attend the Second Vatican Council as a *Peritus* because the Prefect of the Holy Office would not give him authorisation. The Dutch bishops nonetheless relied on Schillebeeckx for advice and since he was not officially a *Peritus*, he was not required to take any oaths of confidentiality and was thereby able to convene his own press conferences at will. His interpretations of the Conciliar debates and documents became synonymous with the 'spirit of the Council'. Throughout the 1960s and beyond he was a leading proponent of the correlationist project, that is, the project of correlating the Catholic faith to the culture of modernity. Boeve observes that this project is contrary to the whole orientation of the *Communio* circle of theologians as well as the Radical Orthodoxy scholars and other decidedly non-liberal Protestant theologians.

Correlating the faith to modernity

Like Boeve, David Tracy notes that the *Communio* theologians, in particular Balthasar and Ratzinger, oppose the correlationist methodology believing that 'Catholic theology, above all, needs to clarify and affirm its own unique identity as such and not in correlation with the ever-shifting and dangerous contours of the contemporary situation.[54] While Balthasar and Ratzinger happily consult scholars outside their own Catholic ecclesial orbit, such consultations are ad hoc, not undertaken in a systematically correlational manner.[55] Ratzinger famously ridiculed the idea of correlating the Catholic faith to popular elements within modern culture with his statement that the Church is not a haberdashery shop that updates its windows to attract customers with the arrival of a new fashion season.

Tracy and Schillebeeckx both defended the correlationist project by arguing that what they were seeking to do in the twentieth century was the same kind of exercise as that undertaken by Aquinas in the thirteenth. They read Aquinas as a proto-correlationist, concretely someone whose project was one of correlating the Catholic faith to that of Aristotelian philosophy. As the argument goes, in the thirteenth century it was Aristotelianism, in the twentieth century it was elements of the culture of Modernity and Frankfurt School Critical Theory. Ironically such a reading of the Thomist project is actually closer to Stream One Strict Observance Thomism (abhorred by scholars like Rahner, Tracy and Schillebeeckx) than to the Stream Three-type of Thomism with which Balthasar and Ratzinger were more comfortable (Balthasar and Ratzinger do not read Aquinas as someone who was trying to correlate the Catholic faith to Aristotelianism). This underscores Mark Jordan's point about how one's reading of what Aquinas does with Aristotle is quite fundamental to one's whole understanding of how to approach the discipline of Catholic theology.

The affirmation of secularism

Not only do *Communio* and *Concilium* theologians have a different position on Frankfurt School Critical Theory, Feminism and New Left philosophy in general (which morphs into postmodernism in 1989) but underlying these differences are different attitudes on secularism.

In his *Theological Investigations* Rahner defined 'secularization' as 'the growing influence of the "world" (as the outcome of human ingenuity) and the process by which it becomes increasingly autonomous and separates itself more and more from the Church considered as a social entity in the world.'[56]

In his article unpacking this understanding Patrick J. Lynch noted that Rahner's ideas on secularisation are strikingly similar to Max Weber's notion of the elimination of magic from the world.[57] Lynch wrote:

As a Thomist, Rahner believes that the world is rational and that God communicates himself indirectly to humanity through the world's rationality. Humanity must therefore probe for the rational basis of activity in the world and try to uncover all the dimensions of its (the world's) evolutionary development. Rahner calls this process the 'secularization of attitudes', since it entails the gradual removal of animistic and sacral interpretations from the world. ... Although Rahner is aware that such development could go astray and ultimately lead to the world's and humanity's destruction, he also recognises that God no longer needs to be involved to maintain the world's stability. Such stability may be achieved, he writes, 'by consciously aiming to develop psychic mechanisms and social methods of training, and finally by the police' (TI 11.173). He also thinks that public morality in a society that does not invoke God as the source of its stability probably would not be much different from one which does (TI 11.174).[58]

Lynch further suggested that Rahner believed that 'the expanding realm of knowledge helps the church both in her doctrinal formulation and in her pastoral ministry'. He observed that in *Theological Investigations* 13.93 Rahner argued that the social sciences assist the Church in acquiring concrete knowledge about human nature:

On the one hand, they aid her in formulating a 'political theology' which discloses the relevance of God's saving message for the social, economic and political orders; on the other, they form the backdrop against which the church's current 'political theology' may be criticised through concrete historical information on the ways in which God's salvation is currently appearing in the world. The discoveries of the natural sciences, especially about relativity and evolution, have brought the church to a richer – and more authentic – interpretation of the Christian world view (*Theological Investigations* 11.222-3). The growth of philosophy as a discipline distinct from theology has given the church a more comprehensive understanding of the nature of the human person and the processes of human thought. (*Theological Investigations* 13.73-76)[59]

Lynch concluded that whether or not a particular aspect of the secularisation process is authentic, or one might say, a good development, depends on what Rahner called a 'global moral instinct', which he discussed in volume nine of his *Theological Investigations* and distinguished from the more well-known category of prudential judgement.

Schillebeeckx's understanding of secularisation is similarly positive and closely follows the trajectory of Rahner. Schillebeeckx wrote:

The process of secularization seems to me to be fundamentally the dis-covery of man's rational sphere of understanding, a self-understanding of man which naturally takes place in history, with the result that secularization is given with the growth of humanity itself. In this respect, the process of secularisation is clearly a positive achievement.[60]

In his essay on 'Secularisation and Christian Belief in God', published in *God and the Future of Man* (1969), Schillebeeckx identified four major turning points in the process of secularisation. He located the first turning point in the Middle Ages with the development of the idea of natural law and what he calls the 'principle of the legitimacy of the rational sphere of understanding'. He cited St Albert the Great and St Thomas Aquinas as the chief instigators of this development. To emphasise this point he wrote that 'more and more historians are rightly coming to see the thirteenth century as fundamentally a century of laicizing rather than as a century of the cathedrals under whose towers this secularisation took place'.[61] Schillebeeckx's second turning point occurs in the sixteenth century with the arrival of the concept of a 'pure nature'. This is not an idiosyncratic judgement. Almost every intellectual and social historian has made this point, though scholars differ over which particular sixteenth-century author should be given the credit/blame for this. According to Schillebeeckx, St Robert Bellarmine SJ (1542–1621) was the first to teach this concept. Schillebeeckx then identified the Reformation as the third turning point, specifically the Protestant opposition to philosophy and its associated 'fideism', which had the effect of marginalising God from intellectual life. This marginalisation is then radicalised by Immanuel Kant (1724–1804) who completely separates faith and reason.

From this genealogy a significant question arises: how does it differ from the analysis of the *Communio* scholars? The *Communio* scholars would certainly agree that the concept 'pure nature' with its associated two-tiered approach to human reality, the Reformation and Kant are all big players in the narrative. They would however have a different reading of the medieval contribution. For the *Communio* scholars it is Scotus with his notion of the univocity of being, not St Albert the Great or his 'dumb ox' companion St Thomas Aquinas with their understanding of the relationship between faith and reason and between the eternal law and the natural law, who takes the first move in the secularising process.

Different readings of the Classical Thomist synthesis thus lie at the root of the differences between Schillebeeckx and de Lubac and others. Schillebeeckx reads what he calls the 'legitimisation of the rational sphere of understanding' as a positive development and in the end he and his associates find no difficulty in appropriating elements of the Critical Theory of the Frankfurt School as an exercise in the work of this rational sphere of understanding. While Schillebeeckx regards the post-Kantian marginalisation or even ghettoisation of the faith as a bad thing, his strategy for liberating faith from the ghetto is to tie it up to the 'insights' of Critical Theory and thereby make the faith acceptable to its dialogue partner, the 'Modern world'. The *Communio* scholars however have no faith in either Kantian rationality or Frankfurt School Critical Theory. For *Communio* scholars the solution to the sociological phenomenon of secularism is not the project of correlating the faith to the culture of modernity with reference to the political 'insights' of Critical Theory, but to valorise the Christocentric Trinitarianism of Catholic theological anthropology, to remind the faithful that the meaning of human life is found in the sanctification of the person in preparation for eternal life with the Trinity. In doing so they set out to restore the 'tapestry' (to use Hans Boersma's metaphor) of a sacramental world, which has been in a state of decay since Scotus started to unravel the intricate synthesis of Aquinas.

Moreover, the *Communio* theologians, unlike proponents of 'Critical Theory', are not perturbed by the concept of hierarchies. Whereas the typical *Concilium* theologian is keen to democratise ecclesial discernment, the typical *Communio* theologian gives priority to what Weber called 'charismatic authority' over 'rational-bureaucratic' authority. This is strongly evident in the following statement of Ratzinger:

> Authority in the Church stands on faith. The Church cannot conceive for herself how she wants to be ordered. She can only try ever more clearly to understand the inner call of faith and to live from faith. She does not need the majority principle, which always has something atrocious about it. ... The sacramental order guarantees more freedom than could be given by those who would subject the Church to the majority principle.[62]

Recontextualising the faith to postmodernity

In his essay on 'Experience According to Schillebeeckx: The Driving Force of Faith and Theology' Boeve described Schillebeeckx's goal as one of constructing a 'plausible and relevant theology within a modern context proceeding from a critical dialogue with this context', which resulted in a 'critical-hermeneutical, *praxis*-oriented theology that places Christians in the midst of an emancipatory and liberating struggle of humanity for a more just and human society'.[63] With this assessment Boeve noted the close relationship between the projects of Schillebeeckx and Metz. Both are very world-orientated.

Boeve affirms these projects but he also recognises the sociological fact that between the late 1960s and the late 1980s the European intellectual avant-garde changed its attitude from one of embracing the culture of modernity to one of critiquing it. After the fall of the Berlin Wall in 1989 New Left academics abandoned Marxism for varieties of postmodern philosophy and Catholic theologians focused on correlating the faith to the culture of modernity according to modern canons of rationality found themselves holding a baby nobody wanted.

While accepting the postmodern critiques of modernity and concluding that they mean that the significance of *Gaudium et spes* as an attempt to reconcile Christianity and modernity is a defunct project, Boeve nonetheless wants to preserve what he calls the method of *Gaudium et spes*, which he defines as entering into the critical consciousness of an era. The critical consciousness is now postmodern rather than modern. Instead of correlating the Catholic faith to the culture of modernity, Boeve's project is one of recontextualising the faith to the culture of postmodernity. This is consistent with what Borgman identified as Schillebeeckx's principle that 'believers here and now are not asked to imitate what Jesus said or did, rather they are to relate to their context as Jesus related to his'.[64] It is not the content that matters but the mode of contextualisation.

In outlining his recontextualisation project Boeve begins from the principle that those who inherit a Tradition are not only its heirs but also its testators, and that Tradition develops when there has been a change in context by those who receive it.[65] Boeve then argues that both the correlation-to-modernity theorists and Catholic traditionalists generate problems because they only adhere to a single pole of the relationship with Tradition – either to the pole of being an heir, or to the pole of being a testator:

> Traditionalists over emphasise the idea of being heirs: the inheritance is preserved and passed on as a whole, undifferentiated; a creative and life-giving reception of the tradition is rarely mentioned. The modernizing tendency emphasized the idea of being contextual benefactors: the inheritance was streamlined, adapted, and where necessary, corrected in the light of the modern critique of tradition. In the first instance, the tradition as a dynamic process of recontextualisation was abandoned. In the second instance, the tradition as bestower of meaning was neglected; the Christian narrative ran the risk of becoming a (legitimating) reduplication of the modern master narratives.[66]

This is a very different understanding of Tradition from that of the *Communio* scholars. Ratzinger's understanding of Tradition is indebted to the work of Josef Pieper. Although Pieper died before Boeve's recontextualisation project began, he anticipated the use of the testator-beneficiary metaphor. Contrary to the position now taken by Boeve, Pieper argued that what a student learns through his own efforts is his own property, but what he receives from Tradition is something more like the loan of a gift. Pieper also endorsed St Augustine's maxim *quod a patribus acceperunt, hoc filiis tradiderunt*. This means that the last child in line receives from his father exactly the same thing as the first in line handed over to his 'son'. The *traditum* is something that in the accomplishment of the process of Tradition does *not* grow.[67] Doctrines clarifying the *traditum* might grow, but not the *traditum* itself.

In his essay *La Révélation Divine* de Lubac was quite emphatic about this principle. De Lubac argued that 'whether we are talking about profane or ecclesiastical history, by themselves, historical events bring us no increase in supernatural revelation'.[68] This stance was also taken by Cardinal Paul J. Cordes in a 2009 address in Sydney to Catholic academics and representatives of Church agencies. Cordes stated that 'the theologian misinterprets the concept of Revelation when he suggests that human life situations might acquire the quality of Revelation. The Church holds that Revelation is complete with the death of the last Apostle.'[69]

Contrary to Ratzinger, Pieper, de Lubac, Cordes and others, Boeve argues that 'Christian faith and tradition are not only contained in a specific historico-cultural context, but are also co-constituted by this context'.[70] This is a significantly different position that means that each new generation, each new beneficiary, can add to the 'testamentary benefit', the deposit of the faith as it were, new accretions. This is not the same thing as Newman's idea of the organic development of doctrine. For Newman any new doctrinal developments had to grow out of the original deposit of the faith. He did not envisage a process whereby some element of the original deposit of the faith might find itself grafted onto stock from another narrative.

Where *Communio* scholars talk about the organic development of doctrine, which is a clarification of some element of the *traditum*, Boeve talks about the *interruption* of the narrative and its recontextualisation. He writes:

> Being a Christian as such calls one to a praxis of both being interrupted and interrupting – respecting the very otherness of the other while at the same time also becoming the other of the other, questioning and challenging the other, criticising him or her where he or she tends to become hegemonic. The category of interruption in fact subsequently appears to be a good avenue to conceive of God's salvific engagement with history – including our involvement in history and the way we perceive God's relation to it. As a particular narrative, the Christian narrative is interrupted by the God it testifies to as the One who interrupts closed narratives, and, by doing so, is called to become itself a narrative interrupting closed narratives.[71]

The concept of interruption comes from Metz's sixth thesis on Christian hope. Boeve adopts the concept and argues that narratives are interrupted and recontextualised by changing social conditions. According to Boeve, the Catholic faith is but one narrative among a plurality of narratives. It is not, and should not be, a 'master narrative'. The concept 'Master Narrative' comes from Jean-François Lyotard's work *The Postmodern Condition: A Report on Knowledge* (1979). Lyotard used the French '*grand récit*' and this was transposed into English as 'master narrative'. The concept refers to a narrative about narratives of historical meaning, experience or knowledge, which offers a society legitimation through the anticipated completion of a (as yet unrealised) master idea. For example, the postmoderns claim that 'progress' was the master narrative of the culture of modernity. The celebration of 'difference' is a kind of master narrative of the culture of postmodernity. Although the postmoderns regard all master narratives as oppressive, the celebration of difference is regarded as an exception to this principle because it does not really affirm or privilege anything – nothing is normative, except the principle that nothing can be normative. If the Catholic Church claims to be the repository of all truth regarding God's Revelation to humanity (as the CDF document *Dominus Iesus* of 2000 asserts), then it is presenting the Catholic faith as a master narrative – a story that can explain and contain all other stories – with the master project of restoring all things in Christ. This is deemed to be oppressive because it violates the principle that nothing can be normative. It privileges the Catholic narrative over non-Catholic narratives.

Boeve believes that the Church should eschew the temptation to present the Catholic faith as a master narrative. As he writes:

> In the post-modern context, Christianity as a master narrative has also lost much of its credibility – in spite of the fact that many see the fall of the modern master narrative as an opportunity for narrating a new Christian master narrative. Christianity, however, has no future as an all-encompassing meta-narrative, but only as a small narrative, or better still as an open narrative, as a narrative that offers orientation and integration without thereby being determined to integrate everything in its own narrative in a totalitarian way.[72]

The project of recontextualising the Catholic faith to postmodern culture means in effect that every area of theology must be altered to make it capable of a defence before a tribunal of postmodern philosophers. For example, after rejecting the sacramental theology of St Thomas Aquinas, Rahner, Balthasar and Ratzinger for its interest in ontology, Boeve suggests that if theology is 'to regain contextual plausibility', the sacramentality of life celebrated in the sacraments must no longer be thought of as 'participation in a divine being, nor as an anticipation of a self-fulfilling development, but as being involved in the tension arising from the interruption of the divine Other into our human narratives'.[73] Boeve concludes that 'it goes without saying that such a recontextualisation will have serious consequences for Christian self-awareness, and that such a sacramental structuring of human existence has implications which go beyond a theology of the sacraments'.[74]

The implications of a Boevian approach to Tradition and its recontextualisation to postmodern culture are well summarised in the following paragraph by Thomas Guarino:

> Catholic 'foundationalist' thinkers like Rahner and Lonergan ... thought that some foundationalist ontology is necessary if one is adequately to defend fundamental Catholic positions on doctrine. If one accepts postmodernity more fully, thereby abandoning some form of foundationalist ontology, one's entire understanding of revelation, especially the role of Christian doctrine, is deeply affected. Either the truth of the gospel must simply be asserted, breaking its link with a rationally elaborated infrastructure. Or, by opening a fissure between ontology and theology, one develops a quite different understanding of what the deposit of faith is, how it develops, and the type of continuity and identity proper to it. Particularly affected is the type of truth mediated by it.[75]

Boeve's project is a classic example of one that opens a fissure between ontology and theology. Guarino goes on to observe that 'the theological concern raised by theories of communicative praxis, such as those of Jürgen Habermas, is that Revelation is now seemingly discovered by the consensual community of discourse, attenuating at least to some extent the idea that Revelation is primarily the Word of God, the gift of God to the Church'.[76] This has far-reaching consequences for the notion of the Magisterium, the authority of the episcopacy and the papacy and, indeed, for most topics in Fundamental Theology. This is particularly evident in the field of religious education where the recontextualisation project has been applied in Catholic schools with the aim of producing a new generation of 'post-critical believers'.

Boeve versus Ratzinger

Boeve acknowledges that the recontextualisation project is in radical opposition to the new evangelisation or reevangelisation projects of the *Communio* theologians, including and especially, Joseph Ratzinger/Benedict

XVI. He summarises the 'options' available to Catholic scholars contending with the issue of secularism as (i) the *correlation project* (in shorthand terms, the pastoral projects of Rahner, Schillebeeckx, Küng and Tracy), (ii) the stance of *Communio* and Radical Orthodoxy scholars, highly critical of secularism, or what Boeve calls the *project of rupture*, and (iii) *interruption* (his own project).

In his memoriam for Schillebeeckx Boeve argued that 'every reflection on the relevance of Schillebeeckx for today's theology will be obliged to declare its position with regard to this evolution' (where the evolution is that of the confluence of *Communio* and Radical Orthodoxy critiques in opposition to the correlation and recontextualisation projects). Specifically, Boeve asserts that for Ratzinger,

> it is not dialogue with the world that one should expect to find on the theological agenda, but rather conversion of a world characterized by the absence of faith and declining values. The current context, certainly the European context, has alienated itself to such a degree from the Christian faith that an emphasis on the Christian alternative as a rupture with the world is the only approach that can claim legitimacy.[77]

Ratzinger would probably argue that in his mind the expression 'the world' simply refers to the part of humanity that remains unconverted to Christ and that he is not at all opposed to the idea of representatives of the Catholic faith, theologians, teachers, priests, etc. entering into conversations and relationships with such persons. However, from his perspective, the purpose of such conversations is conversion. Moreover, the Church herself, according to the ecclesiology of Vatican II, is nothing less than the Universal Sacrament of Salvation. Her whole reason for being is to mediate Christ to the world. This is what she does in her dialogue with the world. Ratzinger would also probably emphasise that he does believe in the *organic* development of Tradition. However he and Boeve have a different idea about development itself. For Ratzinger Christianity is *the* master narrative in the sense that other narratives are either pre-figurements or post-Christian mutations of the Christian narrative. He approaches dialogue with the proponents of other traditions from within the horizon of Christian Revelation. As he expressed the point in the context of Jewish-Christian dialogue:

> To be sure, the point of this dialogue was not simply to repeat nineteenth and early twentieth century scholarship in comparative religion, which, from the lofty height of a liberal-rationalistic standpoint, had judged the religions with the self-assurance of enlightened reason. Today there is a broad consensus that such a standpoint is an impossibility,

and that, in order to understand religion, it is necessary to experience it from within, indeed, that only such experience, which is inevitably particular and tied to a definite historical starting-point, can lead the way to mutual understanding and thus to a deepening and purification of religion.[78]

To extend Boeve's testator metaphor, one might say that Ratzinger is highly sensitive to the intentions of the deceased as expressed in the testamentary document. Ratzinger would acknowledge that new historical contexts may exercise an influence over the appropriation of the Tradition. Some elements of the Tradition may be more or less easily appropriated in different cultural contexts. However Ratzinger rejects the proposition that history or culture itself constitutes the Tradition. He also rejects the idea that cultures are 'shells' to clothe the faith. He believes that cultures are built on practices and practices embody meanings, and it is therefore important that cultures are built on practices that embody Christian meanings. As +Robert Barron has expressed the principle: 'Philosophy, ethics and cultural forms do not position Christ, rather Christ positions them' and 'to understand this principle is to grasp the nettle of the Christian thing'.[79]

Conclusion

The combined effect of the *Concilium* scholars' various new understandings of how to approach theological reflection is that of an affirmation of many of the presuppositions of the Enlightenment project. In particular they take on board the criticisms of hierarchical institutions to be found in contemporary social theory, especially Critical Theory. This affirmation also informs their view of secularisation and what the Dutch and Belgians call 'de-confessionalisation', the sociological phenomenon of people in formerly Christian countries disassociating themselves from the institutional Church in which they were baptised, and learning to think for themselves as 'post-critical believers' without recourse to institutions like the papacy or the Congregation of the Doctrine of the Faith. For *Concilium* scholars, this is ultimately a positive development.

Whereas the *Communio* scholars tend to start with the Trinitarian dogmas and work on developing the territories of theological anthropology and moral theology with reference to Patristic-era Christology, the *Concilium* scholars tend to start with contemporary social theory and work on what they can learn from sociologists about such topics as freedom and justice and equality. They then seek to apply the knowledge thus gained to a restructuring of the Church, including her teaching and practices. Whereas the deification or sanctification of the human person is a core *Communio* interest, the abolition of non-democratic social practices, structures and attitudes is a core *Concilium* interest. *Concilium*-style scholars also manifest a strong desire for the Church to be accepted by the world and believe that the world is more likely to accept the Church if the Church retreats from her centuries-long practice of presenting the Catholic faith as the master narrative. In contrast, *Communio* scholars regard the world as simply the part of humanity that remains unconverted to Christ. For them Christianity makes no sense at all, is not worth any bother at all, *unless* it is *the master narrative*. For *Communio* scholars it is the task of the Church and her theologians to teach the faith in an unadulterated form, handing on the same faith in the twenty-first century as they claim their forefathers received in the twentieth, tenth, fifth and so on, receding back to the Apostles. For *Concilium* scholars it is the task of the Church and her theologians to engage in dialogue with the world from a position where the Catholic faith is presented merely as one of many inadequate or incomplete narratives, and to recontextualise this incomplete narrative many times over in accord with changing social conditions. This includes making significant changes to the understanding of sacramental theology, ecclesiology, moral and liturgical theology.

At the time of the Second Vatican Council all the leading *Periti* who were later to split into the different *Concilium* and *Communio* camps were in agreement that Catholic intellectual life operated too much in a ghetto. There was an almost universal desire to break free of the neo-scholastic straitjacket and to enter into serious intellectual engagements with non-Catholic scholars. This comes across very strongly in many of Rahner's statements, though he was not alone in this. Even Balthasar wrote a book called *Razing the Bastions*. However the same Balthasar who wrote *Razing the Bastions* also wrote:

> According to the speech of Christ in Matthew 10:20 – 'For his name's sake they will be hated by all', persecution constitutes the normal condition of the Church in her relation to the world, and martyrdom is the normal condition of the professed Christian.[80]

Underneath all the many fault lines one can enumerate, which distinguish the *Communio* from the *Concilium* approaches to Catholic theology, perhaps the most fundamental is a different attitude to issues in eschatology. There is nothing in the *Communio* framework that is in any sense sympathetic to the project of Bloch and Metz to focus on building utopia on earth. While *Communio* theologians do believe that principles of social morality flow from belief in Christ, they do not believe that paradise on earth can ever be achieved, and especially not through the vehicle of politics. As a *caricature* one might say that *Communio* theologians want to help people to become aristocrats in heaven, while *Concilium* theologians want Catholics to be the vanguard of the Left on earth. Neither side is much into what it criticises as 'bourgeois Christianity' – a kind of selfish use of ecclesial institutions and ecclesial networks for purposes of social self-promotion.

Liberation Theology and
the Papacy of Francis

In an interview published in 1985 Karl Rahner was asked whether he was of the opinion that 'European theology cannot be exported to other parts of the world, but that in Africa an independent, autonomous theology must come into being that can totally differentiate itself from our European theology'. He replied, 'Yes, of course' and added that 'in time, an African, an Asian and a South American theology must arise'.[1] When further questioned as to whether the moral theology would be different and whether he would allow an African chief his harem, Rahner replied, 'I don't know, I don't know enough about Africa ... [but] obviously, the Church doesn't need to revitalise old ethical life-styles that are now disappearing on their own.'[2]

While Liberation Theology first bursts onto the theological scene in the early 1970s with the publication of *Teologia de la Liberación* by Gustavo Gutiérrez in Lima, and *Jesus Christo Libertador* by Leonardo Boff in Petrópolis, it arrives internationally some three decades after Rahner's interview with the pontificate of Francis. In this chapter an attempt will therefore be made to outline the major methodological presuppositions of the various currents of Liberation Theology and to situate Pope Francis within the particular current of Argentinian 'People's Theology'.

The European contribution

Ironically, Liberation Theology is a late-twentieth-century product of the European intelligentsia planted in the countries of Latin America by priests who had been sent to Europe for their postgraduate studies. As Ph. I. André-Vincent wrote in a review in 1976, Liberation Theology carries the label 'Made in Germany'.[3]

While it might be a little overstated to ascribe the entire enterprise to the Germans, it is certainly the case that the leading scholars in the movement were all educated somewhere in Europe and that more of the ingredients for this intellectual cocktail could be sourced in Germany than anywhere else, though Belgium was also a strong supplier. Leonardo Boff obtained his doctorate from the University of Munich in 1970; his brother, Clodovis Boff, obtained his doctorate from the Catholic University of Leuven in 1968; the Uruguayan Jesuit Juan Luis Segundo (1925–96) obtained his Licentiate from the University of Louvain and then his doctorate from the Sorbonne; the Peruvian Dominican Gustavo Gutiérrez studied philosophy at Leuven, then theology at the Catholic University of Lyon; the Barcelonia-born Jesuit Jon Sobrino, who has spent most of his life in El Salvador, studied for his doctorate in Frankfurt; Lucio Gera (1924–2012), the Italian-born professor of Dogmatic Theology at the Catholic University of Argentina, studied in Bonn; Juan Carlos Scannone, the Argentinian Jesuit, obtained his doctorate from the University of Munich.

There is also a close link between late-twentieth-century German 'Political Theology' and Liberation Theology, though the two movements have distinctive springboards and methodologies. An excellent analysis of the relationship between the two may be found in Francis Schüssler Fiorenza's essay 'Political Theology: an Historical Analysis'.[4] Fiorenza notes that the expression 'Political Theology' (of which the theology of Johann Baptist Metz is the flagship) 'was coined to express a theological reaction to the individualism of existential theology' and it thus 'sought to underscore the public, societal and political dimensions of the Christian faith'.[5] Specifically, 'the German political theologians argue that the response to the secularized situation made by existentialism and by transcendental theology [i.e. Karl Rahner's solution] is inadequate. Faith is reduced to the private sphere of individual existence or to transcendental subjectivity'.[6] German 'Political Theologians' such as Metz demanded a political interpretation of the Gospel rather than an existential interpretation. Metz argued that faith is not something purely private, it has an accompanying *praxis*, and that it is the role of a political ethics to link the two. The precise dynamics of the mediation of political ethics was not, however, well developed.

The Liberation Theologians take up the theme of the inadequacy of existential theology. They criticise it for being 'too bourgeois' and for presupposing that the pastoral problems to be addressed are all those of middle-class Europeans. This criticism is especially strong in relation to the Conciliar document *Gaudium et spes*. José Comblin has stated that 'if one tries to learn what specific agenda *Gaudium et spes* was putting forward, one has to recognise that it contributed nothing new and repeated what everyone was saying. The light of faith was unable to provide anything that was original or might offer guidance to the modern world. In the end, the teaching on the signs of the times boiled down to acceptance of the modern world'.[7]

Nonetheless, the Liberation Theologians *do like* any statement in *Gaudium et spes*, or elsewhere, that exhorts Catholics to be aware of the signs of the times. According to Comblin, 'faith does not consist in intellectual acceptance of specific truths drawn from the Bible. Faith consists in recognizing God's plan, or the coming of the kingdom of God. It is a matter of recognizing the march of the people of God in our times'.[8] Therefore the problem with *Gaudium et spes* (from the perspective of Liberation Theologians) was not its exhortation to read the signs of the times, but the fact that the majority of the bishops at the Council *misread* the signs. Specifically the Liberation Theologians complain that the bishops of the Council affirmed the culture of modernity without taking account of the effect of this culture on the countries of Latin America and the Third World.

The Liberation Theologians thus take up the Political Theologians' critique of what they regard as bourgeois/liberal Catholicism and their interest in social practices, but they argue that in Latin America, the problem is not, as it is in Europe, the death of God, or the problem of the credibility of the Christian narrative after successive centuries of wars between ostensibly Christian countries, Nazi death camps and General Franco's peculiar form of fascism, but rather the problem of grinding poverty. Their solution is to turn to social theory for an analysis of Latin America's social and economic predicament. Contemporary social theory, bred of the different varieties of Marxism, became the philosophical partner(s) of the Liberation Theologians, as an alternative to the classical Greek philosophical partners of Stream One-type Thomism, the German Idealist and Heideggerian partners of Stream Two-type Thomism or the German and French Personalist partners of much of Stream Three-type Thomism and the works of the *Communio* theologians.

Notwithstanding Liberation Theology's eschewal of bourgeois Christianity and so-called 'first-world' or 'dead white male' theology, John Milbank has argued that Liberation Theology does nonetheless owe a significant intellectual debt to the theology of Karl Rahner because it presupposes something like Rahner's 'supernatural existential' in its treatment of the grace–nature relationship.[9] Specifically Milbank argues that Liberation Theology shares the Rahnerian tendency to naturalise the supernatural, rather than to sacralise the natural. Ratzinger has argued something similar. He suggested that Rahner unwittingly influenced the rise of Liberation Theology by arguing that that which is 'rational' is 'Christian'. In the 1960s the Liberation Theologians took the view that Marxism represents the most rational account of social realities and applying the Rahnerian idea that the rational is the Christian, even if only implicitly or anonymously, they defended a project of baptising elements of Marxist social theory. According to these readings of the intellectual history both the theologies of Metz and Rahner were significant German influences on the rise of Liberation Theology.

There also appears to have been some Russian involvement in fostering the movement. Ion Mihai Pacepa, the highest ranking KGB defector from the Soviet Union in the 1970s, claims that the Liberation Theology movement was 'born in the KGB and it had a KGB-invented name'. According to Pacepa:

> The birth of Liberation Theology was the intent of a 1960 super-secret 'Party-State Dezinformatsiya Program' approved by Aleksandr Shelepin, the Chairman of the KGB, and by Politburo member Aleksey Kirichenko, who coordinated the Communist Party's international policies. This program demanded that the KGB take secret control of the World Council of Churches (WCC), based in Geneva, Switzerland, and use it as cover for converting Liberation Theology into a South American revolutionary tool. The WCC was the largest international ecumenical organization after the Vatican, representing some 550 million Christians of various denominations throughout 120 countries. ... The KGB began by building an intermediate international religious organization called the Christian Peace Conference (CPC), which was headquartered in Prague. Its main task was to bring the KGB-created Liberation Theology into the real world.[10]

Whatever of the reliability of Pacepa's statement (an issue that is almost impossible to judge without access to KGB archives), it is certainly the case that the World Council of Churches was a strong promoter of Liberation Theology, as Schillebeeckx observed.[11]

Many have commented that Latin American societies in the 1960s were media-ripe for the promotion of Liberation Theology and that significant clerical leaders of the Vatican II generation were uncomfortable with the Church's establishment status in these countries. José Comblin has revealed that towards the end of the Second Vatican Council, a group of bishops were secretly meeting at *Domus Mariae* and that on 16 November 1965, some forty bishops met in the catacomb of St Domitila and signed the 'Catacomb Pact of the "servant and poor Church" in which they pledged to live a simple life, refuse to hold private property in their own names, refuse honorary titles such as Monsignor or Your Excellency, and promised not to be lured into corruption by the rich and powerful'.[12]

The Liberation Theology movement was therefore the result of a confluence of factors: (i) post-Second World War European theological trends, which focused on the social dimensions of the faith, (ii) the political and economic instability of the Latin American countries, (iii) the fact that the intellectual life of these countries was in many ways a battle between seventeenth-century scholasticism and twentieth-century Marxism, (iv) the fact that a new generation of clerics wanted to break free of both the scholasticism and the class system imported from Spain and Portugal, and (v) the opportunism of Marxist ideologues and their friends in the World Council of Churches.

History as the locus of Revelation

In addition to the above influences, a very significant intellectual foundation stone of the Liberation Theology movement is the idea that history is the 'locus of revelation'. This might be called the Belgian contribution. It rests on a different reading of 'the signs of the times' from eschatological and Christocentric interpretations, favoured by Balthasar and Ratzinger, and others in the *Communio* circles. As Christopher Rowland writes: 'The emphasis is on experience as a prior "text" which must condition the way in which scripture and tradition are read and the "signs of the times" interpreted'.[13] It is an approach to Revelation that is very Schillebeeckxian, and an approach to soteriology that is driving on themes in the work of Léopold Malevez SJ (1900-73) who was a professor of Dogmatic Theology at the Jesuit seminary in Egenhoven for some thirty years (1931-61). Malevez drew a distinction between what he called the incarnational and eschatological approaches to salvation history. For those who favour the eschatological approach, the emphasis is on the discontinuity between profane history and the final reign of God after the renewal of the cosmos, while for those who favour the incarnational approach, the emphasis is on how all good human actions prepare for the coming age beyond the consummation of the world. Abbot Christopher Butler of Downside Abbey (1902–86), a *Peritus* of the Second Vatican Council, made the point that Christian eschatology and Christian incarnationalism are not mutually exclusive and that the division identified by Léopold Malevez between the two should not be a separation. Rather, the relationship should be yet another example of a Catholic 'critical couplet' – two poles held in tension with the word 'and' rather than with the options 'either/or'. Butler wrote:

> Eschatology without Incarnation is not Christian at all, but Jewish. Incarnation without eschatology is – I know not what; Buddhism, perhaps, or Platonism. Born within the Jewish tradition and of Jewish spiritual stock, Christianity has been eschatological from the beginning. ... But its novelty was not that it simply lodged the idea of incarnation within an eschatological framework, but that it proclaimed a real, 'mystical', 'sacramental' anticipation of the Last

Things as the unique gift that God was bestowing on man in the Gospel – and of this real anticipation the Incarnation is the epitome and the fountainhead. ... Incarnation, for us, is eschatological, and eschatology is incarnated.[14]

Segundo's Liberation Theology has been criticised for a lopsided emphasis on the incarnational. According to Michael R Candelaria:

Common to Segundo and Scannone [who will be discussed later in this chapter], and a basic theological *fundamentum* of Liberation Theology in general, is the unitary view of history, *una sola historia*. This idea affirms the unity of salvation and liberation, redemption and earthly progress, the sacred and the profane. Reality is one. There is no supernatural realm outside of and above the natural realm of human history.[15]

For Segundo, secularisation moves humanity closer to total human liberation. In his mind, secularisation is a 'central postulate of the Christian message'. Seen in terms of theology's task, secularisation means shifting the focus of our intellectual endeavours from the realm of the heavenly to the realm of the earthly. Secularisation does not necessarily imply forsaking sacred reality. Rather, it implies recognising the sacred in the world, and translating worship into social action. At bottom, secularisation means that everything in the Church must be translated from 'religious' terms into man's tasks in history.[16]

In *Our Idea of God*, Segundo wrote: 'We could say that a presentation of Christianity is adequate only when it moves from the history of salvation to the salvation of history in man, i.e., to the building up of history by man, whom God has prepared and commissioned for this task'.[17] The focus is therefore on the 'world' rather than eternal life. Segundo claimed to have sourced these ideas in the works of Malevez. He declared: 'What I have always understood as my own "theology of liberation" began with him [Léopold Malevez] – a theology I amplified once I returned to Latin America [from Louvain]'.[18]

Consistent with his tendency to conflate the secular or profane with the sacred, Segundo was critical of Metz for rejecting any causal connection between the kingdom of God and social-political systems. Metz was still trying to hold a place for the eschatological dimension.

In his *The Liberation of Theology*, Segundo offered the following four principles for his methodology:

First, there is a way of experiencing reality, which leads us to ideological suspicion. Secondly there is the application of our ideological suspicion to the whole ideological superstructure in general and to theology in particular. Thirdly, there comes a new way of experiencing theological reality that leads us to exegetical suspicion, that is, to the suspicion that the prevailing interpretation of the Bible has not taken important pieces of data into account. Fourthly, we have our new hermeneutic, that is, our new way of interpreting the fountainhead of our faith (i.e. Scripture) with the new elements at our disposal.[19]

Stephan van Erp has commented that although Liberation Theologians 'share with correlation theologians [e.g. Schillebeeckx] the need for an analysis of experience, they refer to the specific experience of socio-political oppression and human suffering, rather than to experience as a general epistemological category'.[20] Such an experience of sociopolitical oppression becomes the primary experience from which all of Segundo's subsequent hermeneutics of suspicion cascade.

According to this reading, Liberation Theology (especially in the style of Segundo) is a sub-branch of Schillebeeckxian theology fused with Rahnerian-style secularism and Frankfurt School Marxism, the latter operating as a philosophical partner to the theological ideas stemming from Metz, Rahner, Malevez and Schillebeeckx.

The central importance of *Praxis*

According to Schillebeeckx, 'an authentic faith in God only seems to be possible in the context of a *praxis* of liberation and of solidarity with the needy. It is in that *praxis* that the idea develops that God reveals himself as the mystery and the very heart of humanity's striving for liberation, wholeness and soundness'.[21] Similarly, in *A Theology of Liberation,* Gutiérrez argued that instead of using only Scripture and Tradition as starting points, theologians needed to start with facts and questions derived from the world and from history.[22] Segundo went further and argued that 'not a single dogma can be studied under any other final criterion than that of its social impact on the praxis'.[23] Jon Sobrino is of the view that this orientation must extend all the way to the study of Christology, which must begin with the so-called historical Jesus, rather than with the Jesus of the Chalcedonian doctrines.[24]

Behind these moves lies the Marxist principle of giving priority to *praxis* over theory. As Zoë Bennett put the proposition: 'The commitment and practice of liberation theology requires three moments: the moment of *praxis*, the moment of reflection on *praxis*, and the moment of return to a renewed *praxis*. It begins and ends in *praxis*'.[25] Louis Dupré has highlighted the irony that the alleged priority of *praxis* over theory is itself an *idea*.[26]

For a very comprehensive overview of the relationship between theory and practice in contemporary Christian (predominately Catholic) theology, recourse can be had to Chapter Three of Matthew Lamb's *Solidarity with Victims: Towards a Theology of Social Transformation*. Lamb makes the important observation that the relationship between theory and practice raises such fundamental issues as 'the relations of faith to love, of church to the world, of orthodoxy to orthopraxy, of salvation to liberation, of religion to political concerns, of historical and systematic to moral and pastoral theology'.[27] Specifically he identifies five common models of the theory–praxis relationship: (i) the primacy of theory, (ii) the primacy of *praxis*, (iii) the primacy of faith-love, (iv) critical theoretic correlations and (v) critical *praxis* correlations.

Under the primacy of *praxis* heading, Lamb offered a further three subdivisions. He distinguished between *praxis* understood as (i) cultural-historical activity, (ii) liberal sociopolitical reform activity, and (iii) radical Marxist revolutionary activity. He traced the cultural-historical primacy of *praxis* to Luther's repudiation of speculative theology and the Enlightenment's rejection of metaphysics. (Luther claimed that speculative theology comes from the devil in hell!). Lamb then traced the notion of *praxis* as socio-political reform activity to a marriage between 'the Kantian relation of religion to morality and the Ritschlian distinction between the speculative judgements of science and the value judgments of religion'. The Marxist theories of *praxis* are of course exactly that, theories rooted in the dialectical materialism of Karl Marx, which holds that class conflict is the dynamic of human history and that the ideological superstructure is determined by the economic substructure.[28] Crudely this means that all thought is tied to economics. The choice is therefore between a *praxis* à la Luther-Kant, a *praxis* à la Kant-Ritsch or a *praxis* à la Hegel-Marx.

Lamb summarised his analysis of these three types of primacy of *praxis* theories with the statement:

These primacy of praxis types agree in rejecting classical metaphysics. If Christianity is to be faithful to its task, it must be intrinsically involved in historical, cultural, political, social and/or revolutionary praxis. Doctrinal theory is at best extrinsic and secondary. The reflex character of theory-praxis tends toward a reduction of theory to reflection on praxis as variously understood. The normativity tends toward an identification of Christianity with modern, secular (liberal or Marxist) processes.[29]

Finally, in terms of Lamb's five categories, Balthasar is offered as an example of the primacy of faith-love type (and this would hold true of most, if not all,

Communio scholars), Rahner is offered as an example of the critical theoretic correlations type (in his case the correlating partners are the philosophies underpinning liberal modernity) and Metz is offered as an example of a critical *praxis* correlations type (who occupies a position between Rahner on the one side and Liberation Theologians on the other).

The single most systematic treatment of the place of *praxis* within Liberation Theology is however Clodovis Boff's *Theology and Praxis: Epistemological Foundations* published in English in 1987. In this work Boff offered no less than ninety-eight principles for a correct understanding of the *praxis* process, which perhaps underscores Dupré's point about just how theoretical the notion of the priority of *praxis* is.

Aidan Nichols has described Clodovis Boff as 'the most sophisticated methodologist among the liberation theologians' and he suggests that Boff's *magnum opus* is an attempt 'to reach an understanding of the relationship between theory and *praxis* which will at one and the same time resemble that of Marxism, in requiring the theologian to situate himself epistemologically within a given *praxis*, and yet depart from Marxism by limiting the significance of such practical engagement vis-à-vis other epistemological factors in the making of good theology'.[30]

The Battle of the Boffs

Clodovis Boff's early concern with reconciling Marxist epistemology with what Nichols irenically called 'other epistemological factors in the making of good theology' (one assumes here the factors of Scripture and Tradition) reached a turning point in October 2007 with the publication of an article titled 'Teologia da Libertação e volta ao fundamento' (Liberation Theology and the Return to the Essentials) in *Revista Eclesiástica Brasileira*. In this article he complained of an inversion of the epistemological primacy of God over the poor.[31] He suggested that Liberation Theology had lost its way because the poor have been given epistemological primacy over Divine Revelation. Leonardo Boff (Clodovis's brother and fellow liberation theologian) responded to Clodovis's essay in May 2008 with his own article entitled 'Pelos pobres, contra a estreiteza do método' (For the Poor and Against the Poverty of Method). In this he accuses his brother of not understanding the Incarnation, not understanding the theology of the Holy Spirit and not understanding the theological significance of the poor. Specifically, he wrote:

> Clodovis' text is concentrated too heavily upon the figure of Christ, in fact upon an incarnate Christ who does not yet know the changes

which are brought about by the resurrection. As we have seen, however, through the resurrection Christ has attained cosmic omnipresence and pushes human development towards the kingdom of the Trinity. At base, Clodovis formulates christomonistically, as though Christ were everything, thereby forgetting the Father and the Holy Spirit.[32]

In an earlier article published in 1975, Leonardo Boff had enumerated five characteristics for a Christology of Liberation Theology. They were, first, the primacy of anthropology over ecclesiology; secondly the priority of utopian perspectives over factual ones; thirdly an emphasis on a critical element over a dogmatic element; fourthly the priority of the social over the personal; and finally, the priority of orthopraxis over orthodoxy.[33]

The degree of divergence between Clodovis and Leonardo's Christology was even starker in Leonardo's 2007 *Concilium* essay entitled 'Is the Cosmic Christ Greater than Jesus of Nazareth? In this paper Leonardo wrote:

> Before appearing in human history, Jesus, Siddhartha Guatama, Chuang Tzu, and others were in gestation within the universe. On account of what they did they were called Christ, in Jesus' case, or Buddha, in Siddhartha Guatama's. All of them have cosmic dimensions to the extent that the entire universe worked to make their appearance possible. What emerged in them did not become a personal monopoly. They gave archetypal shape to potentialities inherent in the universe. So we can say that Jesus emerges as a singular expression of the cosmic Christ. The cosmic Christ does not exhaust all the possible forms of his manifestation in Jesus, a man from the Mediterranean, limited in time and space.[34]

Boff went on to assert that 'the actual content of 'Christ' or 'Buddha' refers to the same reality. Both reveal God. Siddhartha Guatama is a manifestation of the cosmic Christ in the same way as Jesus of Nazareth. Or Jesus of Nazareth is an 'Enlightened One', like Buddha'.[35] Boff concluded his paper by quoting the following statement from the Brazilian Yoga master Hermógenes: 'I asked a blessing from Krishna and it was Christ who blessed me. I prayed to Christ and it was Buddha who heard me. I called on Buddha and it was Krishna who answered me'.[36]

Given such conclusions it is not surprising that Leonardo Boff found himself in trouble with the Congregation for the Doctrine of the Faith. In 1985 he was silenced for a year after the publication of his book *Church, Charism and Power: Liberation Theology and the Institutional Church*. An unrepentant Boff accused Cardinal Ratzinger, then the Prefect of the CDF, of 'religious terrorism' and he later left the Franciscan Order and his priestly ministry.

Leonardo Boff's position is similar to that of the Spanish Claretian Missionary priest José Maria Vigil. Vigil is critical of the Roman Missal for its failure to acknowledge religious pluralism and for its prayer that all may be united in a single flock under a single shepherd. He calls for a revision of the theology of Revelation in such a way that Catholics would have to 'renounce the concept of being chosen' since 'only religions that move beyond their self-conviction of being "the chosen ones" can come together in an "alliance of civilisations" (and of religions) to tackle together the practical tasks of saving the human race and saving the planet'.[37] Vigil prefers the term Jesuanity to Christianity because in his reading, the Jesus of the Gospels 'poses no problems to a pluralist Christianity' unlike 'the image of God elaborated in the Christological dogmas of the fourth to fifth centuries that turn out to be the *punctum dolens* for devising a pluralist Christology'.[38] Vigil also endorses the efforts of EATWOT – the Latin American Ecumenical Association of Third World Theologians – for their work on 'devising an encounter between its liberation theology and the theology of religious pluralism'.[39] Vigil exhorts his readers to set the 'sights of theology on the salvation of the poor and the salvation of the earth' and he acknowledges that this would imply 'a theological revolution the like of which has not been seen in twenty centuries of Christianity'.[40] His work has been criticised by the Spanish Episcopal Commission for the Doctrine of the Faith, especially those elements dealing with religious pluralism and theological methodology.

Feminist Liberation Theology

The Liberation Theology movement has also fused with some circles of Feminist Theology. Elaine Wainwright notes that the *praxis* model, as it functions in Liberation Theology, 'assumes that interpretation of Scripture can be undertaken by all readers' and that biblical interpretation is moving from the 'control of its dominant practitioners who have been white, western, male, academic and in many instances clerical, to contexts in which scholars from a range of locations are engaged with grass-roots readers in *praxis* toward transformation'.[41] She specifically endorses the work of Elisabeth Schüssler Fiorenza, 'one of the foremothers of contemporary feminist biblical criticism' and her way of engaging readers in the 'twirling, moving, spiral dance of feminist biblical interpretation'.[42] The following paragraph is an excerpt from an essay by Schüssler Fiorenza:

A feminist theology that conceives of itself as a critical theology of liberation must sustain a creative but often painful tension. In order to remain feminist and faithful to women's experiences it must insist that Christian theology, Biblical tradition, and the Christian churches are guilty of the structural sin of sexist-racist patriarchy which perpetuates and legitimates the societal exploitation and violence against women. Patriarchal religion and theology perpetuate and legitimate rape, wife-battering, child-abuse, sexual exploitation of women, second-class citizenship and many more injustices against women. At the same time a critical feminist theology of liberation must be able to show that Christian faith, tradition and Church are not inherently sexist and racist, if it wants to remain a Christian theology. In order to sustain this creative tension such a feminist theology has to move critically beyond androcentric texts, traditional teachings of men, and patriarchal structures by centring on the historical struggle of self-identified women and women-identified men against sexist-racist-militarist patriarchy and for liberation in the power of the Spirit.[43]

In another article 'The New Vision of Feminist Theology', Anne E Carr writes that according to Elisabeth Schüssler Fiorenza, the 'only adequate criterion for feminist theology is the women themselves who struggle for liberation, transcendence, and selfhood in remembrance of their heritage. They are Women-Church, the *ekklesia* of women, the "movement of self-identified women and women-identified men" who judge theological claims according to whether they serve to oppress or liberate women.'[44] She acknowledges that the logic of this stance is that the locus or place of Divine Revelation and grace is therefore not the Bible or the Tradition of a patriarchal church but the *ekklesia* of women and the lives of women who live the 'option for our women selves'. The aim of this church is women's religious self-affirmation and power, their freedom from 'all patriarchal alienation, marginalization and oppression'.[45]

A subfield of feminist Liberation Theology is eco-feminism. An exposition of its theoretical orientations may be found in an essay by Mary Judith Rees published in *Concilium* in 2009. Rees speaks of analysing the cultural and psychological need for myth and of 'the significant new insight' that 'it is possible to situate the Christian myth within the broader sweep of our evolution as a species and to gain a much larger sense of the history of the universe and of the antiquity of our roots'.[46] Included in this process is the rediscovery of feminine images of the Divine as *Pachamama*, Earth Mother.[47] Rees suggests that the 'post-patriarchical way of being' of eco-feminists is most visible in their epistemology. The body and bodily experience, including women's sexual, sensual, abused and wounded bodies, is the locus for understanding. The associated *praxis* includes the promotion of women's rituals, the hallmark of which is the celebration of women's bodies through dance. Rees states that 'many of these rituals are inspired by indigenous cosmologies' and that the 'great shift' is the turn to the natural world.[48]

Eco-feminism tends to be popular with certain communities of women religious who usually begin by embracing First World feminist paradigms with their focus on an analysis of power relationships within the Church (understood through the prism of liberal managerial theory) and then there is a fusion of First World Feminism with Third World Liberation Theology and often an additional element of pre-Christian mythology or what Rees called 'indigenous cosmologies'. Such cosmologies often include an interest in feminine deities. For example, eco-feminist theology came to the attention of the national press in Australia in the late 1990s when a group of nuns were sighted by fishermen dancing naked on Tennyson's Beach in South Australia to celebrate the Summer solstice. This was an incidence in a First World country of what Rees called 'the celebration of women's bodies through dance' and 'the turn to the natural world'.

Popular culture as *Locus Theologicus*

Not all Liberation Theologians, however, take on such gender-exclusive hermeneutical frameworks or the openness to pagan mythology. In particular no less an authority on the movement than Gutiérrez has noted the existence of different subspecies of Liberation Theologians, some more or less connected to creedal Christianity than others. Thus, he writes:

> Our discussion of Latin America as a whole is not intended to imply that life and reflection does not vary from one national context to another. The intense political experience of Peronism, for example, has led certain theologians to distinguish, within LT [Liberation Theology] in recent years, a particular current, having its own traits, which they call the 'theology of popular pastoral ministry'. Juan Carlos Scannone has systematized this approach with clarity and penetration, centering it on the category people.[49]

Juan Carlos Scannone SJ, professor emeritus of the University of Savior-San Miguel in Buenos Aires, is an Argentinian philosopher and luminary of the Argentinian school of Liberation Theology. He is also famously a former spiritual advisor to the young Fr Jorge Bergoglio, now Pope Francis. Scannone wrote his doctorate on the philosophy of Maurice Blondel at the University of Munich and he later became interested in the thought of the French

Jewish phenomenologist Emmanuel Lévinas (1905–95). Scannone was also influenced by Rudolfo Kusch (1922–79), an Argentinian anthropologist who is little known outside of Latin America, though one of his works has been published in English under the title *Indigenous and Popular Thinking in Latin America*.[50] In his introduction to the translation Walter D. Mignolo wrote:

> Kusch identifies a connection between indigenous thought and interiority, affectivity and attention to emotional experience, as well as a resistance to prioritizing the rational over the affective, the exterior world over the interior of the human being. By so doing Kusch uncovers European philosophy's repressed subjectivity, its drive to situate logic before subjectivity, and its inclination to place the person at the service of the institution, instead of the other way around.[51]

The idea that European philosophy situates logic before subjectivity is certainly true of some strains of European philosophy, though it was precisely this problem that nineteenth-century European Romanticism sought to address, and which Existential Thomism, and in particular Lublin Thomism, sought to address. These remedial efforts and alternatives are often overlooked in the Latino literature where there is a tendency to read for 'European' Suárezian and other varieties of scholasticism, since these were part and parcel of the Spanish colonial legacy.

Scannone has distinguished four currents in Liberation Theology: first, a theology from the pastoral *praxis* of the Church; secondly, a theology from the *praxis* of revolutionary groups; thirdly, a theology from historical *praxis*; and fourthly, a theology from the *praxis* of the Latin American peoples.[52] His own contribution, badged 'People's Theology' is most closely associated with the fourth current – the *praxis* of the Latin American peoples – and with the political philosophy of Peronism. Candelaria outlines the general methodology of 'People's Theology' in the following paragraph:

> For exponents of the Theology of the People, people implies nationalist and populist undercurrents. People means primarily the nation and takes on a quasi-sacred quality: 'the people are good'. The San Miguel statement of 1968, issued by the Argentinian Bishops, utilizes this meaning of people. When speaking of Church-world relations it identifies the people as a national community. Lucio Gera, one of the theological architects of the document, in the fashion of Herder, associates the people with homeland, religion, autochthonous tradition, and folklore. The Argentine people, in Gera's estimation, have 'integrated the Catholic faith with nationalism, from the cry of Facundo the gaucho, "religion or death", to the socio-political philosophy of Peronism'.[53]

Candelaria concludes:

> Scannone's unique theology is geared toward an interpretation of
> popular culture. The key elements of this theology include making
> a break or epistemological rupture with conventional ways of doing
> theology; positing popular culture as the locus of interpretation; and
> conceiving the people as the authentic subject of theology.[54]

One of the hallmarks of 'People's Theology' is therefore a strong affirmation
of popular religious devotions found among the poor and uneducated. Other
schools of Liberation Theology (for example, those associated with Segundo)
regard pious devotions as superstitious practices designed by a hierarchical
clergy to distract the common folk from political action.

In an essay published in 1977 entitled 'Popular Culture: Pastoral and
Theological Considerations', Scannone claimed that his theology 'regards both
the popular culture and the pastoral care of the people as the hermeneutic
locus, that is, the sphere of critical reflection, interpretation and knowledge,
of the Christian message'.[55] Specifically, he refers to the cultural ethos of the
'Juan Pablos' (Joe Blows) as a source of wisdom which has not been subject
to 'the distortions which, among the privileged, stem from ownership, power
and learning'.[56] Scannone posits this as a general theological principle, not
limited to Argentinian 'Juan Pablos'. It is, he asserts, 'the poor of all the
nations to which the people of God is sent who most naturally possess the
living wisdom which, in either case, constitutes the kernel of the Christian
ethos and that of the cultural *ethos* of each people'.[57]

Scannone also enlists the precedent of Thomas Aquinas's assimilation
of Aristotelian philosophy to defend his project of treating the culture of
the 'Juan Pablos' as a *locus theologicus*. He draws an analogy between the
mediating function of philosophy in theological knowledge and what he
perceives to be the mediating function of popular culture in relation to 'the
understanding of faith (theology) and pastoral action'.[58] Specifically he writes:

> The practical folklore which accompanies the history and historical
> praxis of the Latin American peoples can be reflexively and critically
> formulated in theory or in science. The theological moment of this
> *praxis*, insofar as it is the *praxis* of the inculturated people of God
> can – for that reason – theoretically be formulated into a theology
> which ought to be a critical reflection on the praxis in light of the
> Word of God, as it is interpreted in the Church. The culture, in which
> this people incarnates its faith and its liberating *praxis* of the love
> of neighbour, thus serves as the 'Manuductio' for the perspective of
> faith. That ought not to astonish, for in the establishment of the Latin

American cultural ethos evangelisation historically played a decisive role. From thence we believe that the hermeneutical space for the Latin American theoretical conception of liberation (as well as its theological conception) is the *praxis* and culture of the Latin American people.[59]

Argentinian 'People's Theology' thus includes the rather novel element of giving a privileged epistemological standing to the 'people' in a manner similar to that given to the proletarian class by Marxist theorists and to the 'Volk' by the German National Socialists. For example, one finds scattered references throughout Marxist works to the 'bourgeois mystification of knowledge' or the middle-class 'sin' of using a superior education as a tool in the class war. People's Theology follows in this trajectory with its hermeneutic of suspicion regarding the ideas of those who are socially privileged or learned (without of course acknowledging the irony that the theory itself was composed by people educated at elite European universities). The theory also carries affinities with the ideas of the 'cultural caudillo of the Mexican revolution' José Vasconcelos (1882–1959). In an essay published in 1925 entitled *La Raza Cósmica,* Vasconcelos promoted the idea that the peoples of Latin America, since they are a genetic mix of old and new world races, can be bearers of a new era of universal brotherhood, a new civilisation known as Universópolis. To 'European ears', the notion of 'the people' enjoying some kind of special epistemological status is strongly evocative of the National Socialist concept of the *Volk,* the idea that the common folk are bearers of a historic mission and charism. Scannone would argue of course that in the case of the Argentinian 'Juan Pablos' their spirituality is based on Christian beliefs, not Norse mythology.

The closest First World articulation of such a notion may be found in Alasdair MacIntyre's articles about the practices of 'plain persons' (those not philosophically educated) on Scottish islands relatively unspoiled by modernity. MacIntyre finds in the practices of the Scottish crofters, for example, a cultural embodiment of the Aristotelian virtues and suggests that such practices may assist plain persons to discern the principles of the natural law more easily than those who work in professions such as stockbroking or merchant banking where the connection between the workplace practices and the practice of virtue is not so intrinsic. Both Scannone and MacIntyre share a sense that the cultural practices of modernity can have a corrupting effect on their practitioner's receptivity to Christian Revelation.

MacIntyre's respect for the life-forms of those relatively untouched by Modernity is however significantly different from the Marxist idea of the 'bourgeois mystification of knowledge'. It is not a case of arguing that the middle classes deliberately mystify knowledge to keep the working class out of positions of cultural power, as Antonio Gramsci (1891–1937) argued, or that their ideas are self-interested justifications of their own economic advantages (the line of Vladimir Lenin (1870–1924) and the luminaries of the Frankfurt School) but rather that the underlying logic of the practices themselves is hostile to the instantiation of virtue and sets up barriers to the work of grace. For example, MacIntyre is critical of the underlying logic of many bureaucratic practices that preclude administrators from exercising their prudential judgement and developing the virtue of prudence.

Cardinal Francis George of Chicago (1937–2015) made a similar point to MacIntyre when he said that a problem with American Catholics is that they tend to be 'Catholic in theory, but Protestant in practice' by which he meant that the culture of the United States has such strong Calvinist roots that Catholics tend to fall into the trap of bifurcating their social and private selves to accommodate to the strongly Calvinist culture or the religion of 'getting on'.

Nothing in the thought of MacIntyre or Cardinal George is however remotely hostile to education as such or to the fact of being a middle-class Catholic. There is merely the recognition that there is an important two-way link between social practices and human cognition. There is also the understanding that social practices carry within them different theological presuppositions, different theo-logics. Cardinal George's point was that there are social practices associated with a Calvinist theo-logic and social practices associated with a Catholic theo-logic. A Catholic theo-logic is hostile to the bifurcation of the person into a separate private and public self.

For an in-depth account of how Scannone understands the place of *praxis* within his theology, recourse can be had to his article '*Das Theorie-Praxis Verhältnis in den Theologie der Befreiung*' (The Theory-Praxis Relationship in Liberation Theology), published in a collection of essays edited by Karl Rahner in 1977.[60] In this he states:

> The *praxis* of liberation, which aims at formulating theology reflexively and critically, cannot be any arbitrary praxis that ascribes the name 'liberation' to itself. Rather, it must be a truly liberating praxis, *corresponding to the judgment of faith in light of the Word of God.*[61]

Scannone goes on to differentiate between three streams of Christian practice: (i) the liberating *praxis* of the Church as an institutional body, particularly her episcopacy, (ii) the *praxis* of Christian laity who are politically active and (iii) the *praxis* of the Latin American people in its totality. Each stream has its strengths and temptations and Scannone argues that all three are necessary to serve as a reciprocal critique through mutual mediation. He does however conclude that the 'historical accent must lie on the third stream' and that 'the hermeneutical space for the Latin American theoretical conception of liberation (as well as its theological conception) is the *praxis* and culture of the Latin American people'.[62]

Other names associated with Argentinian 'People's Theology' include Lucio Gera (1924–2012), already mentioned above by Candeleria, and Rafael Tello. These two are said to have set about 'Peronizing' Liberation Theology, and thus making it less Marxist, but more Nationalist, and less intellectual and more popularist. Either way, it applies a strong hermeneutic of suspicion to the ideas of the middle class and the highly educated. This mentality is something of a Peronista hallmark. 'Work Boots not Books' was a Peronista slogan.

Congregation for the Doctrine of the Faith interventions

Given the revolutionary nature of many of the ideas expressed above it is not surprising that during the papacy of John Paul II, the Congregation for the Doctrine of the Faith issued two major documents dealing with the methodology of Liberation Theology. In the Preliminary Notes that preceded the *Instruction on Certain Aspects of Liberation Theology* published in 1984, the CDF described Liberation Theology as a 'phenomenon with an extraordinary number of layers' and, further, that 'there is a whole spectrum from radically Marxist positions, on the one hand, to the efforts which are being made within the framework of a correct and ecclesial theology, on the other hand, a theology which stresses the responsibility which Christians necessarily have for the poor and oppressed, such as we see in the documents of the Latin American Bishops' Conference (CELAM) from Medellin to Puebla'. Referring to those manifestations of Liberation Theology at the Marxist end of the spectrum, the CDF observed that Liberation Theology is a universal phenomenon in three ways: first, 'it does not intend to add a new theological treatise to those already existing, that is, it does not wish to develop new aspects of the Church's social ethics. Rather it sees itself as a new hermeneutics of the Christian faith, a new way of understanding Christianity as a whole'. As such 'it affects theology at its basic constitution, not merely in aspects of its content'. It 'alters all forms of Church life: the Church's constitution, liturgy, catechesis, moral options'. Secondly, it is not confined to Latin America but is commonly found across the entire Third World and even reaches into the First World, and thirdly, it is universal in the sense of operating beyond denominational boundaries. In terms of its actual content the CDF *Notes* located at the heart of the subject of Liberation Theology the idea that 'nothing lies outside political commitment, everything has a political colour'.

The CDF document explained the theoretical attraction of Liberation Theology by reference to three sociological developments after the Second Vatican Council. The first was the view that the existing theological Tradition was inadequate, the second was a 'naïve belief in science which accepted the human sciences as a new gospel without wanting to see their limitations and endemic problems'. Specifically, 'psychology, sociology and the Marxist interpretation of history seemed to be scientifically established and hence to become unquestionable arbiters of Christian thought'. Thirdly, 'the criticism of tradition applied by modern Evangelical exegesis, in particular by Rudolf Bultmann and his school, similarly became a firm theological authority, cutting off the path to theology in its prior form and so encouraging people all the more to produce new constructions'. The crucial concepts become 'people', 'community', 'experience' and 'history'. Whereas previously it was 'the Catholic Church in her totality – a totality that spanned time and space and embraced laity (*sensus fidei*) and hierarchy (Magisterium) – that constituted the hermeneutical criterion', with the Liberation Theologians influenced by Marxism it became simply the community. The biblical horizon was then fused with the Marxist idea of history such that faith is replaced by 'fidelity to history', hope becomes confidence in the future elimination of class conflict, and love consists in the 'option for the poor'. Above all, it is axiomatic for Liberation Theologians that truth is realised in history and its praxis and hence 'the only true orthodoxy is orthopraxy'.

In the actual *Instruction on Certain Aspects of the Theology of Liberation*, the following statement of principle is to be found:

> The ultimate and decisive criterion for truth can only be a criterion which is itself theological. It is only in the light of faith, and what faith teaches us about the truth of man and the ultimate meaning of his destiny, that one can judge the validity or degree of validity of what other disciplines propose, often rather conjecturally, as being the truth about man, his history and destiny.

The *Instruction on Certain Aspects of Liberation Theology* was followed in 1986 by an *Instruction on Christian Freedom and Liberation*. Paragraph three of the 1986 document tied both freedom and liberation to the Incarnation, Cross and Resurrection of Christ. Paragraph sixty further addressed the issue of the difference between incarnational and eschatological approaches to the theology of history with the statement that an important distinction needs to be made between earthly progress and the growth of the Kingdom, which do not belong to the same order, though they are not completely separate. Paragraph seventy also addressed the issue of the theological significance of human experience with the following statement:

> A theological reflection developed from a particular experience can constitute a very positive contribution, inasmuch as it makes possible a highlighting of aspects of the Word of God, the richness of which had not yet been fully grasped. But in order that this reflection may be truly a reading of the Scripture and not a projection on to the Word of God of a meaning which it does not contain, the theologian will be careful to interpret the experience from which he begins in the light of the experience of the Church herself. This experience of the Church shines with a singular brightness and in all its purity in the lives of the saints. It pertains to the pastors of the Church, in communion with the Successor of Peter, to discern its authenticity.

In the conclusion of the 1986 *Instruction* reference is made to the need for the development of a theology of freedom and liberation that 'faithfully echoes Mary's *Magnificat*', rather than a 'criminal' misdirection of popular piety in the direction of a 'purely earthly plan of liberation' which would simply cause 'new forms of slavery'.

The central message of the document is that liberation must be Christocentric, as John Paul II himself indicated in an address delivered early in his pontificate in 1979:

> Christ himself links liberation particularly with knowledge of the truth. ... Liberation means man's inner transformation, which is a consequence of the knowledge of the truth. ... Truth is important not only for the growth of human knowledge, deepening man's interior life in this way; truth has also prophetic significance and power. ... The theology of liberation must, above all, be faithful to the whole truth on man, in order to show clearly, not only in the Latin-American context but also in contemporary contexts, what reality is this freedom 'for which Christ set us free'.[63]

Other criticisms of Liberation Theology

In his book *Liberation Theology* James V. Schall SJ noted that in contrast to modern political theory, classical and medieval political theory was aware that one's expectations of politics needed to be moderate.[64] In particular, Schall pointed out that according to Aquinas, 'efforts to achieve the essential effects or conditions of the Divine republic [heaven in other words] through the earthly peace were not only impossible of achievement but blasphemous'.[65] This 'moderation' of classical theory was designed 'precisely to prevent man's ultimate metaphysical and religious desires from seeking a political expression'.[66] Moreover, Schall argued:

> The medieval relation of theology to politics was always that theology was the queen of the sciences, the ultimate judge of the truly human, such that it provided a check on the aberrations of politics. Theology is now looking upon itself in a rather opposite fashion. It is a partisan advocate for political well-being. Theology tests its validity by the criterion of political performance or, even more fundamentally, theology is claiming to be the vision which establishes the Kingdom politically.[67]

Schall goes on to say that theology is 'turning to politics as a matrix discipline' and that what is new in modern political theory is the transformation of politics into an aspect of eschatology. Balthasar made similar observations. As he put the proposition: 'The kingdom of God cannot be coerced into existence by any amount of political effort. It remains the gift of God and of the returning Lord to a world that cannot perfect itself by its own efforts.'[68]

While Schall focused his criticisms on the tendency of Liberation Theology to 'immanentize the eschaton', John Milbank has been critical of an array of projects that seek to subvert the standing of theology as the queen of the sciences by the promotion of putatively 'theologically neutral' social theory. Specifically he criticises Liberation Theology for this kind of subversion and for trapping itself in the cage of secular reason. Milbank suggests that the early Clodovis Boff, whom he regards as typical of Liberation Theologians in this regard, simply renames Kant's categorical imperative as 'faith', which is to say that faith becomes 'the impulse of the heart to love one's neighbour'.[69] Specific questions about how to love one's neighbour, the precise form that one's actions towards one's neighbour might take, are left unasked. They are presupposed to be obvious. Theological beliefs are reduced to the status of a 'feint regulative gloss upon Kantian ethics and a somewhat eclectic, though basically Marxist, social theory'.[70] Milbank also criticises Liberation Theology for its circular reasoning:

> All that theology can do is to give these principles of liberation another name: salvation. Theology is able to declare that natural, human ethics is approved by God. It is able to do this because natural, human ethics

has the goal of liberation – the setting free of the human capacity for transcendence, which is precisely the supposed source and foundation for our knowledge of God's existence. All revolves within this futile circle. This is all very circular.[71]

Cardinal Angelo Scola shares Milbank's concern with the occlusion of the primacy of Christian Revelation and certain secularising approaches to the role of experience in Liberation Theologies. Specifically, he has warned against the tendency to attempt an analysis of human experience outside the framework of Christian Revelation. While he accepts that there is a place for the analysis of human experience in theological work, he argues that 'the truth-criterion of Christian experience is inside this experience itself, not outside or beyond it' and further, that 'theology stimulates experience to measure itself against the totality of the datum of Revelation as it is attested by the Bible and authentically interpreted by the Magisterium'.[72] As a consequence,

> the 'communional' nature of the subject of Christian experience absolutely precludes confusing it with *praxis*. This is because the original and archetypal experience belongs to the primordial subject, Jesus Christ, and, in him, to all who are 'his own'. Every authentic human experience of the Christian God is, therefore, objectively included in, and formed by, the experience of Jesus Christ. As a result, the Christian experience of the individual takes the form of a tension towards the totality, hence, of an opening, of a way. Any temptation to lock ourselves into a human measure reduces experience to something partial. This partialness can be overcome only by the 'gift from on high', in the Spirit and in faith. Faith bestows the opening towards the totality that is the incarnate Son of God.
>
> We therefore realise that from the methodological point of view the relationship between theology and experience is not, and cannot be identified with, the relationship between theory and praxis. Nor can the theologian understand himself as a kind of Christian 'organic intellectual' a la [the Italian Marxist Antonio] Gramsci. In point of fact, the priority of experience over theology is ontological, and this priority reveals plainly that man is primarily and essentially the receiver, not the producer of truth.[73]

The 'special interest' nature of Liberation Theology has also drawn academic criticism. Balthasar argued that 'any theology which is coloured by a specific culture or epoch must, if it is Catholic, be acceptable in its central concerns to all other local churches' – 'it must be so shaped, that, in essence, it could be considered relevant and be proclaimed in every satellite of the [former]

Soviet Union or the People's Republic of China'.[74] While it is legitimate for different theologies to have different accents, or a focus on different images and concepts, Balthasar asserted that such images and concepts 'must be open to and commune with one another within the universe of the *Catholica*'.[75] He noted that while 'Liberation' is a central point of Revelation, 'revelation would suffer a drastic contraction if everything without exception were to be traced back to the concept of liberation'.[76] Balthasar also warned that God through the Incarnation of Christ, 'delivered his own hermeneutic' and thus, contemporary fashionable hermeneutical frameworks 'can quite distort God's self-interpretation in Christ to the point of unrecognizability'.[77] Specifically Balthasar stated:

> Whenever a form of Christianity which considers itself enlightened forgets that Christ's Cross and Resurrection have wholly fulfilled the Old Testament's 'utopian' promise ('God with us'), the result is not a lapsing back into paganism (which, in any event, is irretrievable), but a drifting into a Judaizing mentality that now reads the New Testament through the filter of a master-slave ideology and which, consequently, takes into its own control the business of mankind's total politico-religious liberation, entirely contrary to the Old Testament's original understanding of Israel.[78]

Taken together the criticisms of the Congregation for the Doctrine of the Faith, John Paul II, Schall, Milbank, Scola and Balthasar combine to make essentially the same point, that any understanding of the meaning of liberation must take place within the framework of Christian Revelation or what Balthasar called 'God's own hermeneutic', not secular social theory.

Gustavo Gutiérrez and Gerhard Cardinal Müller

In an interview given in 1996 Cardinal Ratzinger spoke of having entered into a dialogue with Gustavo Gutiérrez that had helped the scholars at the CDF to better understand his work and which had also helped Gutiérrez to see the one-sided character of his earlier publications, with the result that he had subsequently developed a form of Liberation Theology with the right content.[79] Like Clodovis Boff, there is an early and a more mature Gutiérrez.

In 2015 Gutiérrez jointly published *On the Side of the Poor: The Theology of Liberation* with Cardinal Gerhard Müller, the current Prefect for the Congregation of the Doctrine of the Faith. The book consists of a series of essays alternating between the two authors. Gutiérrez refers to the twin errors of a 'verticalism of a disembodied spiritual union with God' (which recognises God's transcendence but not His immanence) and a 'socioeconomic-political horizontalism' (focused on the immanence and neglectful of the transcendence). In other words, there are Catholics who focus on their personal spiritual lives caring little about the social (horizontal) dimensions of their faith, and Catholics who focus on social issues rather than their personal relationship to God (the vertical dimension), when the two dimensions should be integrated.

Müller strongly affirms this notion of their being twin errors and links them to the neo-scholastic construction of the nature and grace relationship, which fosters the dualistic idea that the State governs the body, and the Church, the soul. Müller concluded that 'we can understand liberation theology on the whole to be a socially applied *nouvelle théologie*, as formulated by Henri de Lubac, or, also to be a theology of grace, as developed by Karl Rahner, now applied to history and society'.[80] What Müller does not do is offer a suggestion about which Liberation Theologians have followed Rahner and which ones have followed de Lubac. Moreover, he says nothing about the significance of this difference. Others think that this difference goes to the very root of post-Conciliar theological conflict and is hugely significant. The choice of Rahner places one on the *Concilium* track, while the choice of de Lubac places one on the *Communio* track. The tracks begin at the same junction (opposition to neo-scholasticism) but they do not converge or cross, and they end in very different places. Milbank, for example, makes the following observation:

> The Rahnerian version of integralism can only make the social the real site of salvation by a dialectical baptism of secular society. It has to annex Christian 'orthodoxy' to the practical rejection of Christian truth. And its assumption that there is a universally available social ethic ignores the historical genesis of morality. By contrast, the integralism which 'supernaturalises the natural' [the Lubacian version], is able to expound the difference of supernatural charity as the historical, though incomplete insertion of a different community, and a different ethical practice.[81]

Milbank's judgement is that Liberation Theology got bogged in a secularist mire precisely because it took the Rahner–Schillebeeckx bus rather than the de Lubac–Balthasar bus.

Although Müller glosses over the significant differences between de Lubac and Rahner, he nonetheless addressed Milbank-type criticisms of Liberation Theology with his statement, 'when something is said about the primacy of *praxis*, there is intended no reduction of Christian belief to ethics. Rather, the emphasis is on our participation in the *praxis* of God in love, which can be recognised only through faith in the Word of God's self-revelation'.[82] Such a statement is music to Lubacian and Balthasarian ears. However, to what extent real, on the ground, practitioners of Liberation Theology actually make this distinction is a moot point. It is nonetheless significant that the current Prefect for the Congregation of the Doctrine of the Faith has acknowledged this issue.

With reference to the criticism (made by Balthasar and others) of the limited regional applicability of even the most benign forms of Liberation Theology, Müller acknowledges that Liberation Theology is what he calls a 'regional theology' and he warns against theology 'splintering into an innumerable set of regional theologies'. Without addressing the question of just how many the Church can support before having too many, Müller says that these regional theologies need to be oriented to the universal Church and there needs to be a communications network of such regional theologies, which will have the effect of orienting them to the universal Church.

Müller also makes the significant claim that the terms 'capitalism' and 'socialism' mean something different in Latino parlance from the common understanding of these terms in Europe and the Anglosphere. In this context he writes:

> Liberation theology uses the term capitalism to name the financial structure that produces oppression and exploitation in Latin America. What is meant here is not simply an economic system in which free enterprise has an important place. In this context, capitalism means the combination of money and material means of power in the hands of an oligarchy and the international centres of business and power. As an alternative, liberation theology speaks of socialism. With this proposal, there is clearly intended not a planned and ordered economy. What is intended here is an economic system with the goal of the active participation of all people in the economies of their respective countries and also of the active participation of the underdeveloped nations in the global economic process.[83]

Again, Müller's nuances may not in fact be acknowledged by all 'on the ground' proponents of Liberation Theology, but his interventions can nonetheless be read as correcting some of the more extreme tendencies within the movement.

Situating Pope Francis

While much has been written about Pope Francis's agenda for his pontificate and his personal history as a Jesuit Provincial and Archbishop, little has been written on his attitudes to the practice of theology as an intellectual discipline. This is because with Francis the accent is on social problems, not ideas, *praxis* rather than *theoria*. As he said to a Jesuit student who explained that he was studying Fundamental Theology: 'I can't imagine anything more boring.'[84] When a person says that he 'can't imagine anything more boring than Fundamental Theology', it is not likely that his publications will be full of treasure to be mined for a book on how to do theology. In an article published in *The Atlantic*, Ross Douthat observed:

> Francis is clearly a less systematic thinker than either of his predecessors, and especially than the academically-minded Benedict. Whereas the previous pope defended popular piety against liberal critiques, Francis *embodies* a certain style of populist Catholicism – one that's suspicious of overly academic faith in any form. He seems to have an affinity for the kind of Catholic culture in which mass attendance might be spotty but the local saint's processions are packed – a style of faith that's fervent and supernaturalist but not particularly doctrinal. He also remains a Jesuit-formed leader, and Jesuits have traditionally combined missionary zeal with a certain conscious flexibility about doctrinal details that might impede their proselytizing work.[85]

Nonetheless, it has been suggested by several academics and papal commentators that if Pope Francis has sympathy for any particular approach to Catholic theology, it is that of 'People's Theology'. One of the most extensive articles on this subject is Juan Carlos Scannone's 'El papa Francisco y la teologia del pueblo' published in the journal *Razón y Fe*.[86] In this paper Scannone claims that not only is Pope Francis a practitioner of 'People's Theology' but also that Francis extracted his favourite four principles – time is greater than space, unity prevails over conflict, reality is more important than ideas, and the whole is greater than the parts – from a letter of the nineteenth-century Argentinian dictator, Juan Manuel de Rosas (1793–1877) sent to another Argentinian caudillo, Facundo Quiroga (1788–1835), in 1834. These four principles, which are said to govern the decision-making processes of Pope Francis, have their own section in his Apostolic Exhortation *Evangelii Gaudium* and references to one or other of them can be found scattered throughout his other papal documents. Pope Francis calls them principles for 'building a people'.

A common thread running through each of these principles is the tendency to give priority to *praxis* over theory. There is also a sense that conflict in itself is not a bad thing, that 'unity will prevail' somehow and that time will remove at least some of the protagonists in any conflict. The underlying metaphysics is quite strongly Hegelian, and the approach to *praxis* itself resembles what

Lamb classified as 'cultural-historical' activity and is associated primarily with Luther and Kant rather than Marx.

Professor Loris Zanatta of the University of Bologna has published an article entitled '*Un papa peronista*?' in which he makes the claim that Pope Francis has used the word *pueblo* or people some 356 times in his papal speeches, that Pope Francis believes that poverty bestows upon people a moral superiority, and accordingly, that for Pope Francis, the 'deposit of the faith' is to be found preserved among the poor living in 'inner city neighbourhoods'.[87] Such a reading situates Pope Francis squarely in the territory of Scannone's 'People's Theology'. The fact that Pope Francis as the Archbishop of Buenos Aires used his authority to have Lucio Gera's body buried in the crypt of his cathedral is taken as further evidence of his strong endorsement of Argentinian 'People's Theology'.

Notwithstanding the fact that Bergoglio/Francis is certainly not a fundamental or a dogmatic or systematic theologian in anyone's estimation, there is nonetheless one book review, published in the Argentinian journal *Stromata* in 1984, in which he addresses the topic of theological method. It is a review of Balthasar's *Truth is Symphonic: Aspects of Christian Pluralism* and Karl Lehmann's *Die Einheit des Bekenntnisses und der theologische Pluralismus* (The Unity of the Confession of Faith and Theological Pluralism). In this review Bergoglio endorses Balthasar's criticisms of the reduction or 'domestication' of mystery to the dimensions of a human concept. Bergoglio writes:

> The reality of the greater distance and greater proximity of God to man, which is given in Jesus Christ, this being *in similitudine maior dissimilitudo*, offers von Balthasar the basis for an elaboration of the criteria in which he will centre his reflection concerning the possibility of ecclesial pluralism: the *criteria of proximity and of maximality (distance)*.[88]

The section of *Truth is Symphonic* from which Bergoglio took this statement is entitled 'The treatment of the criterion of dogma'. It runs to some nine very dense pages. Here the unnamed target of Balthasar's reflections is the neo-scholastic attachment to dialectics and the corresponding impatience with paradox.

Balthasar begins his analysis by stating that 'every Christian act of faith embraces, not the formula or theorem, but the *res*, the matter referred to'. (St Thomas Aquinas would agree, but many neo-scholastics got so hooked on the formulae that this fact was often occluded in their publications.) Balthasar goes on to argue that for the encounter to take place, that is, the encounter between the human person and the *res*, the expression or dogmatic formula, must 'cause the act of God's love for us to appear more Divine, more radical, more complete and at the same time more unimaginable and improbable'.[89] Balthasar then criticises those who approach two apparently contradictory statements of Christ and instead of accepting the paradox, latch on to one or other statement and give it priority. This he argues is a recipe for heresy.[90] Balthasar concludes his reflections on orthodoxy with the statement: 'Orthodoxy is God's orthopraxy, making the believer's "doxy" the affirmation of and participation in God's "praxy", praxis.'[91]

Later in the same work, Balthasar develops the concept of 'abiding', which he defines as 'faith, receiving in constant thankfulness, the amazed realization of the superabundance of divine gifts, the attempt to understand as much of it as possible'.[92] Balthasar describes abiding as both the continual spur to right action and its regulating principle. He argues that this 'abiding' means the primacy of reception over response and transmission and he ties this to the Pauline warnings about 'works' and what he describes as 'overhasty undertakings and attempts to change the world'. Balthasar concludes this section by stating that the importance of this disposition of 'abiding' and its primacy of reception over response and transmission entails the primacy of *logos* over *ethos*, a principle that was also emphasised by Romano Guardini.[93]

Balthasar suggests that in the lives of the saints, when this receptivity to the *logos* is strong, through the gifts of Holy Spirit, 'believing and doing are perfected in each other and become one'.[94] His succinct maxim is: 'Faith becomes instrumental and action attracts belief'.[95] This construction of the relationship is prototypically Chalcedonian in the sense that *logos* and *ethos*, faith and action, are distinct but not separated. Receptivity to the *logos* leads to a Marian disposition of 'abiding', pondering the glory of Revelation in one's heart and allowing the *logos* to take possession of one's soul, forming it and infusing it with the Gifts of the Holy Spirit such that 'believing and doing are perfected in each other and become one'. This is a very different construction of the *logos–ethos* relationship from the one that starts with the concrete facts of social injustice and reflection upon such conditions in the Marxist-inspired *praxis* models.

Unfortunately, in his review of *Truth is Symphonic,* Bergoglio did not say anything about Balthasar's endorsement of Guardini's principle of the priority of *logos* over *ethos*. Had he done so he would have found himself contending with a core issue in *Communio*-style critiques of Liberation Theology. The fact that Guardini's theology was to have been the subject of Bergoglio's aborted doctoral dissertation indicates that Bergoglio regarded Guardini as, at least, an interesting scholar. However, Bergoglio did not address this issue at all; he merely summarised sections of Balthasar's book on theological pluralism and then turned his attention to Lehmann's work from which he culled the following idea:

> The tension between plurality and unity is not only irresolvable by accentuating just one of the sides and by displacing the pole of synthesis in that direction. It is also irresolvable ecclesially by experimenting with a kind of balance of partial aspects, the formal unity of which would amount to a syncretism. In such a case, one could only manage to achieve a caricature of authentic pluralism, and the inspired options in such a syncretistic attitude would only be of use for 'the moment' not for 'the time', since they lack the capacity to bring harmony to the whole process and to growth. ... The unity of confession invites us to preserve undiluted the original richness of the Word of God in its differences, and to discard the claim that we ourselves create the perfect and controllable synthesis.[96]

The above statements were made in the context of a book review and thus do not provide anything like an extensive treatment of the topic of Bergoglio/ Francis's preferred theological method, but they do indicate that he had read both Balthasar and Lehmann on the subject of theological pluralism, that he was sympathetic to Balthasar's frustration with neo-scholastic conceptualism ('the domestication of the mystery' or reduction of the *intellectus fidei* to a mere *intellectus rationis humanae* as Balthasar put it), and one gathers the impression (from his treatment of Lehmann's book) that theological tensions do not concern him because he believes that such tensions are a natural result of the human intellect's inability to master the mystery and are merely the 'war-room' or one might say, cabinet-debating room, of the Church. However, with both Lehmann and Balthasar, Bergoglio is clear that the tensions can only be held together fruitfully when theologians identify themselves as belonging to the Church. As he expressed the idea:

> To share in the unity of confession presupposes an acceptance of belonging, and of the consequences of belonging, which bear this kind of unity, in us, from the ecclesial point of view. It is the whole Church who has the whole truth of faith; it is only possible to participate in this totality to the extent that ecclesial belonging becomes complete.[97]

Precisely what Bergoglio meant by the statement 'it is the whole Church who has the whole truth of faith' is not however clear. He certainly sees a link between ecclesiology and the issue of theological pluralism but he does not offer any account of his understanding of the powers and responsibilities of the office of Peter, of the nature of magisterial authority (including the relationship of the Petrine Office and the episcopacy) and of how these relationships in turn relate to the *sensus fidelium*. With Benedict XVI one could comb through his publications on these issues and see, for example, that he regarded the pope as a constitutional (not absolute) monarch, whose powers were circumscribed by the deposit of the faith and whose duty it was to uphold, teach and defend. With Francis however one can only try and deduce his understanding of these critical relationships from his actions.

The case study in which all this theory became relevant was the debate over Cardinal Kasper's proposal to grant Communion to the divorced and the remarried. Notwithstanding the fact that such a change in the teaching of the Church would alter 2,000 years of Tradition, and that it was *prima facie* inconsistent with the teaching of Scripture as well, that Cardinal Kasper's arguments based on alleged Patristic-era antecedents were heavily criticised by eminent Patristic scholars, and that the idea was strongly opposed by both of his papal predecessors, Pope Francis allowed a very public debate on the issue. The debate made it obvious that support for this proposal was coming from Belgium and Germany, in particular from clerical leaders who came of age during the 1960s (a significant number of the younger German bishops were strongly opposed to Cardinal Kasper's theological agenda). Many Poles interpreted the project as yet another German attack on something they had heroically defended, in this instance, John Paul II's teaching on this specific issue in *Familiaris consortio*, and the Africans did not see that Church teaching should be changed because the Church was in crisis in Europe. The attitude of a number of leaders was that the countries of Germany, Austria, Belgium and Holland are disaster zones for the Church precisely because their intellectual leaders of the generation of 1968 put their energies into accommodating the pastoral practices of the Church to the zeitgeist rather than challenging the zeitgeist with the perennial truths of the Gospel. This argument was made at the 2015 Synod by Dr Anca-Maria Cernea, President of the Association of Catholic Doctors of Bucharest. In her address to the Synod she specifically mentioned the influence of Frankfurt School philosophy on Catholic theology as a cause of the crisis of family life in Western Europe.[98] (The Church tax or '*Kirchensteuer*' issue has also been mentioned as a significant sociological factor underlying the low rates of Church attendance in Germany.)

In an extensive interview published as *God or Nothing*, Cardinal Robert Sarah of Guinea offered an analysis of the spiritual pathologies operative in post-Christian countries, affirmed what he described as the 'definitely sealed' teaching of John Paul II in *Familiaris consortio* and concluded that bishops should stop discussing the Communion for the divorced and remarried issue 'like disrespectful intellectuals, giving the impression of disputing the teaching of Jesus and the Church'.[99]

In his article in *The Atlantic*, Ross Douthat summarised the two positions thus:

> The argument, from Kasper and others, is that this [Communion to the divorced and remarried] would be strictly a pastoral change, a gesture of welcome and forgiveness rather than an endorsement of the second union, and so it wouldn't alter the Church's formal teaching on the indissolubility of marriage. The possible implication is that the post-sexual-revolution landscape is now as culturally foreign to the Church as China was in the age of Matteo Ricci, and that some cultural accommodation is needed before missionary work can thrive.
>
> [However] the problem for Francis is that Kasper's argument is not particularly persuasive. Describing Communion for the remarried as merely a pastoral change ignores its inevitable doctrinal implications. If people who are living as adulterers can receive Communion, if the Church can recognise their state of life as non-ideal but somehow tolerable, then either the Church's sacramental theology or its definition of sin has been effectively rewritten. And the ramifications of such a change are potentially sweeping. If ongoing adultery is forgivable, then why not other forms of loving, long-standing sexual commitment? Not only same-sex couples but cohabiting straight couples and even polygamous families (a particular concern among African cardinals) could make a plausible case that they deserve the same pastoral exception, rendering the very idea of objective sexual sin anachronistic in one swift march.[100]

Proposition twelve of the 1977 ITC Document 'Propositions on the Doctrine of Christian Marriage' expressed the established theological teaching in this way:

> Without refusing to examine the attenuating circumstances and even sometimes the quality of a second civil marriage after divorce, the approach of the divorced and remarried to the Eucharist is plainly incompatible with the mystery of which the Church is the servant and the witness. In receiving the divorced and remarried to the Eucharist, the Church would let such parties believe that they can, on the level of signs, communicate with him whose conjugal mystery they disavow on the level of reality. To do so would be, moreover, on the part of the Church to declare herself in accord with the baptised at the moment when they enter or remain in a clearly objective contradiction with the life, the thought, and the being itself of the Lord as Spouse of the Church. If the Church could give the sacrament of unity to those who

have broken with her on an essential point of the mystery of Christ, she would no longer be the sign of the witness of Christ but rather a countersign and a counter-witness. Nevertheless, this refusal does not in any way justify any procedure that inflicts infamy and that contradicts in its own way the mercy of Christ toward us sinners.

The end result of this battle was the promulgation of the Apostolic Exhortation *Amoris Laetitia* in 2016. The document was affirming of the Nuptial Mystery theology found in John Paul II's *Catechesis on Human Love* and in the works of cardinal-theologians such as Carlo Caffarra of Bologna, Angelo Scola of Milan and the Quebecois Marc Ouellet, in the sense that elements lifted from this theology were presented in the earlier sections of the Exhortation. The family was described as an icon of the Holy Trinity (which is vintage Ouellet) and aspects of the theological anthropology of John Paul II and Benedict XVI were flagged. So too was the Church's perennial teaching against contraception. However, chapter eight of the document, or what might be described as the *praxis* chapter rather than a theory chapter, emphasised that those who find themselves in 'irregular situations' (what were formerly described as situations of mortal sin or morally disordered situations) should be spiritually and emotionally accompanied along the path of a gradual reintegration into the life of the Church. Whereas in previous Church teaching emphasis was on how the person's rational intellect makes it possible to discern the true and the good and the beautiful, the subtext of this document was that many contemporary people are in effect so far post-Christian as to be pre-Christian. The cultural environment in which they breathe, in which their wills and intellects develop, is so toxic to a Christian understanding of sexuality and marriage that their levels of moral culpability in what is an objectively sinful situation are not easily amenable to judgement, and thus the Church has to be for them a 'field hospital' when their life choices, based on subjective conceptions of the good, detached from Christian Revelation, cause all manner of damage. Notwithstanding the earlier endorsements of selected teachings of John Paul II, chapter 8 gives the impression that the role of the Church as 'teacher of the Truth' and 'guardian of the deposit of the faith' should be muted so as not to scare people away from the Church operating in her capacity as a 'field hospital'. The change of language from 'morally disordered' or 'mortally sinful' to an 'irregular situation' is symptomatic of this muting.

The document is likely to be the subject of ongoing hermeneutical analysis and theological debate as it neither expressly rejected nor expressly affirmed Cardinal Kasper's position. Within days of its release an international debate broke out over the correct interpretation of the very ambivalent footnote 351. It has been described as the most famous footnote in the history of the

Church. The debate is over, first, what precisely is meant by footnote 351, and secondly, if footnote 351 is construed to mean that in certain circumstances (other than situations of a so-called Josephite or non-sexual relationship) a person who is divorced and repartnered may take Communion, how this can be consistent with previous magisterial teaching. For example, how can it be consistent with paragraph eighty-four of John Paul II's Apostolic Exhortation *Familiaris consortio* and paragraph twenty-nine of Benedict XVI's Apostolic Exhortation *Sacramentum Caritatis*? A pastoral crisis may arise if the lay faithful and their priests have to choose between the judgements of two popes (John Paul II and Benedict XVI) on the one side, and a third pope (Pope Francis) on the other.

According to the journalist Sandro Magister, the more ambivalent passages in chapter eight of *Amoris Laetitia* were probably written by Fr Victor Fernández, an Argentinian theologian famous for his 1995 book on the subject of kissing.[101] Fr Fernández is widely regarded as a member of Pope Francis's inner circle and passages from his published works on moral theology bear striking similarities to statements found in *Amoris Laetitia*.

Pope Francis avoided taking questions from journalists on how some of the ambivalent passages of *Amoris Laetitia* are to be interpreted and suggested that they consult Cardinal Christoph von Schönborn of Vienna. Schönborn has said, in the context of an address to a Catholic academy, that the situation of a couple living together without sexual intimacy would be covered by the footnote but he left open the issue of whether other situations might also come under the footnote 351 umbrella.

If one ponders the two Synod debates and the Apostolic Exhortation that followed, from the perspective of the "Four Principles" of de Rosas, then it would appear that the indeterminate nature of the outcome is to be taken in Hegelian terms as simply a pointer to the political reality that dialectical progress continues unabated; while for the moment the *magisterium* of the Petrine Office appears to have been deputed to the Archbishop of Vienna.

The Aparecida document

In an article published in the journal *Nova et Vetera* Keith Lemna and David H. Delaney suggest that the best way to get a sense of where Pope Francis stands theologically (in a broader sense, not on specific questions of moral and sacramental theology) is to read the Aparecida document – a joint declaration of the bishops of Latin America and the Caribbean (CELAM) after the fifth general conference in Aparecida, Brazil, in 2007. Cardinal Bergoglio was the head of the editorial commission for the document.

As Pope Francis he cited this document sixteen times in his Post-Synodal Apostolic Exhortation, *Evangelii Gaudium*.

The Aparecida document links the preferential option for the poor to the task of evangelisation, inserts a large dose of Trinitarian Christocentrism and bleaches out the Marxist elements typical of the early years of Liberation Theology. One might say that this document took the criticisms of the CDF into account and produced a statement that would not fall foul of any of the principles enunciated by the CDF under the leadership of Cardinal Ratzinger. Like every official document Bergoglio/Francis has produced it is quite long and attempts to address every conceivable issue possibly relevant to the topic under review. It could be summed up as a call to reevangelise the peoples of Latin America in Communion with the Persons of the Trinity, to pay particular attention to the reevangelisation of those who have fallen away from participation in the life of the Church, to be acutely sensitive to the social effects of globalisation and to affirm popular piety.

The document is prefaced by the address given by Pope Benedict XVI to the Aparecida Conference delegates on the Feast of Our Lady of Fatima, 2007. In this address Benedict was highly critical of projects to 'breathe life into the pre-Columbian religions', which separate people from Christ and the universal Church, strongly affirming of the 'great mosaic of popular piety which is the precious treasure of the Catholic Church in Latin America', strongly in favour of catechesis, in particular a catechesis based on the *Catechism of the Catholic Church* and the *Compendium of the Social Doctrine of the Church*, utterly hostile to Marxism's 'sad heritage of economic and ecological destruction' and 'oppression of souls', and desirous of linking Eucharistic theology to the commitment to evangelisation and the work of building bonds of social solidarity.

Conclusion

In an interview given to the BBC in 1984 Leszek Kołakowski was asked by a journalist why Marxism was so popular. He replied:

> I think that Marxism was transformed in such a way that it has become a sort of convenient jargon in which all kinds of claims and grievances can be expressed, many of them of a kind which has absolutely nothing to do with those Marx identifies himself with. ... It has become really an idiom in which you can express any sort of claim. Marxism has become a syncretic mixture ... what the Germans call an *eklektische Bettlesuppe* – a mixed beggars' broth. It is incoherent, not codified and

in many ways using only vague hints and allusions for things which cannot be spoken.[102]

Reading this interview, one gets a sense that the *eklektische Bettlesuppe* metaphor is also apt for Liberation Theology. When one immerses oneself in this field one realises that it is very difficult to find two Liberation Theologians who are following the same methodology and who have the same understandings of key concepts such as *praxis* and liberation. There are also marked differences between the Peruvians, the Brazilians and the Argentinians. What is shared is a common grievance about the effects of the Iberian colonisation and shared concerns about how to pastorally care for people who are stricken by grinding poverty. There is also a common belief that the concerns of middle-class Catholics in Europe and the Anglosphere are radically different from those of Catholics in the former Spanish and Portuguese colonies. In one half of the globe there is material poverty, in the other half spiritual poverty. As +Fulton Sheen (1895–1979) once described the difference between people living under the yoke of Communism and those in the affluent free world, one side (people caught behind the Iron Curtain) have the cross without Christ, the other side (those living to the west of Berlin) have Christ without the cross (in the sense that their Christ is a wet social worker, not a Divine redeemer).

The CDF interventions, officially under Cardinal Ratzinger and unofficially under Cardinal Müller, sought to acknowledge the real pastoral problems driving Liberation Theology. They attempted to address these without recourse to Marxism or novel Christologies. Müller's judgement that the whole Liberation Theology project is based on an account of the relationship between nature and grace, which is either Rahnerian or Lubacian, is also quite a significant theoretical point. What each of these accounts of nature and grace tried to overcome was the two-tiered neo-scholastic system where grace and Revelation are viewed as 'top ups' for Aristotelian nature and post-Kantian philosophy. What de Lubac certainly understood is that there is an inescapable social dimension to Christian life, that Catholics are their brother's keepers. Benedict XVI made reference to precisely this point, citing de Lubac, in his encyclical *Spe Salvi*. Applied de Lubac however is very different from applied Rahner. *Communio* scholars are much more comfortable with a Liberation Theology built on de Lubac's understanding of the grace–nature relationship and Scola's understanding of the role of experience in theological study than one built on Rahner's understanding of the grace–nature relationship and a Schillebeeckxian understanding of the role of experience in theological study, both of which are more appealing to those in the *Concilium* circles.

In this context, in his essay 'Theological Method: The Southern Exposure', Alfred T Hennelly SJ recounted the story of how Cardinal Jean Daniélou (a former student of de Lubac), after a visit to Buenos Aires, described Liberation Theology as a 'sub-sub-sub-division' of moral theology. Hennelly explained that by this Daniélou meant that Liberation Theology 'was a part of theology that studied the moral act, a part of moral theology which studied the social act, a part of that area which studied the political act, and a part of the latter which studied the problem of underdeveloped nations'. Hennelly noted that Daniélou was 'profoundly mistaken', that what is at issue is 'not merely the ethics of development (or of liberation) but the entire structure, method, and content of contemporary theology'.[103]

While Hennelly was undoubtedly correct in his judgement about the revolutionary significance of Liberation Theology, Daniélou's comment is nonetheless a good illustration of how someone from the *ressourcement/ Communio* milieu might look at the problems of Latin America and situate them within a theological framework. Arguably a Lubacian engagement with Liberation Theology would much more closely resemble that of Daniélou than the versions of Liberation Theology that are running along a Rahnerian-Schillebeeckxian route.

Almost all First World theologians are likely to acknowledge that Catholic spirituality has had a deep effect on the uneducated classes in formerly Spanish or Portuguese colonies, and thus that this is a relevant factor to take into account for those interested in the evangelisation of such peoples. However the idea that uneducated people in general have some kind of epistemic virtue or epistemic virginity that is lost once they step over the entrance to a university is taking the Frankfurt School's hermeneutic of suspicion to an extreme not likely to sit comfortably with more mainstream Catholic anthropology. It has been a consistent Catholic teaching that all persons, of all classes, are born with a free will, and that the Divine distribution of graces, including the Gifts of the Holy Spirit, is not class dependent. A roll call of the martyred intellectuals and aristocrats who stood up to Adolf Hitler when the 'people' marched along to his tunes would provide ample counterexamples to the proposition that it is always the elite who have the oppressive ideas and the so-called 'ordinary people' who are reliable. It is a historical fact that both Nazis and communists, cognizant of the sociological reality that it is harder to control intellectuals than to control a mob, pursued policies of 'de-capitating' the countries they conquered, liquidating the intellectuals from whom resistance might be expected, and above all, executing the most talented priests.

Whether a person's culture is high or popular is not the significant theological question. The significant theological question is how far and how much the grace of the Incarnation has penetrated his or her social milieu and his or her very personality. Assuming this as a general principle, the answer to the question of whether or not the cultural practices of poor people can be a *locus theologicus* is that it depends on how far and how much these practices are rooted in the Divine *logos*. Some Catholic Scottish crofters, including a few Orcadian fishermen, may in fact have a deeper understanding of the Catholic faith and a closer relationship to the Trinity than someone with a degree from the theology faculty of the University of Leuven, but not because they are poorer than middle-class professionals at Europe's elite universities. The 'both/and' hallmark of Catholic theology is here highly relevant. The Catholic world view is sufficiently rich to affirm the works of the saintly scholars as well as the saintly fishermen, farmers, labourers, lawyers and so on. In the architectonic world of a Catholic culture, each has a place, and each social and vocational group has its particular responsibilities, and even particular patron saints.

In the final analysis, the most significant achievement of the Liberation Theology movement is that it has drawn attention to what Gutiérrez and Müller have described as the twin errors of the 'verticalism of a disembodied spiritual union with God' (which recognises God's transcendence but not His immanence) and a 'socioeconomic-political horizontalism' (focused on the immanence and neglectful of the transcendence).

Conclusion

In the Introduction reference was made to the judgement of Joseph Ratzinger that the 'fundamental crisis of our age' is that of coming to an understanding about the mediation of history in the realm of ontology. One could rephrase this and say that the fundamental problem for Catholic theology is dealing with the Romantic movement issue (history) without doing violence to classical theology's favourite realm of ontology (nature and grace). The relationship between nature, grace and history is therefore central to this crisis. Different theological schools represent different accounts of this relationship. Key determinants of where scholars end up are the positions they take on (i) the nature and grace relationship – Do they support Suárez or not? If not, do they take their lead from Rahner, Balthasar, de Lubac or someone else? (ii) the position they take on the faith and reason relationship – do they support Kant or not? If not, do they take the approach of Classical Thomism, or Aristotelian Thomism, some form of Augustinianism, the perspectives of John Henry Newman, Josef Pieper and Étienne Gilson, or those of Karl Rahner or Bernard Lonergan, or someone else?; (iii) the position they take on the cultures of modernity and postmodernity – are these cultures fertile soil for Christianity or not? Should the emphasis be on critiquing these cultures or correlating the faith to them? (iv) the position they take on Heidegger – is there any place for metaphysics or not? Is nature itself entirely historical, or not? (v) if there is a place for metaphysics, which metaphysicians do they prefer? (vi) the position they take on the concept of Tradition – should the *traditum* develop with reference to the spirit of the times, or not? And consequently, whether the Catholic faith is an 'open narrative' or not. Included in this last fault line is the whole territory of the relationship of Scripture to Tradition, and in particular whether one reads the teachings in Scripture as normative for all times, or not. There is further the question of (viii) whether a particular theologian believes in the priority of *logos* over *ethos*, or not? If the answer to this question is 'no', then a further set of questions arise about the scholar's preferred understanding of the concept of 'praxis'. Does the particular scholar, for example, follow the anti-intellectual orientation of Luther or the anti-metaphysical orientation of Kant or some kind of dialectical metaphysics borrowed from Hegel or Marx? If the scholar belongs to the milieu of Liberation Theology, then question

(ix) becomes: Which particular version of Liberation Theology does this scholar follow?

Theologians influenced by postmodern philosophy have also raised a variety of questions in the territory of linguistic philosophy that impact upon the understanding of how meaning is mediated and the use of doctrinal formulae to this end.

The ITC document *On the Interpretation of Dogma* observed that in the matter of dogmas, the certitude that Catholic revealed truth, transmitted by the *Paradosis* of the Church, is universally valid and unchangeable in substance was called into question during the Reformation and today, in 'a vastly more acute fashion and in entirely different conditions, the situation is now of global proportions as a result of the ideology of the Enlightenment and the modern demands for liberty'. The document goes on to mention radical Liberation Theology and radical Feminist Theology as two approaches to theology for which dogmas function only as an inspiring force in the process of an alleged liberation. Chapters 4 and 5 of this work highlighted the hallmarks of these approaches to theology, which are 'radical' because they are at their roots different from the approaches outlined in Chapters 1, 2 and 3, which might be described as the more 'classical' approaches to the task of doing Catholic theology.

In addition to the above divisions, which revolve around the fundamental building blocks of any theological framework, there is the division between the accommodating to modernity and/or recontextualising to postmodernity First World theologians and the critical of modernity (and often innocent of postmodernity) Latino and Third World theologians. As Alfred T. Hennelly SJ explained in relation to Sobrino's Liberation Theology:

> Sobrino utilizes for his comparison the two 'moments' of the Enlightenment. He believes that the major emphasis in European theology has been a response to the challenge of the first moment, symbolized by Kant, where liberation is seen as the freeing of reason from all authoritarianism and where its basic interest is rationality. The Latin Americans, by contrast, orient themselves to the second moment of the Enlightenment, symbolized by Marx, where liberation is seen as the freeing of reality from suffering and where the basic interest is not rationality but transformation.[1]

There are also theologians who are interested in responding to both Kant and Marx for whom the Critical Theory of the Frankfurt School is highly important and serves as the bridge between these two 'moments'. These theologians can be found in both *Concilium* and Liberation Theology academic circles.

Finally, in the context of the modernity/postmodernity fault line, there is then the position of the *Communio* scholars, Radical Orthodoxy scholars and the large majority of Thomist scholars. These types are equally critical of Kant and Marx and highly critical of the idea of appropriating contemporary social theory as a modern analogue for the classical philosophy appropriated by Patristic and medieval authors. As John Milbank has expressed the mentality:

> Theology does not require the mediation of the social sciences since, were this the case, then theology would only be left with the most vacuous of tasks: announcing the empty, algebraic equation liberation = salvation, or: all is as modern human beings, and especially social scientists, think it is, but what we have to announce is that God (as he cannot but) agrees with this analysis, and also 'values', this state of affairs. Theology is supposed to extract 'meaning' and 'significance', yet it is only permitted to extrapolate regulatively the significance already implied by the social scientific account.[2]

Milbank concluded that the fundamental question is this: 'Can there be theology, *tout court*, without mediation by the social sciences? Because only if the answer is yes ... can one go on upholding the fundamentally historical character of salvation: in other words, orthodoxy.'[3]

The stance one takes on the question of whether or not theology requires the mediation of the social sciences, and if so, what ones, in which context, and to what end(s) is thus yet another highly significant fault line.

As stated in the beginning, this work has been written primarily for the millennial generation of Catholic scholars, as an aid to identifying the different species of theologians they are likely to encounter in their academic 'zoos'. The hope is that this work might help them to overcome a rather large amount of confusion in these times of chaos and crisis. For this reason, there has been an emphasis on the divisions and the hallmarks so that younger scholars might quickly come to an understanding of what the 'big issues' are that require their judgement. It should also be clear from the analysis offered in the chapters that there is a strong affinity between most species of Thomists (though certainly not Stream One types) and the *Communio* scholars, on the one hand, and the *Concilium* scholars and Liberation Theologians, on the other.

In chapter 14 of his *De Trinitate*, St Augustine concluded that the only merit of this science is that from it a saving faith is 'begotten, nourished, defended and strengthened'. If he was right, the stakes are very high for those entrusted with the vocation of making the judgements.

Notes

Introduction

1 P. Trower, *Turmoil and Truth: The Historical Roots of the Modern Crisis in the Catholic Church* (San Francisco: Ignatius, 2003), p. 32.
2 J. Ratzinger, *Principles of Catholic Theology* (San Francisco: Ignatius, 1987), p. 160.
3 A. Esolen, 'Piety? Who Needs Piety?', insidecatholic.com, 28 February 2008.

Chapter 1

1 V. Lossky, *Orthodox Theology: An Introduction* (New York: S. Vladimir's Press, 2001), p. 15.
2 Ibid.
3 H. de Lubac, cited in A. Nichols, *Beyond the Blue Glass: Catholic Essays on Faith and Culture* (London: St. Austin Press, 2002), p. 43. Nichols was relying on a citation in E. Fouilloux, 'Dialogue théologique? (1946-1948)', in S-T. Bonino OP (ed.), *Saint Thomas au XXe Siècle: Actes du colloque Centenaire de la 'Revue Thomiste'*, Toulouse 25–28 mars, 1993 (Paris, 1994), p. 174.
4 R. Voderholzer, 'Dogma and History: Henri de Lubac and the Retrieval of Historicity as a Key to Theological Renewal', *Communio: International Catholic Review* 28 (Winter 2001), pp. 648–68 (649).
5 T. Weinandy, 'Doing Christian Systematic Theology: Faith, Problems and Mysteries', *Logos* 5 (Winter 2002), pp. 120–39 (127).
6 M. X. Moleski, *Personal Catholicism: The Theological Epistemologies of John Henry Newman and Michael Polanyi* (Washington, DC: Catholic University of America Press, 2000), pp. 187–8.
7 A. Nichols, *Lovely like Jerusalem: The Fulfilment of the Old Testament in Christ and the Church* (San Francisco: Ignatius, 2007).
8 John Paul II, 'The Old Testament is Essential to Know Jesus: Address to the Pontifical Biblical Commission', *L'Osservatore Romano*, 23 April 1997, p. 2.
9 Ibid.
10 J. Ratzinger, *Daughter Zion* (San Francisco: Ignatius, 1983), pp. 12–13.
11 John Paul II, *Fides et Ratio*, #21.
12 N. Ormerod, 'Faith and Reason: Perspectives from MacIntyre and Lonergan', *Heythrop Journal* 46(1) (2005), pp. 11–22 (11). The published version of the paper substituted the adjectives 'long and troubled' for 'complex and tortuous'.

13 J. Pieper, *Leisure as the Basis of Culture* (San Francisco: Ignatius, 2009), pp. 11–12.

14 F. Kerr, 'Knowing God by Reason Alone: What Vatican I Never Said', *New Blackfriars* 91 (May 2010), pp. 215–28.

15 A. Scola, *The Nuptial Mystery* (Grand Rapids: Eerdmans, 2005), pp. 348–9.

16 J. Ratzinger, 'Sources and Transmission of the Faith', *Communio: International Catholic Review* 10 (1983), pp. 17–34 (29).

17 J. Ratzinger, *Jesus, the Apostles and the Early Church* (San Francisco: Ignatius, 2007), p. 24.

18 Ibid., pp. 24–5.

19 International Theological Commission, *Unity of the Faith and Theological Pluralism*, #7 (Vatican City, 1972).

20 J. Ratzinger, *Nature and Mission of Theology* (San Francisco: Ignatius, 1995), p. 95.

21 Ibid., p. 84.

22 J. H. Newman, *Essay on the Development of Christian Doctrine* (London: Longmans, Green & Co, 1903), pp. 169–80.

23 C. Gnilka, *Die Methode der Kirchenvater im Umgang mit der Antiken Kultur* (Basel: Schwabe & Co Ag-Verlag, 1993).

24 J. Ratzinger, 'Christ, Faith and the Challenge of Cultures', *Address to the Presidents of the Bishops' Conferences of Asia*, 2–5 March 1993.

25 M. Levering, *The Feminine Genius of Catholic Theology* (London: Bloomsbury, 2012).

26 See, for example, John Milbank's seminal work: *Theology and Social Theory: Beyond Secular Reason* (Oxford: Blackwell, 1990).

27 J. Keating, 'Theology as Thinking in Prayer', *Chicago Studies* 53(1) (Spring 2014), pp. 70–83 (74).

28 A. Nichols, *The Shape of Catholic Theology: An Introduction to its Sources, Principles and History* (Collegeville, MN: Liturgical Press, 1991), p. 252.

29 Ibid., p. 253.

30 K. Barth, 'Interview with Tanneguy de Quénétain', *Gespräche 1959-62* (Zürich: TVZ, 1995), pp. 530–1.

31 S. Caldecott, 'The Science of the Real: The Renewal of Christian Cosmology', *Communio: International Review* 25 (Fall 1998), pp. 462–79 (477).

32 G. Müller, *The Hope of the Family: A Dialogue with Gerhard Cardinal Müller* (San Francisco: Ignatius, 2014), pp. 85–6.

33 R. Barron, *Vibrant Paradoxes: The Both/And of Catholicism* (Skokie: Word on Fire Publications, 2016).

34 E. L. Mascall, *Christ, the Christian and the Church: A Study of the Incarnation and its Consequences* (London: Longmans, 1946), p. 1.

35 A. Riches, *Ecce Homo: On the Divine Unity of Christ* (Grand Rapids: Eerdmans, 2016).

36 J. Ratzinger, *Mary: The Church at the Source* (San Francisco: Ignatius, 2005), p. 31.

37   M. I. Naumann, 'Mariology at the Beginning of the Third Millennium',
     Keynote Address to the Mariology conference of the University of Notre
     Dame (Sydney campus), 3 March 2016, forthcoming in K. Wagner,
     I. Naumann, P. J. McGregor and P. Morrissey (eds), *Mariology at the
     Beginning of the Third Millennium* (Eugene, OR: Pickwick Publications,
     2017).
38   H. U. von Balthasar, *Elucidations* (San Francisco: Ignatius, 1998), p. 72.
39   C. Journet, *The Primacy of Peter* (Westminster, MD: Newman Press, 1954),
     p. 33.
40   Ibid.
41   T. Guarino, 'Postmodernity and Five Fundamental Theological Issues',
     Theological Studies 57(4) (December 1996), pp. 654–90 (658).
42   M. D'Arcy, *The Sense of History: Secular and Sacred* (London: Faber and
     Faber, 1959), pp. 172–3.
43   Ibid., p. 173.
44   R. Millare, 'The Primacy of *Logos* over *Ethos*: The Influence of Romano
     Guardini on Post-Conciliar Theology', *The Heythrop Journal* 54(6) (2013).
45   J. Ratzinger, *Principles of Catholic Theology* (Ignatius: San Francisco, 1982),
     p. 70.
46   G. Müller, *The Hope of the Family*, p. 60.
47   J. Ratzinger, 'Sources and Transmission of the Faith', *Communio:
     International Catholic Review* 10(1) (1983), pp. 17–34 (23).
48   Material for this section on Scripture and Tradition has been taken from
     the author's chapter on 'Tradition' in the *Oxford Handbook on Modern
     European Thought* (Oxford: Oxford University Press, 2013), pp. 277–300.
49   P. Casarella, Introduction to the 2000 edition of *Scripture in the Tradition*
     (New York: Herder and Herder, 2000), p. xvi.
50   J. Ratzinger, *Revelation and Tradition* (New York: Herder and Herder,
     1966), p. 46.
51   Benedict XVI, *Verbum Domini*, #35.
52   M. Reiser, *Der Unbequeme Jesus* (Neukirchen-Vluyn: Verlag Neukirchener,
     2013), p. 25.
53   Paul VI, 'Address to the International Congress on Theology of Vatican II',
     1 October 1966, *AAS* 58 (1966), p. 891.

Chapter 2

1   F. C. Bauerschmidt, *Thomas Aquinas: Faith, Reason and Following Christ*
    (Oxford: Oxford University Press, 2013), pp. 24–5.
2   A. Nichols, *Discovering Aquinas: His Life, Work and Influence* (Grand
    Rapids: Eerdmans, 2003), p. 4.
3   F. C. Bauerschmidt, *Holy Teaching: Introducing the Summa Theologiae of
    St. Thomas Aquinas* (Grand Rapids: Brazos, 2005).

4   D. D. Novotný, 'In Defense of Baroque Scholasticism', *Studia Neoaristotelica* 6(2) (2009), pp. 209–33 (222).

5   F. Copleston, *A History of Philosophy, Vol III* (New York: Doubleday, 1985), p. 355.

6   J. Milbank, *Theology and Social Theory: Beyond Secular Reason* (Oxford: Blackwell, 1990), p. 9.

7   J. Borella, *The Sense of the Supernatural* (Edinburgh: T & T Clark, 1998), p. ix.

8   R. Spaemann, *Philosophische Essays* (Stuttgart: Reclam, 2008), pp. 26–7.

9   Ibid., pp. 26–7.

10 N. J. Healy Jr, 'Henri de Lubac on Nature and Grace', *Communio: International Catholic Review* 35 (Winter 2008), pp. 535–65 (546).

11 L. Bouyer, *Cosmos: The World and the Glory of God* (Petersham, MA: St. Bede's Publications, 1988), pp. 131–2.

12 J. Montag, 'The False Legacy of Suárez', in J. Milbank, G. Ward and C. Pickstock (eds), *Radical Orthodoxy* (London: Routledge, 1999), pp. 38–64.

13 Ibid., p. 57.

14 Ibid., p. 5.

15 J. Ratzinger, 'Dogmatic Constitution on Divine Revelation: Origin and Background', in H. Vorgrimler (ed.), *Commentary on the Documents of Vatican II* (London: Burns & Oates, 1967–9), p. 176.

16 Bauerschmidt, *Thomas Aquinas*, p. 300.

17 A. MacIntyre, *Three Rival Versions of Moral Enquiry* (London: Duckworth, 1990), p. 73.

18 Ibid., p. 75.

19 A. Di Noia, 'Thomism after Thomism: Aquinas and the Future of Theology', in Deal W. Hudson et al. (eds), *The Future of Thomism* (Mishawaka, IN: University of Notre Dame Press, 1992), pp. 231–45 (236).

20 Ibid., p. 234.

21 Ibid., p. 234.

22 Ibid., pp. 234–5.

23 M. D. Jordan, *Rewritten Theology: Aquinas after his Readers* (Oxford: Blackwell, 2006), p. 88.

24 Ibid.

25 Ibid.

26 Ibid., p. 62.

27 F. Kerr, 'Ambiguity in Thomas Aquinas: Reflections After Aquinas', *Providence: Studies in Western Civilisation* 8(1) (Spring/Summer 2003), pp. 1–20.

28 A. MacIntyre, 'Aquinas's Critique of Education', in A. O. Rorty (ed.), *Philosophers on Education: New Historical Perspectives* (London: Routledge, 1998), p. 96.

29 G. Valente and P. Azzorro, 'A New Beginning Among the Ruins: An Interview with Alfred Läpple', 01/02 (2006), available at www.30giorni.it/articoli_id_10125_13.htm.

30 Ibid.

31   T. O'Meara, *Church and Culture: German Catholic Theology 1860-1914* (Indiana: University of Indiana Press, 1991), p. 50.

32   S-T. Bonino, 'To Be a Thomist', *Nova et Vetera* 8(4) (Fall 2010), pp. 763–75 (770).

33   F. C. Bauerschmidt, *Thomas Aquinas*, p. 311.

34   J. Milbank, 'On "Thomistic Kabbalah"', *Modern Theology* 27 (January 2011), pp. 147–85 (154–5).

35   Ibid., p. 155.

36   R. Peddicord, *The Sacred Monster of Thomism: An Introduction to the Life and Legacy of Reginald Garrigou-Lagrange* (South Bend, IN: St. Augustine's Press, 2005), p. 54.

37   A. Dru, 'From the *Action Française* to the Second Vatican Council: Blondel's 'La Semaine sociale de Bordeaux'', *Downside Review* (July 1963), pp. 226–45.

38   R. Peddicord, *The Sacred Monster of Thomism*, p. 84.

39   J. Ratzinger, 'The Dignity of the Human Person', in Vorgrimler (ed.), *Commentary on the Documents of the Second Vatican Council*, p. 157.

40   A. Vincelette, *Recent Catholic Philosophy: The Twentieth Century* (Milwaukee: Marquette University Press, 2011), p. 82.

41   I. S. Markham (ed.), *The Student's Companion to the Theologians* (Chichester: Wiley-Blackwell, 2013).

42   F. J. Michael McDermott, 'Vatican II', in Ian S. Markham (ed.), *The Student's Companion to the Theologians* (Chichester: Wiley-Blackwell, 2013), p. 537.

43   Vincelette, *Recent Catholic Philosophy*, p. 87.

44   D. Coffey, 'The Whole Rahner on the Supernatural Existential', *Theological Studies* 65 (2004), pp. 95–118.

45   A. G. Cooper, *Naturally Human, Supernaturally God: Deification in Pre-Conciliar Catholicism* (Minneapolis: Fortress Press, 2014), p. 113.

46   Ratzinger, *Principles of Catholic Theology*, p. 166.

47   A. Nichols, *Beyond the Blue Glass: Catholic Essays on Faith and Culture* (London: St. Austin Press, 2002), p. 112.

48   K. Rahner, *Foundations of Christian Faith* (New York: Crossroad, 1982), p. 451.

49   K-H. Weger, *Karl Rahner: Ein Einführung in sein theologisches Denken* (Freiburg: Herder, 1978), p. 4. Cited by Paul Imhof and Hubert Biallowons (eds), translation edited by Harvey D. Egan, *Karl Rahner in Dialogue: Conversations and Interviews 1965-1982* (New York: Crossroad, 1986), p. 3.

50   B. J. Lonergan, *Philosophical and Theological Papers: Collected Papers (1958-64)*, 17, edited by R. C. Croken et al. (Toronto: Toronto University Press, 1996), pp. 352–83. See also A. Kennedy, 'Christopher Dawson's Influence on Bernard Lonergan's Project of "Introducing History into Theology"', *Logos: A Journal of Catholic Thought and Culture* 15(2) (Spring 2012), pp. 138–65 (151).

51   R. M. Doran, 'System and History: The Challenge to Catholic Systematic Theology', *Theological Studies* 60(4) (December 1999), pp. 652–78.

52 G. B. Sala, *Lonergan and Kant: Five Essays on Human Knowledge*, trans. Joseph Spoerl and ed. Robert M Doran (Toronto: University of Toronto Press, 1994).

53 B. J. Lonergan, *Insight: A Study of Human Understanding* (London: Darton, Longman and Todd, 1958).

54 R. Barron, *Exploring Catholic Theology: Essays on God, Liturgy and Evangelisation* (Grand Rapids: Baker Academic, 2015), p. 184.

55 B. J. Lonergan, *The Way to Nicea: The Dialectical Development of Trinitarian Theology* (London: Darton, Longman and Todd, 1976); *Verbum: Word and Idea in Aquinas* (Notre Dame: University of Notre Dame Press, 1946); *Grace and Freedom: Operative Grace in the Thought of St. Thomas Aquinas* (London: Darton, Longman and Todd, 1970).

56 K. B. Nielsen, 'Bernard Lonergan', in Staale Johannes Kristiansen and Svein Rise (eds), *Key Theological Thinkers from Modern to Postmodern* (Farnham: Ashgate, 2013), pp. 239–47 (243).

57 B. J. F. Lonergan, 'Functional Specialities in Theology', *Gregorianum* 50 (1969), pp. 485–505 (490).

58 Ibid., p. 491.

59 Ibid., p. 243.

60 K. Rahner, 'Kritische Bemerkungen zu B.J.F. Lonergan's Aufsatz: "Functional Specialities in Theology"', *Gregorianum* 50 (1969), pp. 485–505.

61 Ibid.

62 Ibid.

63 Ibid., p. 505.

64 A. Nichols, *Scribe of the Kingdom*, vol. 2 (London: Sheed and Ward, 1994), p. 63.

65 W. Norris Clarke, *Person and Being* (Milwaukee: Marquette University Press, 1993).

66 C. Fabro, *La Nozione Metafisica di Participazione Secondo S. Tommaso d'Aquino* (Torino: Società Editrice Internatiozionale, 1950); L-B. Geiger, *La participation dans la philosophie de saint Thomas d'Aquin* (Paris: Vrin, 1953); and J. de Finance, *Être et agir* (Paris: P.U.F., 1945).

67 F. Copleston, *A History of Philosophy Vol III* (New York: Doubleday, 1985), p. 379.

68 W. Hankey, 'From Metaphysics to History, from Exodus to Neoplatonism, from Scholasticism to Pluralism: The Fate of Gilsonian Thomism in English-speaking North America', *Dionysius* XIV (1998), pp. 157–88.

69 Ibid., p. 169.

70 Ibid., p. 161.

71 W. Norris Clarke, 'The Integration of Person and Being in Twentieth Century Thomism', *Communio: International Review*, Fall (2004), pp. 435–47 (441).

72 J. Kupczak, *The Human Person in the Philosophy of Karol Wojtyła/John Paul II: Destined for Liberty* (Washington, DC: Catholic University of America, 2000), p. 28.

73 J. Daniélou, 'Les orientations presents de la Pensée religieuse', *Études* 249 (1946), p. 14.

74 F. Lescoe, *Philosophy Serving Contemporary Needs of the Church* (New Britain: Mariel Publications, 1979).

75 J. W. Gałkowski, 'The Place of Thomism in the Anthropology of Karol Wojtyła', *Angelicum* 65 (1988), pp. 181–2.

76 V. Sliuzaite, *The Notion of Human Experience in the Thought of Karol Wojtyła: A Study of the Notion of Experience in the Light of an Adequate Anthropology* (Roma: Pontificiam Universitatem Lateranensem, 2013), p. 38.

77 G. F. McLean, 'Karol Wojtyła's Mutual Enrichment of the Philosophies of Being and Consciousness', in Nancy Mardas Billias et al. (eds), *Karol Wojtyła's Philosophical Legacy* (Washington, DC: The Council for Research in Values and Philosophy, 2008). Cited in Sliuzaite, p. 53.

78 J. Kupczak, *The Human Person in the Philosophy of Karol Wojtyła/John Paul II: Destined for Liberty* (Washington, DC: Catholic University of America Press, 2000), p. 83.

79 Ibid., pp. 83–4.

80 R. A. Spinello, 'The Enduring Relevance of Karol Wojtyła's Philosophy', *Logos* 17(3) (Summer 2014), pp. 17–48 (19).

81 Ibid., p. 21.

82 K. Wojtyła, 'Thomistic Personalism', *Person and Community: Selected Essays*, trans. Theresa Sandok, OSM (New York: Peter Lang, 1993), pp. 165–75 (170).

83 M. Novak, Preface to *The Human Person in the Philosophy of Karol Wojtyła/John Paul II: Destined for Liberty* (2000).

84 Ibid., p. xvii.

85 W. Norris Clarke, *The Creative Retrieval of Saint Thomas Aquinas: Essays in Thomistic Philosophy, New and Old* (New York: Fordham, 2009), p. 227.

86 R. P. Kraynak, *Christian Faith in Modern Democracy: God and Politics in a Fallen World* (Indiana: University of Notre Dame, 2001), p. 98.

87 Ibid., p. 113.

88 D. L. Schindler, *Heart of the World, Center of the Church: Communio Ecclesiology, Liberalism and Liberation* (Edinburgh: T & T Clark, 1996), p. 79.

89 Ibid., p. 81.

90 E. Fortin, 'The New Rights Theory and Natural Law', *The Review of Politics* 44(4) (October 1982), pp. 590–612 (605).

91 I. Markham, *Truth and the Reality of God: An Essay in Natural Theology* (Edinburgh: T & T Clark, 1998), p. 115.

92 R. Black, 'Is the New Natural Law Christian?', in Nigel Biggar and Rufus Black (eds), *The Revival of Natural Law: Philosophical, Theological and Ethical Responses to the Finnis-Grisez School* (Aldershot: Ashgate, 2000), p. 158.

93 L. Melina, 'Christ and the Dynamism of Action: Outlook and Overview of Christocentrism in Moral Theology', *Communio: International Catholic Review* 28 (Spring 2001), pp. 112–40 (115).

94   Ibid., p. 124.

95   Ibid., p. 130.

96   Ibid., p. 131.

97   A. MacIntyre, 'Community, Law and the Idiom and Rhetoric of Rights', *Listening* XXVI(2) (1991), pp. 96–110 (104–5).

98   Ibid., p. 105.

99   Ibid., p. 105.

100 UNESCO, *Human Rights: Comments and Interpretations: A Symposium* with an introduction by Jacques Maritain (Paris: UNESCO, 1948), pp. i–ix. Note: paragraphs in this section of the chapter on human rights are taken from the author's article: 'A Schallian Guide for the Perplexed', in M. D. Guarra (ed.), *Jerusalem, Athens and Rome: Essays in Honour of James V Schall* (South Bend, IN: St. Augustine's Press, 2013).

101 S. B. Twiss, 'History, Human Rights and Globalisation', *Journal of Religious Ethics* 32(1) (2004), pp. 39–70 (58).

102 John Paul II, cited in Mary Ann Glendon, 'Foundations of Human Rights: The Unfinished Business', *American Journal of Jurisprudence* 44 (1999), pp. 1–14.

103 J. V. Schall, *Jacques Maritain: The Philosopher in Society* (Oxford: Rowman and Littlefield, 1998), pp. 84–6.

104 T. Kozinski, *The Political Problem of Religious Pluralism: And Why Philosopher's Can't Solve It* (New York: Rowman and Littlefield, 2010), 109.

105 J. V. Schall, *Jacques Maritain*, p. 95.

106 B. Ashley, 'The River Forest School and the Philosophy of Nature Today', in R. James Long (ed.), *Philosophy and the God of Abraham: Essays in Memory of James A. Weisheipl, OP* (Toronto: PIMS, 1991), pp. 1–15.

107 C. Hovey, 'Alasdair MacIntyre's Hermeneutics of Tradition', in Craig Hovey and Cyrus P. Olsen (eds), *The Hermeneutics of Tradition: Explorations and Examinations* (Eugene: Cascade, 2014), pp. 144–73 (152).

108 S-T. Pinckaers, in 'Scripture and the Renewal of Moral Theology', J. Berkman and C. S. Titus (eds), *The Pinckaers Reader: Renewing Thomistic Moral Theology* (Washington, DC: Catholic University of America Press, 2005), p. 52.

109 Ibid.

110 Ibid.

111 Ibid., p. 28.

112 Ibid., p. 29.

113 C. Leget, 'Doing Theology Today with "master" Aquinas: Interview with Gilles Emery', *Thomas Institute Utrecht*, 2002.

114 S-T. Boninio, Foreword to *Surnaturel: A Controversy at the Heart of Twentieth Century Thomistic Thought* (Naples, Florida: Ave Maria Press, 2009), pp. vii–viii.

115 J. Milbank, 'On "Thomistic Kabbalah"', p. 157.

116 O-T. Venard, 'On the Religious Imagination and Poetic Audacity of Thomas Aquinas', in Francesca Bugliani Knox and David Lonsdale (eds),

Poetry and the Religious Imagination (Ashgate: Aldershot, 2015), pp. 67–91 and 'Extending the Thomist Movement from the Twentieth to the Twenty-First Century: Under what Conditions could there be a "Literary Thomism?"', in Simon Oliver, Karen Kilby and Thomas O'Loughlin (eds), *Faithful Reading: New Essays in Theology in Honour of Fergus Kerr OP* (London: T & T Clark, 2012), pp. 91–112.

117 Venard, 'Extending the Thomist Movement', p. 98.
118 Ibid., p. 92.
119 Ibid., p. 112.
120 Ibid., p. 112.
121 J. A. Di Noia, 'American Catholic Theology at Century's End: Postconciliar, Postmodern and Post-Thomistic', *The Thomist* 54 (July 1990), pp. 349–518 (513–14).
122 M. Jordan, *Rewritten Theology: Aquinas after His Readers* (Oxford: Blackwell, 2006), p. 60.

Chapter 3

1 H. Küng, *Disputed Truth: Memoires*, vol. 2 (London: Bloomsbury, 2008), pp. 157–8.
2 Ibid., p. 158.
3 C. Ernst, 'The Concilium World Congress', *New Blackfriars* 51 (607) (December 1970), pp. 555–60 (558).
4 H. de Lubac, *Meine Schriften im Rückblick* (Einsiedeln: Joannes Verlag, 1996), p. 482. (English translation provided by Sebastian Condon).
5 P. Trower, *Turmoil and Truth*, p. 32.
6 J. Comblin, 'The Signs of the Times', *Concilium* 4 (2005), pp. 73–85 (80).
7 Ibid., p. 74.
8 H. U. von Balthasar, *Wer ist ein Christ?* (Einsiedeln: Johannes Verlag, 1965), p. 30.
9 J. Ratzinger, *Salt of the Earth: The Church at the End of the Millennium* (San Francisco: Ignatius, 1997), p. 66.
10 J. Martinez, 'Christ of History, Jesus of Faith', in Adrian Pabst and Angus Paddison (eds), *The Pope and Jesus of Nazareth* (London: SCM Press, 2009), pp. 26–7.
11 K. J. Vanhoozer, *The Cambridge Companion to Postmodern Theology* (Cambridge: Cambridge University Press, 2003), pp. 21–2.
12 Huby, J. 'Henri de Lubac, *Surnaturel: Etudes Historiques*', *Etudes* 251 (1946), pp. 265–8. English translation taken from H. de Lubac, *At the Service of the Church*, pp. 205–6. For a comprehensive analysis of the treatment of the nature and grace and related anthropological questions in de Lubac, see M. Figura, *Der Anruf der Gnade: Über die Beziehung des*

Menschen zu Gott nach Henri de Lubac (Einsiedeln: Johannes Verlag, 1979).

13 J. Martinez, 'Christ of History, Jesus of Faith', p. 29.

14 B. Lambert, '*Gaudium et spes* and the Travail of Today's Ecclesial Conception', in J. Gremillion (ed.), *The Church and Culture since Vatican II* (South Bend, IN: Notre Dame University Press, 1985), p. 36.

15 Ibid., p. 36.

16 P. J. Lynch, 'Secularisation Affirms the Sacred; Karl Rahner', *Thought* 61(242) (September 1986), pp. 381–93 (381).

17 J. Milbank, 'The New Divide: Classical versus Romantic Orthodoxy', *Modern Theology* 26 (1) (January 2010), pp. 26–38.

18 P. Tillich, *Time* 73, 11 March 16 (1959), p. 47. Quoted in Douglas John Hall, 'The Great War and the Theologians', in Gregory Baum (ed.), *The Twentieth Century: A Theological Overview* (New York: Orbis, 1999), pp. 3–14 (6).

19 V. Ern, 'Od Kanta do Kruppa', quoted by A. Mrówczyński-Van Allen in *Between the Icon and the Idol* (Oregon: Cascade Publications, Oregon, 2014), p. 130. Material from this section of chapter 3 has also been published in 'Henri de Lubac's Engagements with Neo-Scholasticism of the Strict-Observance' in *The Companion to Henri de Lubac*, Jordan Hillebert (ed), (London: T & T Clark, 2016).

20 L. Kołakowski, 'Reprodukcja kulturalna I zapominanie', in Czy diabel moze byc zbawiony i 27 innych kazan, Znak, 2006. Quoted in A. Mrówczyński-Van Allen in *Between the Icon and the Idol* (Oregon: Cascade Publications, 2014), p. 130.

21 J. Pieper, *The End of Time: A Meditation on the Philosophy of History*, trans. Michael Bullock (New York: Pantheon Books, 1954); reprinted (San Francisco: Ignatius, 1999), p. 16.

22 J. Ratzinger, 'The Dignity of the Human Person: Commentary on *Gaudium et spes*', in H. Vorgrimler (ed.), *Commentary on the Documents of Vatican II*, vol. III (New York: Herder & Herder, 1969), p. 155.

23 J. Ratzinger, *Truth and Tolerance: Christian Belief and World Religions* (San Francisco: Ignatius, 2004), p. 136.

24 A. Vincelette, *Recent Catholic Philosophy: The Twentieth Century* (Milwaukee: Marquette University Press, 2011), p. 94.

25 M. Hanby, *Augustine and Modernity* (London: Routledge, 2003).

26 Ibid., p. 135.

27 For recent discussions of this issue see N. Healy, Jr, 'Natural Theology and the Christian Contribution to Metaphysics: On Thomas Joseph White's Wisdom in the Face of Modernity', *Nova et Vetera* 10 (2012), pp. 539–62 and '*Preambula fidei*: David L Schindler and the Debate over "Christian Philosophy"', in *Being Holy in the World: Theology and Culture in the Thought of David L Schindler* (Grand Rapids: Eerdmans, 2011).

28 F. Kerr, 'Knowing God by Reason Alone: What Vatican I Never Said', pp. 215–28.

29 Ibid., p. 222.

30   J. Ratzinger, 'The Dignity of the Human Person: Commentary on *Gaudium et spes*', p. 153.

31   Ibid., p. 153.

32   F. Kerr, *After Aquinas: Versions of Thomism* (Oxford: Blackwell, 2002).

33   E. Sillem, *Ways of Thinking about God: Thomas Aquinas and Some Recent Problems* (London: Darton, Longman and Todd, 1961).

34   W. Hankey, 'Making Theology Practical: Thomas Aquinas and the Nineteenth Century Religious Revival', *Dionysius* 9 (1985), pp. 85–127.

35   A. Sicari, 'For a Reflection on the Ideals of Communio', *Communio: International Catholic Review* 16 (Winter 1989), pp. 495–8 (498).

36   H. U. von Bathasar, *Henri de Lubac. Sein organisches Lebenswerk* (Einsiedeln: Johannes Verlag), p. 58.

37   H. de Lubac, *La revelation divine* (Paris: Cerf, 1983), pp. 100–1. English translation found in R. Voderholzer, 'Dogma and History: Henri de Lubac and the Renewal of Historicity as a Key to Theological Renewal', *Communio: International Catholic Review* 28 (Winter 2001), pp. 648–68 (663).

38   H. de Lubac, *Corpus Mysticum: The Eucharist and the Church in the Middle Ages*, trans. Gemma Simmonds with Richard Price and Christopher Stephens (South Bend, IN: University of Notre Dame Press, 2006), p. 246.

39   J. Zimmermann, *Incarnational Humanism: A Philosophy of Culture for the Church in the World* (Downers Grove, IL: IVP Academic, 2012), p. 87.

40   Ibid., p. 129.

41   L. Feingold, *The Natural Desire to See God According to St. Thomas and His Interpreters* (Naples, Florida: Sapientia Press, 2010). See also S. A. Long, *Natura Pura: On the Recovery of Nature in the Doctrine of Grace* (New York: Fordham University Press, 2010).

42   N. J. Healy, 'Henri de Lubac on Nature and Grace: A Note on Some Recent Contributions to the Debate', *Communio: International Catholic Review* 35 (Winter 2008), p. 557.

43   A. Riches, 'To Rest in the Infinite Altitude of the Divine Substance: A Lubacian Response to the Provocation of Lawrence Feingold and the Resurgent Attack on the Legacy of *Surnaturel*', forthcoming in *Synesis*. Riches was quoting from de Lubac's *Catholicism: Christ and the Common Destiny of Man*, p. 250.

44   Ibid.

45   R. Voderholzer, *Meet Henri de Lubac: His Life and Work* (San Francisco: Ignatius, 2008), p. 120.

46   A. von Speyer, *Erde und Himmel. Ein Tagebuch: Zweiter Teil. Die Zeit der grossen Diktate*, ed. and with introduction by Hans Urs von Balthasar (Einsiedeln: Johannes Verlag, 1975), p. 195.

47   M. Blondel, 'The Latent Resources in Tom Burns (ed.), St. Augustine's Thought', in *A Monument to Saint Augustine* (London: Sheed and Ward, 1930), pp. 319–53 (326).

48   Ibid., pp. 326–7.

49 J. Ratzinger, 'Guardini on Christ in our Century', *Crisis Magazine* (June 1996), pp. 14–15 (14).

50 J. Ratzinger, Introduction to *The Lord* by Romano Guardini (Washington, DC: Regnery Gateway, 2011), p. ix.

51 J. Ratzinger, 'Dalla Liturgia alla Cristologia. Il Principio Teologico di Romano Guardini e la sua Forza Assertiva', in *Perché siamo Ancora nella Chiesa* (Milan: Rizzoli, 2005), pp. 239–64 (251–2). English translation by S. Zucal in 'Benedict XVI Has a Father, Romano Guardini', http://chiesa. espresso.repubblica.it/articolo/207016?eng=y.

52 Ibid.

53 H. U. von Balthasar, *Romano Guardini: Reform from the Source* (San Francisco: Ignatius, 1995), p. 21.

54 S. Grygiel, *Discovering the Human Person: In Conversation with John Paul II* (Grand Rapids: Eerdmans, 2014), pp. xi–xii.

55 R. Guardini, *Freedom, Grace, Destiny: Three Chapters in the Interpretation of Existence* (Westport: Greenwood Press, 1975), p. 130.

56 H. U. von Balthasar, *Rechenschaft* (Einsiedeln: Johannes Verlag, 1965), p. 35.

57 H. U. von Balthasar, *Convergences: To the Source of Christian Mystery* (San Francisco: Ignatius, 1983), p. 34.

58 This translation is von Balthasar's. In the English version of *The Mysteries of Christianity*, translated by Cyril Vollert (New York: Herder, 1954), the treatment of the Holy Spirit is found in pages 149–89.

59 H. U. von Balthasar, *Explorations in Theology: Vol. 1 The Word Made Flesh* (San Francisco: Ignatius, 1989), p. 201.

60 Ibid., p. 201.

61 Ibid., p. 195.

62 M. Ouellet, 'The Message of Balthasar's Theology to Modern Theology', *Communio: International Catholic Review* 23 (Summer 1996), pp. 270–99.

63 Ibid., p. 271.

64 Ibid., p. 271.

65 Ibid., p. 281.

66 Ibid., p. 281.

67 E. T. Oakes, 'Hans Urs von Balthasar', in C. Meister et al. (eds), *The Routledge Companion to Modern Christian Thought* (London: Routledge, 2013), pp. 196–206 (197).

68 Ibid., p. 197.

69 Ibid., p. 197.

70 T. J. White (ed.), *The Analogy of Being: Invention of the Antichrist or the Wisdom of God?* (Grand Rapids: Eerdmans, 2011), p. 316.

71 M. Ouellet, 'The Message of Balthasar's Theology to Modern Theology', p. 287.

72 H. U. von Balthasar, in Andrzej Wierciński, *Between Friends: The Hans Urs von Balthasar and Gustave Siewerth Correspondence 1954-1963* (Verlag Gustave Siewerth Gesellschaft Konstanz, 2005-7), p. 159 n. 4.

73 Ibid., p. 165.

74 A. Walker, 'Love Alone: Hans Urs von Balthasar as a Master of Theological Renewal', in David L. Schindler (ed.), *Love Alone is Credible: Hans Urs von Balthasar as Interpreter of the Catholic Tradition: Volume 1* (Grand Rapids: Eerdmans, 2008), pp. 16–41 (35 and 37).

75 D. C. Schindler, *Hans Urs von Balthasar and the Dramatic Structure of Truth: A Philosophical Investigation* (New York: Fordham University Press, 2004); D. C. Schindler, *The Catholicity of Reason* (Grand Rapids: Eerdmans, 2013).

76 A. Walker, '"Christ and Cosmology": Methodological Considerations for Catholic Educators', *Communio: International Catholic Review* (Fall 2001), pp. 429–49 (444).

77 H. U. von Balthasar, *Thomas von Aquin. Besondere Gnadengaben und die zwei Wege menschlichen Lebens. Kommentar zur Summa Theologica II-II, 171–82* (German Thomas edition, vol. 23: Heidelberg und Graz: F.H. Kerle/A. Pustet, 1954). Cited in Peter Henrici 'The Philosophy of Hans Urs von Balthasar', in David L. Schindler (ed.), *Hans Urs von Balthasar: His Life and Work* (San Francisco: Ignatius, 1991), p. 162.

78 H. U. von Balthasar, *Herrlichkeit: Eine Theologische Ästhetik*, vol. III/1:1 (Einsideln: Johannes Verlag, 1975), p. 356. Cited in English translation in Peter Henrici, 'The Philosophy of Hans Urs von Balthasar', p. 163.

79 Pope Emeritus Benedict XVI, *Porta Fidei* (2011), 10.

80 H. U. von Balthasar, *Prayer* (San Francisco: Ignatius, 1986), p. 229.

81 J. H. Newman, 'Sermon 12', in James David Ernest et al. (eds), *Fifteen Sermons Preached before the University of Oxford* (London: Longman, Green and Co, 1909), 222–50 (239).

82 P. McGregor, *The Spiritual Christology of Joseph Ratzinger* (Doctoral diss., Australian Catholic University, 2013).

83 M. P. Gallagher, 'Realisation of Wisdom: Fruits of Formation in the Light of Newman', in Deacon James Keating (ed.), *Entering into the Mind of Christ: The True Nature of Theology* (Omaha: The Institute of Priestly Formation, 2014), pp. 127–8.

84 J. Ratzinger, *Jesus of Nazareth* (New York, Doubleday, 2007), p. 95.

85 Ibid.

86 A. Luciano, *Illustrissimi: Letters from John Paul I* (London: Gracewing, 2001), p. 242.

87 M. P. Gallagher, 'Realisation of Wisdom: Fruits of Formation in the Light of Newman', pp. 130–1.

88 H. de Lubac, *Le revelation divine* (Paris: Cerf, 1983), pp. 100–1.

89 J. Milbank, 'Stanton Lecture 1: The Return of Metaphysics in the 21st Century'. Available on-line: www.abc.net.au/religion/articles/2011/01/28/3123584.

90 W. L. Portier, 'Does Systematic Theology have a Future?', in W. J. Collinge (ed.), *Faith in Public Life* (New York: Orbis, 2007), p. 137.

91 G. Ward, 'Radical Orthodoxy/and as Cultural Politics', in Laurence Paul
    Hemming (ed.), *Radical Orthodoxy: A Catholic Enquiry* (Aldershot:
    Ashgate, 2000), p. 104.
92 P. S. Kucer, *Truth and Politics: A Theological Comparison of Joseph
    Ratzinger and John Milbank* (Minneapolis: Fortress Press, 2014).
93 G. Bailie, *Raising the Ante: God's Gamble*, forthcoming.
94 B. Schüller, 'Die Bedeutung des natürlichen Sittengesetzes fur den Christen',
    in G. Teichtweier and W. und Dreier (eds), *Herausforderung Kritik der
    Moraltheologie* (Würzberg: Echter Verlag, 1971), pp. 105–30 (118).
95 J. Ratzinger et al., *Principles of Christian Morality* (San Francisco: Ignatius,
    1986), p. 52 n. 2.
96 Ibid., p. 53.
97 H. U. von Balthasar, *Principles of Christian Morality*, p. 101.
98 Ibid., p. 101.
99 Ibid., pp. 101–2.
100 L. Melina, *Sharing in Christ's Virtues* (Washington, DC: Catholic
    University of America Press, 2001), p. 127.
101 Ibid.
102 Ibid., p. 128.
103 S. Caldecott, 'The Final Mystery', *Logos: A Journal of Catholic Culture*
    3 (Summer 2000), pp. 87–108.
104 A. Scola, *The Nuptial Mystery* (Grand Rapids: Eerdmans, 2005), p. 384.
105 Ibid., p. 386 n. 9.
106 Ibid., p. 394.
107 M. Ouellet, *Divine Likeness: Towards a Trinitarian Anthropology of the
    Family* (Grand Rapids: Eerdmans, 2006), p. 80.
108 M. Ouellet, *Mystery and Sacrament of Love: A Theology of Marriage and
    Family for the New Evangelisation* (Grand Rapids: Eerdmans, 2015), p. 96.
109 M. Ouellet, *Mystery and Sacrament of Love: A Theology of Marriage
    and Family for the New Evangelisation* (Grand Rapids: Eerdmans, 2015),
    p. 111.
110 Ibid., p. 118.
111 Ibid., p. 119.
112 Ibid., pp. 118–20.
113 J. Ratzinger, 'Sources and Transmission of the Faith', *Communio:
    International Catholic Review* 10 (Spring 1983), pp. 17–34.
114 R. Guardini, *The Spirit of the Liturgy* (New York: Aeterna Press, 2015), p. 54.
115 J. Ratzinger, *The Nature and Mission of Theology: Approaches to
    Understanding Its Role in the Light of Present Controversy* (San Francisco:
    Ignatius, 1995), p. 91.
116 H. U. von Balthasar, *The Office of Peter and the Structure of the Church*
    (San Francisco: Ignatius, 1986), p. 310.
117 St John Paul II, *Fides et Ratio* (1998), sec. 31.
118 J. Ratzinger, *On the Way to Jesus Christ*, p. 50.

119   A. Sicari, 'For a Reflection on the Ideals of Communio', *Communio: International Catholic Review* 16 (Winter 1989), pp. 495–8 (498).
120   A. Nichols, *Scribe of the Kingdom: Essays on Theology and Culture*, vol. 2 (London: Sheed and Ward, 1994), p. 24.

Chapter 4

1   Statement taken from the official *Concilium* website at www.concilium.in.
2   K. Rahner, *Theological Investigations*, vol. IX, trans. Graham Harrison (London: Darton, Longman and Todd, 1972), p. 7.
3   Ibid., p. 12.
4   Ibid., p. 13.
5   Ibid., p. 14.
6   Ibid., p. 14.
7   Ibid., pp. 14–16.
8   Ibid., pp. 17–19.
9   Ibid., p. 19.
10   Ibid., p. 20.
11   Ibid., p. 25.
12   Ibid., pp. 17, 20.
13   Ibid., p. 52.
14   Ibid., p. 56.
15   Ibid., p. 60.
16   A. Brighenti, 'Church, Theology and Magisterium in Latin America', *Concilium* 2 (2012), pp. 39–50 (43).
17   Ibid., p. 44.
18   L. Chapp, 'Revelation', in Edward T. Oakes and David Moss (eds), *The Cambridge Companion to Hans Urs von Balthasar* (Cambridge: Cambridge University Press, 2005), pp. 11–24.
19   R. Garaudy, 'What Does a Non-Christian Expect of the Church?' *Concilium* 35 (1968), pp. 44–5.
20   G-R. Horn, *The Spirit of Vatican II: Western European Progressive Catholicism in the Long Sixties* (Oxford: Oxford University Press, 2015), pp. 260–1.
21   M. Hofmeyr, 'Die invloed van Ernst Bloch op die Politieke Teologie van Johann Baptist Metz', *HTS Teologiese Studies* 59(4) (2003), pp. 1199–1222 (1199).
22   J. Marsden, 'The Political Theology of Johannes Baptist Metz', *The Heythrop Journal* LIII (2012), pp. 440–52.
23   Ibid., p. 440.
24   Ibid., p. 440.
25   G. L. Schaab, 'Feminist Theological Methodology: Toward a Kaleidoscopic Model', *Theological Studies* 62 (2001), pp. 341–65.

26 L. Kołakowski, *Main Currents of Marxism Vol III* (Oxford: Clarendon Press, 1978), p. 347.

27 Ibid., p. 353.

28 Ibid., p. 353.

29 W. L. Portier, 'Interpretation and Method', in Robert J. Schreiter and Mary Catherine Hilkert (eds), *The Praxis of Christian Experience: An Introduction to the Theology of Edward Schillebeeckx* (San Francisco: Harper and Row, 1989), pp. 18–35 (26).

30 C. Davis, 'Theology and Praxis', *Cross Currents* 23(2) (Summer 1973), pp. 154–68 (167).

31 Ibid., p. 167.

32 E. Schillebeeckx, 'Critical Theories and Christian Political Commitment', *Concilium* 4(9) (April 1973), pp. 48–61 (49).

33 Ibid., pp. 50–1.

34 J. Habermas, *Protestbewegung und Hochschulreformen* (Frankfurt: Suhrkamp Verlag, 1969), p. 245.

35 E. Schillebeeckx, 'Critical Theories and Christian Political Commitment', p. 54.

36 Ibid., pp. 54–5.

37 E. Schillebeeckx, *The Understanding of Faith: Interpretation and Criticism* (London: Sheed and Ward, 1974), p. 62.

38 E. Borgman, '*Gaudium et spes*: The Forgotten Future of a Revolutionary Document', *Concilium* 4 (2005), p. 54.

39 E. Borgman, 'Theology as the Art of Liberation' – Edward Schillebeeckx's Response to the Theologies of the EATWOT', *Exchange* 32(2) (2003), pp. 98–108 (100).

40 E. Schillebeeckx, *The Understanding of Faith*, p. 68.

41 Ibid., pp. 74–5.

42 E. Borgman, *Edward Schillebeeckx: A Theologian in his History, Volume 1: A Catholic Theology of Culture (1914-1965)* (London: Continuum, 2004), p. 381. Also cited by L. Boeve, in 'The Enduring Significance and Relevance of Edward Schillebeeckx: Introducing the State of the Question in *Medias Res*', in L. Boeve et al. (eds), *Edward Schillebeeckx and Contemporary Theology* (London: T & T Clark, 2010), p. 6.

43 E. Borgman, *Edward Schillebeeckx*, p. 373.

44 B. E. Hinze, 'A Prophetic Vision: Eschatology and Ethics', in Robert J. Schreiter et al., *The Praxis of Christian Experience*, pp. 138–9.

45 Ibid., p. 139.

46 Ibid., p. 142. Citing p. 731 of Schillebeeckx's *Christ the Sacrament of the Encounter with God*.

47 Ibid., p. 145.

48 E. Schillebeeckx, *God the Future of Man* (London: Sheed and Ward, 1969), p. 153.

49 Ibid., p. 126.

50 Private email correspondence between the author and Adam G. Cooper.

51   L. Boeve and B. Vedder in L. Boeve et al. (eds), *Edward Schillebeeckx and Contemporary Theology* (London: T & T Clark, 2010), p. x.
52   Ibid., p. x.
53   Schillebeeckx, *God and the Future of Man*, p. 155.
54   D. Tracy, 'The Uneasy Alliance Reconceived: Catholic Theological Method, Modernity and Post-Modernity', *Theological Studies* 50 (1989), pp. 548–70 (554).
55   Ibid., p. 555.
56   K. Rahner, *Theological Investigations*, vol. 10, p. 318.
57   P. J. Lynch, 'Secularisation Affirms the Sacred: Karl Rahner', *Thought* 61(242) (September 1986), pp. 381–93.
58   Ibid., p. 386.
59   Ibid., p. 389.
60   E. Schillebeeckx, *God the Future of Man* (London: Sheed and Ward, 1969), p. 68.
61   Ibid., p. 58.
62   J. Ratzinger, *Images of Hope: Meditations on Major Feasts* (San Francisco: Ignatius Press, 2006), p. 34.
63   L. Boeve in L. Boeve and L. P. Hemming (eds), *Divinizing Experience* (Leuven: Peeters, 2004), p. 200.
64   E. Borgman, '*Gaudium et Spes*: the Forgotten Future of a Revolutionary Document', *Concilium* 4 (2005), pp. 48–56 (54).
65   L. Boeve, *Interrupting Tradition: An Essay on Christian Faith in a Postmodern Context* (Louvain, Belgium:, Peeters Press, 2003), p. 24.
66   Ibid., p. 49.
67   J. Pieper, *Tradition: Concept and Claim* (Wilmington: ISI Books, 2008), p. 21.
68   H. de Lubac, *La Révélation Divine* (Paris: Cerf, 1968), p. 101.
69   P. J. Cordes, 'Not without the Light of Faith: Catholic Social Doctrine Clarifies Its Self-Understanding', Address at the Australian Catholic University, North Sydney, 27 November 2009, p. 4.
70   G. Hoskins, 'An Interview with Lieven Boeve: "Recontextualizing the Christian Narrative in a Postmodern Context"', *Journal of Philosophy and Scripture* 3(2) (Spring 2006), pp. 31–7.
71   L. Boeve, *Lyotard and Theology* (London: Bloomsbury, 2014), p. 99.
72   L. Boeve, *Interrupting Tradition*, p. 175.
73   L. Boeve, *Lyotard and Theology*, p. 123.
74   Ibid., p. 123. Material for this section has been taken from the author's chapter on 'Tradition' in the *Oxford Handbook on Modern European Thought* (Oxford: Oxford University Press, 2013), pp. 277–300.
75   T. Guarino, 'Postmodernity and Five Fundamental Theological Issues', *Theological Studies* 57(4) (December 1996), pp. 654–90 (660–1).
76   Ibid., pp. 654–90 (667).
77   L. Boeve, *God Interrupts History: Theology in a Time of Upheaval*, (London: Continuum, 2007), p. 6.
78   J. Ratzinger, 'Interreligious Dialogue and Jewish-Christian Relations', *Communio: International Catholic Review* 25 (1998), pp. 29–41 (31).

79 R. Barron, *The Priority of Christ: Toward a Post-Liberal Catholicism* (Grand Rapids: Eerdmans, 2007), p. 341.
80 H. U. von Balthasar, *The Moment of Christian Witness* (San Francisco: Ignatius, 1994), p. 21.

Chapter 5

1   K. Rahner, in *Karl Rahner: I Remember, An Autobiographical Interview with Meinrod Krauss*, trans. Harvey D. Egan (New York, Crossroad, 1985), p. 91.
2   Ibid., p. 92.
3   P. André-Vincent, 'Les Théologies de la liberation', *Nouvelle Revue Théologique* (February 1976), p. 110.
4   F. Schüssler Fiorenza, 'Political Theology: An Historical Analysis', *Theological Digest* 25(4) (1977), pp. 317–34.
5   Ibid., p. 329.
6   Ibid., p. 131.
7   J. Comblin, 'The Signs of the Times', *Concilium* 4 (2005), pp. 73–85 (81).
8   Ibid., p. 83.
9   J. Milbank, *Theology and Social Theory: Beyond Secular Reason* (Oxford: Blackwell, 1990), pp. 206–55.
10 I. M. Pacepa, 'Former Soviet Spy: We created Liberation Theology', Catholic News Agency, 5 May 2015.
11 E. Schillebeeckx, *God and the Future of Man*, p. 206, n. 16.
12 J. Comblin, 'The Holy Fathers of Latin America', *Concilium* 5 (2009), pp. 12–23 (17–18).
13 C. Rowland, *The Cambridge Companion to Liberation Theology* (Cambridge: Cambridge University Press, 2007), p. 11.
14 Abbott Christopher Butler, 'On the Value of History', *Downside Review* 68 (LXVIII) Number 213 (Summer 1950), pp. 290–305 (294).
15 M. R. Candelaria, *Popular Religion and Liberation: The Dilemma of Liberation Theology* (New York: State University of New York Press, 1990), p. 110.
16 Ibid., p. 111.
17 J. L. Segundo, *Our Idea of God* (Dublin: Gill and Macmillan, 1980), p. 37.
18 J. L. Segundo, *Theology and the Church: A Response to Cardinal Ratzinger and a Warning to the Whole Church* (New York: Winston Press, 1985).
19 J. L. Segundo, *The Liberation of Theology* (New York: Orbis, 1976), p. 9.
20 S. van Erp, *The Art of Theology: Hans Urs von Balthasar's Theological Aesthetics and the Foundation of Faith* (Leuven: Peeters, 2004), p. 35.
21 E. Schillebeeckx, 'The Role of History in what is called the New Paradigm', in Hans Küng and David Tracy (eds), *Paradigm Change in Theology* (London: T & T Clark, 1989), p. 318.
22 G. Gutierrez, *A Theology of Liberation: History, Politics and Salvation* (New York: Orbis, 1998), p. 12.

23 J. L. Segundo, 'Capitalism-Socialism: A Theological Crux', in Claude Geffré
    and Gustavo Gutiérrez (eds), *Mystical and Political Dimensions of the
    Christian Faith* (New York: Herder and Herder, 1974), p. 16.
24 J. Sobrino, *Christology at the Crossroads: A Latin American Approach*
    (New York: Maryknoll, 1978).
25 Z. Bennett, 'Action is the Life of All: The Praxis-based Epistemology
    of Liberation Theology', in Christopher Dawson (ed.), *The Cambridge
    Companion to Liberation Theology* (Cambridge: Cambridge University
    Press, 2007), p. 39.
26 L. Dupré, *Marx's Social Critique of Culture* (New Haven: Yale University
    Press, 1983), p. 287.
27 M. Lamb, *Solidarity with Victims: Towards a Theology of Social
    Transformation* (New York: Crossroad, 1982).
28 Ibid., pp. 69–71.
29 Ibid., p. 73.
30 A. Nichols, *Scribe of the Kingdom: Essays on Theology and Culture Vol 2*
    (London: Sheed and Ward, 1994), p. 139.
31 C. Boff, 'Teologia da Libertação e volta ao fundamento', *Revista Eclesiástica
    Brasileira* 67(268) (Outubro 2007), pp. 1001–22.
32 L. Boff, 'Pelos pobres, contra a estreiteza do método', Petrópolis, festa de
    Corpus Christi, 22 de mayo de 2008.
33 L. Boff, *Jesucristo el liberado: Ensayo de cristolgia critica para nuestro tiempo*
    (Buenos Aires: Latinoamerica Libros, 1975), pp. 59–61.
34 L. Boff, 'Is the Cosmic Christ Greater than Jesus of Nazareth?', *Concilium*
    1 (2007), pp. 57–63 (59).
35 Ibid., p. 62.
36 Ibid., p. 63.
37 Jose Maria Vigil, 'The Pluralist Paradigm: Toward a Pluralist Re-reading of
    Christianity', *Concilium* 1 (2007), pp. 31–9.
38 Ibid., p. 34.
39 Ibid., p. 35.
40 Ibid., p. 36.
41 E. Wainwright, 'Many Have Undertaken … and I too Decided: The One
    Story of the Many', *Concilium* 2 (2006), pp. 45–52 (49).
42 Ibid., p. 49.
43 E. Schüssler Fiorenza, 'For Women in Men's Worlds: A Critical Feminist
    Theology of Liberation', *Concilium* 171 (1984), pp. 32–9 (36).
44 A. E. Carr, 'The New Vision of Feminist Theology', in Catherine Mowry
    La Cugna (ed.), *Freeing Theology: The Essential of Theology in Feminist
    Perspective* (San Francisco: Harper, 1993), p. 21.
45 Ibid., p. 21.
46 M. J. Rees, 'Latin American Women: "We are leaving behind patriarchal
    constructs and pushing toward something new"', *Concilium* 3 (2009),
    pp. 86–94 (90).
47 Ibid., p. 91.

48   Ibid., p. 94.
49   G. Gutierrez, *Liberación de la teologia* (Buenos Aires: Ediciones Carlos Lohle, 1975), p. 261. English translation quoted in Candelaria, *Popular Religion and Liberation*, p. 40.
50   R. Kusch, *Indigenous and Popular Thinking in Latin America* (Durham: Duke University Press, 2010).
51   W. D. Mignolo, Introduction to R. Kusch, *Indigenous and Popular Thinking in Latin America*, pp. vi–vii.
52   K. Lemna and D. Delaney, 'Three Pathways into the Theological Mind of Pope Francis', *Nova et Vetera* 12(1) (2014), pp. 25–56 (33).
53   Candelaria, *Popular Religion and Liberation*, p. 17.
54   Ibid., p. 50.
55   J. C. Scannone, 'Popular Culture: Pastoral and Theological Considerations', *Lumen Vitae* 32 (1977), pp. 157–74 (161).
56   Ibid., p. 163.
57   Ibid., p. 170.
58   Ibid., p. 174.
59   J. C. Scannone, 'Das Theorie-Praxis Verhältnis in den Theologie der Befreiung', in K. Rahner (ed.), *Befreiende Theologie: Der Beitrag Lateinamerikas zur Theologie der Gegenwart* (Stuttgart: Kohlhammer, 1977), pp. 77–96 (96).
60   Ibid., p. 96.
61   Ibid., p. 84.
62   For an article that situates Scannone in the broader oeuvre of Latin American intellectuals students can read Michael Schulz's 'Hermeneutics of Identity: Latin American Philosophy's Search for Self-Independence' published in *Philosophy Study* in 2013.
63   John Paul II, General Audience Address, 21 February 1979.
64   J. V. Schall, 'Political Theory and Political Theology', *Laval Theologique et Philosophique* XXXI (Février 1975), pp. 25–45 (25), citing L. Strauss, 'What is Political Philosophy?', *Journal of Politics* 3 (1957).
65   Ibid., p. 26.
66   Ibid., p. 26.
67   Ibid., p. 34.
68   H. U. von Balthasar, 'Current Trends in Catholic Theology Today', *Communio: International Catholic Review* Spring (1978), pp. 84–5.
69   J. Milbank, *Beyond Secular Reason*, p. 236.
70   Ibid., p. 208.
71   Ibid., p. 233.
72   A. Scola, 'Christian Experience and Theology', *Communio: International Theological Review* 23 (1996), pp. 203–6.
73   Ibid., p. 203.
74   H. U. von Balthasar, 'Liberation Theology in the Light of Salvation History', in James V. Schall (ed.), *Liberation Theology* (San Francisco: Ignatius, 1982), pp. 131–47 (132).

75 Ibid., p. 132.
76 Ibid., p. 132.
77 Ibid., p. 133.
78 Ibid., p. 140.
79 J. Ratzinger, *Salt of the Earth: The Church at the End of the Millennium* (San Francisco: Ignatius, 1997), p. 94.
80 G. Gutiérrez and G. Müller, *On the Side of the Poor: The Theology of Liberation* (New York: Orbis, 2015), p. 81.
81 J. Milbank, *Beyond Secular Reason*, p. 232.
82 G. Müller, *On the Side of the Poor*, p. 19.
83 Ibid., p. 69.
84 Pope Francis as quoted by Cardinal Walter Kasper, in 'An Interview with Walter Kasper', *Commonweal*, 8 May 2014.
85 R. Douthat, 'Will Pope Francis Break the Church?' *The Atlantic*, 18 April 2015. Found online at: www.theatlantic.com/magazine/archive/2015/05/will-pope-francis-break-the-church.
86 J. C. Scannone, 'El papa Francisco y la teologia del pueblo', *Razón y Fe* 1395 (2014), pp. 31–50.
87 L. Zanatta, 'Un papa peronista?', *La Rivista il Mulino* 2 (March–April 2016), pp. 240–9.
88 J. Bergoglio, 'Sobre pluralism teologico y ecclesiologia latinoamericana', *Stromata* 40 (1984), pp. 321–31. Article republished in *Humanitas* 79 (2015), pp. 458–75 (462). Translation from Spanish to English provided by Fr Joel Wallace.
89 H. U. von Balthasar, *Truth is Symphonic: Aspects of Christian Pluralism* (San Francisco: Ignatius, 1987).
90 Ibid., pp. 64–5.
91 Ibid., p. 110.
92 Ibid., p. 116.
93 Ibid., p. 117.
94 Ibid., p. 121.
95 Ibid., p. 121.
96 J. Bergoglio, 'El Pluralismo Teológico', *Humanitas* 79 (2015), pp. 458–76 (467). Translation from Spanish to English provided by Fr Joel Wallace.
97 Ibid.
98 A-M. Cernea, 'The World Needs Real Freedom, Liberation from Sin', Says Romanian Doctor at Synod, 17 October 2015. voiceofthefamily.com/the-world-needs-real-freedom-liberation-from-sin-says-romani.
99 R. Sarah, *God or Nothing: A Conversation on Faith with Nicolas Diat* (San Francisco: Ignatius, 2015), p. 249.
100 R. Douthat, 'Will Pope Francis Break the Church?' *The Atlantic*, 18 April 2015. Found online at: www.theatlantic.com/magazine/archive/2015/05/will-pope-francis-break-the-church.

101   S. Magister, 'Amoris Laetitia' Has a Ghostwriter: His Name is
      Victor Manuel Fernández, http://chiesa.espresso.repubblica.it/
      articolo/1351303?eng=y.
102   L. Kołakowski, 'The Eagle and the Small Birds: Interview with Michael
      Charlton', BBC, 1994, p. 132.
103   A. T. Hennelly, 'Theological Method: The Southern Exposure', *Theological
      Studies* 38(4) (December 1977), pp. 709–36 (729).

Conclusion

1   A. T. Hennelly, 'Theological Method: The Southern Exposure', *Theological
    Studies* 38(4) (December 1977), pp. 709–36 (720).
2   J. Milbank, *Beyond Secular Reason*, pp. 248–9.
3   Ibid., p. 246.

Appendix 1: Christological Heresies

Heresy	Details	Condemned
Adoptionism	The pre-existence of Jesus as Christ is denied. Jesus is held to have only been the adopted son of God. Thus Jesus had essentially two sonships: one by generation and nature, and another by adoption and grace. God is held to have adopted the human Jesus either at baptism or at resurrection. Also known as Dynamic Monarchianism.	Council of Nicea, 325 AD / Council of Rome, 798 AD
Apollinarianism	The full manhood of Christ is denied. Using the tripartite understanding of the person accepted by all the early Church Fathers, Apollinarius argued that Jesus had a human body (σῶμα) and soul (ψυχή), but not a human spirit (πνεῦμα). Instead, Jesus's spirit was exclusively divine.	Council of Constantinople, 381 AD
Arianism	The pre-existence of Christ is denied. Arius argued that the Father alone is God in the full sense (ὁ Θεός), and that the Son was a being created by the Father who might be called God (Θεός), and worshipped as God.	Council of Nicea, 325 AD
Docetism	The full Incarnation of Christ is denied. The physical, human form of Jesus is held to have been only apparent or illusory. The Word was not incarnate, but only appeared to be so.	Council of Chalcedon, 451 AD
Modalism	The three Persons of the Trinity are denied. God is held to be one monad who has revealed Himself in various modes throughout history, that is, Jesus and the Holy Spirit. Also known as Patripassianism (in the West), Sabellianism (in the East) and Modalistic Monarchism.	Council of Nicea, 325 AD

(Continued)

Heresy	Details	Condemned
Monophysitism	The two natures of Christ united in His one hypostasis (ὑπόστασις) are denied. Monophysites held that Jesus's natures were fused in such a manner that the Divine nature subsumed the Human.	Council of Chalcedon, 451 AD
Monothelitism	The two wills of Christ, corresponding to His two natures, are denied. Instead, Jesus is understood as having two natures, but only a single will.	Third Council of Constantinople, 681 AD
Nestorianism	The union of Christ's divine and human natures is denied. Nestorius held that Jesus's two natures – human and divine – were separate. Thus two persons, Jesus and the Divine *logos*, dwelt within the one man.	Council of Ephesus, 431 AD
Psilanthropism	The divinity of Christ is denied. Jesus is held to have been the son of human parents, but graced by God as a prophet, spirit-bearer or even the greatest of the saints. Thus, he is not held to be divine.	Council of Nicea, 325 AD

Appendix 2: Documents of the Second Ecumenical Vatican Council

Document	Date Promulgated	Topic Covered
Constitutions		
Sacrosanctum Concilium	4 December 1963	Constitution on the Sacred Liturgy
Lumen Gentium	21 November 1964	Dogmatic Constitution on the Church
Dei Verbum	18 November 1965	Dogmatic Constitution on Divine Revelation
Gaudium et Spes	7 December 1965	Pastoral Constitution on the Church in the Modern World
Declarations		
Gravissimum Educationis	28 October 1965	Declaration on Christian Education
Nostra Aetate	28 October 1965	Declaration on the Relationship of the Church to Non-Christian Religions
Dignitatis Humanae	7 December 1965	Declaration on Religious Freedom, on the Right of the Person and of Communities to Social and Civil Freedom in Matters Religious
Decrees		
Inter Mirifica	4 December 1963	Decree on the Media of Social Communications
Unitatis Redintegratio	21 November 1964	Decree on Ecumenism
Oreintalium Ecclesiarum	21 November 1964	Decree on the Catholic Churches of the Eastern Rite
Optatam Totius	28 October 1965	Decree on Priestly Training
Prefectae Caritatis	28 October 1965	Decree on the Adaption and Renewal of Religious Life
Christus Dominus	28 October 1965	Decree on the Pastoral Office of Bishops in the Church

(Continued)

Document	Date Promulgated	Topic Covered
Apostolicam Actuositatem	18 November 1965	Decree on the Apostolate of the Laity
Ad Gentes	7 December 1965	Decree on the Missionary Activity of the Church
Presbyterorum Ordinis	7 December 1965	Decree on the Ministry and Life of Priests

Appendix 3: Papal Encyclicals

Leo XIII – Francis

Pontiff	Title	Topic Covered
Leo XIII (1878–1903)	Inscrutabili Dei Consilio (1878)	On the Evils of Society
	Quod Apostolici Muneris (1878)	On Socialism
	Aeterni Patris (1879)	On the Restoration of Christian Philosophy
	Arcanum (1880)	On Christian Marriage
	Grande Munus (1880)	On Saints Cyril and Methodius
	Sancta Dei Civitas (1880)	On Mission Societies
	Diuturnum (1881)	On the Origin of Civil Power
	Licet Multa (1881)	On Catholics in Belgium
	Etsi Nos (1882)	On Conditions in Italy
	Auspicato Concessum (1882)	On St Francis of Assisi
	Cum Multa (1882)	On Conditions in Spain
	Supremi Apostolatus Officio (1883)	On Devotion to the Rosary
	Nobilissima Gallorum Gens (1884)	On the Religious Question in France
	Humanum Genus (1884)	On Freemasonry
	Superiore Anno (1884)	On the Recitation of the Rosary
	Immortale Dei (1885)	On the Christian Constitution of States
	Spectata Fides (1885)	On Christian Education
	Quod Auctoritate (1885)	On Proclaiming an Extraordinary Jubilee
	Iampridem (1886)	On Catholicism in Germany
	Quod Multum (1886)	On the Liberty of Church
	Pergrata (1886)	On the Church in Portugal
	Vi è Ben Noto (1887)	On the Rosary and Public Life
	Officio Sanctissimo (1887)	On the Church in Bavaria
	Quod Anniversarius (1888)	On His Sacerdotal Jubilee
	In Plurimis (1888)	On the Abolition of Slavery
	Libertas (1888)	On the Nature of Human Liberty

(Continued)

Pontiff	Title	Topic Covered
	Saepe Nos (1888)	On Boycotting in Ireland
	Paterna Caritas (1888)	On Reunion with Rome
	Quam Aerumnosa (1888)	On Italian Immigrants
	Etsi Cunctas (1888)	On the Church in Ireland
	Exeunte Iam Anno (1888)	On the Right Ordering of Christian Life
	Magni Nobis (1889)	On the Catholic University of America
	Quamquam Pluries (1889)	On Devotion to St Joseph
	Sapientiae Chritianae (1890)	On Christians as Citizens
	Dall'alto dell'Apostolico Seggio (1890)	On Freemasonry in Italy
	Catholicae Ecclesiae (1890)	On Slavery in the Missions
	In Ipso (1891)	On Episcopal Reunions
	Rerum Novarum (1891)	On Capital and Labour
	Pastoralis (1891)	On Religious Union
	Pastoralis Officii (1891)	On the Morality of Duelling
	Octobri Mense (1891)	On the Rosary
	Au Milieu des Sollicitudes (1892)	On the Church and State in France
	Quarto Abeunte Saeculo (1892)	On the Columbus Quadricentennial
	Magnae Dei Matris (1892)	On the Rosary
	Inimica Vis (1892)	On Freemasonry
	Custodi di Quella Fede (1892)	On Freemasonry
	Ad Extremas (1893)	On Seminaries for Native Clergy
	Constanti Hungarorum (1893)	On the Church in Hungary
	Laetitiae Sanctae (1893)	On Commending Devotion to the Rosary
	Non Mediocri (1893)	On the Spanish College in Rome
	Providentissimus Deus (1893)	On the Study of Holy Scripture
	Caritatis (1894)	On the Church in Poland
	Inter Graves (1894)	On the Church in Peru
	Literas a Vobis (1894)	On the Clergy in Brazil
	Iucunda Semper Expectatione (1894)	On the Rosary
	Christi Nomen (1894)	On the Propagation of the Faith and Eastern Churches
	Longinqua (1895)	On Catholicism in the United States
	Permoti Nos (1895)	On Social Conditions in Belgium
	Adiutricem (1895)	On the Rosary

Pontiff	Title	Topic Covered
	Insignes (1896)	On the Hungarian Millennium
	Satis Cognitum (1896)	On the Unity of the Church
	Fidentem Piumque Animum (1896)	On the Rosary
	Divinum Illud Munus (1897)	On the Holy Spirit
	Militantis Ecclesiae (1897)	On St Peter Canisius
	Augustissimae Virginis Mariae (1897)	On the Confraternity of the Holy Rosary
	Affari Vos (1897)	On the Manitoba School Question
	Caritatis Studium (1898)	On the Church in Scotland
	Spesse Volte (1898)	On the Suppression of Catholic Institutions
	Quam Religiosa (1898)	On Civil Marriage Law
	Diuturni Temporis (1898)	On the Rosary
	Quum Diuturnum (1898)	On the Latin American Bishops' Plenary Council
	Annum Sacrum (1899)	On Consecration to the Sacred Heart
	Depuis le Jour (1899)	On the Education of the Clergy
	Paternae (1899)	On the Education of the Clergy
	Omnibus Compertum (1900)	On Unity Among the Greek Melchites
	Tametsi Futura Prospicientibus (1900)	On Jesus Christ the Redeemer
	Graves de Communi Re (1901)	On Christian Democracy
	Gravissimas (1901)	On Religious Orders in Portugal
	Reputantibus (1901)	On the Language Question in Bohemia
	Urbanitatis Veteris (1901)	On the Foundation of a Seminary in Athens
	In Amplissimo (1902)	On the Church in the United States
	Quod Votis (1902)	On the Proposed Catholic University of Eastern Europe
	Mirae Caritatis (1902)	On the Holy Eucharist
	Quae ad Nos (1902)	On the Church in Bohemia and Moravia
	Fin dal Principio (1902)	On the Education of the Clergy
	Dum Multa (1902)	On Marriage Legislation

(Continued)

Pontiff	Title	Topic Covered
St Pius X (1903–14)	E Supremi (1903)	On the Restoration of All Things in Christ
	Ad Diem Illum Laetissimum (1904)	On the Immaculate Conception
	Iucunda Sane (1904)	On Pope Gregory the Great
	Acerbo Nimis (1905)	On Teaching Christian Doctrine
	Il Fermo Proposito (1905)	On Catholic Action in Italy
	Vehementer Nos (1906)	On the French Law of Separation
	Tribus Circiter (1906)	On the Mariavites or Mystic Priests of Poland
	Pieni l'Animo (1906)	On the Clergy in Italy
	Gravissimo Officii Munere (1906)	On French Associations of Worship
	Une Fois Encore (1907)	On the Separation of Church and State
	Pascendi Dominici Gregis (1907)	On the Doctrines of the Modernists
	Communium Rerum (1909)	On St Anselm of Aosta
	Editae Saepe (1910)	On St Charles Borromeo
	Iamdudum (1911)	On the Law of Separation in Portugal
	Lacrimabili (1912)	On the Indians of South America
	Singulari Quadam (1912)	On Labour Organisations
Benedict XV (1914–22)	Ad Beatissimi Apostolorum (1914)	On Appealing for Peace
	Humani Generis Redemptionem (1917)	On Preaching the Word of God
	Quod Iam Diu (1918)	On the Future Peace Conference
	In Hac Tanta (1919)	On St Boniface
	Paterno Iam Diu (1919)	On the Children of Central Europe
	Pacem, Dei Munus Pulcherrimum (1920)	On Peace and Christian Reconciliation
	Spiritus Paraclitus (1920)	On St Jerome
	Principi Apostolorum Petro (1920)	On St Ephrem the Syrian
	Annus Iam Plenus (1920)	On the Children of Central Europe
	Sacra Propdiem (1921)	On the Third Order of St Francis
	In Praeclara Summorum (1921)	On Dante
	Fausto Appetente Die (1921)	On St Dominic

Pontiff	Title	Topic Covered
Pius XI (1922–39)	Uni Arcano Dei Consilio (1922)	On the Peace of Christ in the Kingdom of Christ
	Rerum Omnium Perturbationem (1923)	On St Francis de Sales
	Studiorum Ducem (1923)	On St Thomas Aquinas
	Ecclesiam Dei (1923)	On St Josaphat
	Maximam Gravissimamque (1924)	On French Diocesan Associations
	Quas Primas (1925)	On the Feast of Christ the King
	Rerum Ecclesiae (1926)	On Catholic Missions
	Rite Expiatis (1926)	On St Francis of Assisi
	Iniquis Afflictisque (1926)	On the Persecution of the Church in Mexico
	Mortalium Animos (1928)	On Religious Unity
	Miserentissimus Redemptor (1928)	On Reparation to the Sacred Heart
	Rerum Orientalium (1928)	On the Promotion of Oriental Studies
	Mens Nostra (1929)	On the Promotion of the Spiritual Exercises
	Quinquagesimo Ante Anno (1929)	On the Occasion of His Sacerdotal Jubilee
	Divini Illius Magistri (1929)	On Christian Education
	Ad Salutem Humani (1930)	On St Augustine
	Casti Connubii (1930)	On Christian Marriage
	Quadragesimo Anno (1931)	On Reconstruction of the Social Order
	Non Abbiamo Bisogno (1931)	On Catholic Action in Italy
	Nova Impendet (1931)	On the Economic Crisis
	Lux Veritatis (1931)	On the Council of Ephesus
	Caritate Christi Compulsi (1932)	On the Sacred Heart
	Acerba Animi (1932)	On Persecution of the Church in Mexico
	Dilectissima Nobis (1933)	On Oppression of the Church in Spain
	Ad Catholici Sacerdotii (1935)	On the Catholic Priesthood
	Vigilanti Cura (1936)	On the Motion Picture
	Mit Brennender Sorge (1937)	On the Church and the German Reich
	Divini Redemptoris (1937)	On Atheistic Communism
	Firmissimam Constantiam (1937)	On the Religious Situation in Mexico
	Ingravescentibus Malis (1937)	On the Rosary

(Continued)

Pontiff	Title	Topic Covered
Pius XII (1939–58)	Summi Pontificatus (1939)	On the Unity of Human Society
	Sertum Laetitiae (1939)	On the 150th Anniversary of the Establishment of the Hierarchy in the United States
	Saeculo Exeunte Octavo (1940)	On the Eighth Centenary of the Independence of Portugal
	Mystici Corporis Christi (1943)	On the Mystical Body of Christ
	Divino Afflante Spiritu (1943)	On Promoting Biblical Studies
	Orientalis Ecclesiae (1944)	On St Cyril
	Communium Interpretes Dolorum (1945)	On Appealing for Prayers for Peace during May
	Orientales Omnes Ecclesias (1945)	On the 350th Anniversary of the Reunion of the Ruthenian Church with the Apostolic See
	Quemadmodum (1946)	On Pleading for the Care of the World's Destitute Children
	Deiparae Virginis Mariae (1946)	On the Possibility of Defining the Assumption of the Blessed Virgin Mary as a Dogma of Faith
	Fulgens Radiatur (1947)	On St Benedict
	Mediator Dei (1947)	On the Sacred Liturgy
	Optatissima Pax (1947)	On Prescribing Public Prayers for Social and World Peace
	Auspicia Quaedam (1948)	On Public Prayers for World Peace and Solution of the Problem of Palestine
	In Multiplicibus Curis (1948)	On Prayers for Peace in Palestine
	Redemptoris Nostri Cruciatus (1949)	On the Holy Places in Palestine
	Anni Sacri (1950)	On a Program for Combatting Atheistic Propaganda Throughout the World
	Summi Maeroris (1950)	On Public Prayers for Peace
	Humani Generis (1950)	On Some False Opinions Threatening to Undermine the Foundations of Catholic Doctrine
	Mirabile Illud (1950)	On The Crusade of Prayer for Peace
	Evangelii Praecones (1951)	On Promotion of Catholic Missions

Pontiff	Title	Topic Covered
	Sempiternus Rex Christus (1951)	On the Council of Chaceldon
	Ingruentium Malorum (1951)	On Reciting the Rosary
	Orientales Ecclesias (1952)	On the Persecution of Eastern Churches
	Doctor Mellifluus (1953)	On St Bernard of Clairvaux
	Fulgens Corona (1953)	On Proclaiming a Marian Year to Commemorate the Centenary of the Definition of the Dogma of the Immaculate Conception
	Sacra Virginitas (1954)	On Consecrated Virginity
	Ecclesiae Fastos (1954)	On St Boniface
	Ad Sinarum Gentem (1954)	On the Supra-nationality of the Church
	Ad Caeli Reginam (1954)	On Proclaiming the Queenship of Mary
	Musicae Sacrae (1955)	On Sacred Music
	Haurietis Aquas (1956)	On Devotion to the Sacred Heart
	Luctuosissimi Eventus (1956)	On Urging Public Prayers for Peace and Freedom for the People of Hungary
	Laetamur Admodum (1956)	On Renewing Exhortation for Prayers for Peace for Poland, Hungary and the Middle East
	Datis Nuperrime (1956)	On Lamenting the Sorrowful Events in Hungary and Condemning the Ruthless Use of Force
	Fidei Donum (1957)	On the Present Conditions of Catholic Missions, Especially in Africa
	Invicti Athleae (1957)	On St Andrew Bobola
	Le Pèlerinage de Lourdes (1957)	On Warning Against Materialism on the Centenary of the Apparition at Lourdes
	Miranda Prorsus (1957)	On Cinema, Sound Broadcasting and Television
	Ad Apostolorum Principis (1958)	On Communism and the Church in China
	Meminisse Iuvat (1958)	On Prayers for the Persecuted Church

(Continued)

Pontiff	Title	Topic Covered
St John XXIII (1958–63)	Ad Petri Cathedram (1959)	On Truth, Unity and Peace in a Spirit of Charity
	Sacerdotii Nostri Primordia (1959)	On St John Vianney
	Grata Recordatio (1959)	On the Rosary: Prayer for the Church, Missions, International and Social Problems
	Princeps Pastorum (1959)	On the Missions, Native Clergy and Lay Participation
	Mater et Magistra (1961)	On Christianity and Social Progress
	Aeterna Dei Sapientia (1961)	On Commemorating the 15th Centennial of the Death of Pope St Leo I: the See of Peter as the Centre of Christian Unity
	Paenitentiam Agere (1962)	On the Need for Practice of Interior and Exterior Penance
	Pacem in Terris (1963)	On Establishing Universal Peace in Truth, Justice, Charity and Liberty.
Paul VI (1963–78)	Ecclesiam Suam (1964)	On the Church
	Mense Maio (1965)	On Prayers During May for Preservation of Peace
	Mysterium Fidei (1965)	On the Holy Eucharist
	Christi Matri (1966)	On Prayers for Peace During October
	Populorum Progressio (1967)	On the Development of Peoples
	Sacerdotalis Caelibatus (1967)	On the Celibacy of the Priest
	Humanae Vitae (1968)	On the Regulation of Birth
St John Paul II (1978–2005)	Redemptor Hominis (1979)	On the World at the Present Time
	Dives in Misericordia (1980)	On the Role of Mercy
	Laborem Exercens (1981)	On Human Work on the 90th Anniversary of Rerum Novarum
	Slavorum Apostoli (1985)	Saints Cyril and Methodius and their Preaching to the Slavs
	Dominum et Vivificantem (1986)	On the Holy Spirit in the Life of the Church and the World
	Redemptoris Mater (1987)	On the Blessed Virgin Mary in the Life of the Pilgrim Church

Pontiff	Title	Topic Covered
	Sollicitudo Rei Socialis (1987)	On the 20th Anniversary of Populorum Progressio
	Redemptoris Missio (1990)	On the Permanent Validity of the Church's Missionary Mandate
	Centesimus Annus (1991)	On the 100th Anniversary of Rerum Novarum
	Veritatis Splendor (1993)	The Fundamentals of the Church's Role in Moral Teaching
	Evangelium Vitae (1995)	On the Value and Inviolability of Human Life
	Ut Unum Sint (1995)	On Commitment to Ecumenism
	Fides et Ratio (1998)	On the Relationship between Faith and Reason
	Ecclesia de Eucharistia (2003)	On the Eucharist in its Relationship to the Church
Benedict XVI (2005–13)	Deus Caritas Est (2005)	On Christian Love
	Spe Salvi (2007)	On Christian Hope
	Caritas in Veritate (2009)	On Integral Human Development in Charity and Truth
Francis (2013–)	Lumen Fidei (2013)	On Faith
	Laudato Si (2015)	On the Environment

Appendix 4: Doctors of the Church

Name	Dates	Contribution to Theology and the Catholic Church	Promoted
St Albert the Great	1193–1280	Known as the 'Universal Doctor', he was a Dominican who fostered research in the natural sciences and the philosophy of Aristotle, and famously taught St. Thomas Aquinas. He was the greatest of the German medieval scholastics.	1931
St Alphonsus Liguori	1696–1787	Noted for his work on moral theology. He founded the Congregation of the Most Holy Redeemer (the Redemptorists).	1871
St Ambrose	c.340–397	A staunch opponent of the heresy of Arianism. He baptised St. Augustine and was a major influence on him.	1298
St Anselm	1033–1109	A Benedictine monk, he later became Archbishop of Canterbury. He was an early exponent of the scholastic method in theology, who developed the ontological argument for the existence of God.	1720
St Anthony of Padua	1195–1231	The first theologian of the Franciscan Order, he was called 'Evangelical Doctor' due to the richness of the spiritual teaching in his sermons and writings.	1946
St Athanasius	298–373	He led the Universal Church against the heresy of Arianism and was influential at the First Council of Nicea in 325.	1568
St Augustine	354–430	One of the first within the Latin church to formulate a very clear theological anthropology. His writings helped to establish the Catholic theological Tradition of original sin, the Trinity, grace and free will. He is famous for his autobiographical *Confessions*.	1298
St Basil the Great	330–379	An opponent of both Arianism and Apollinarianism and a supporter of the Nicene Creed. He exerted a key influence on the development of Christian monasticism. His phrases on the Divine nature of the Spirit were added to the creed in 381.	1568

Name	Dates	Contribution to Theology and the Catholic Church	Promoted
St Bede the Venerable	672–735	Known as the 'Father of English History' for his *Ecclesiastical History of the English People*. He also wrote commentaries on books of the Bible and fostered the use of the AD (Anno Domini) dating method.	1899
St Bernard of Clairvaux	1090–1153	A Cistercian abbot renowned for his reform of his Order, his Mariology and promotion of the *Lectio Divina*. He is called the 'Last of the Fathers' (in the West) as an exemplar of the old Monastic Theology.	1830
St Bonaventure	1221–1274	An Italian Franciscan cardinal known as the 'Seraphic Doctor'. He was a key figure within Scholasticism. His works are examples of a strong integration of theology and philosophy and of a strong Christocentrism. His *Journey of the Mind into God* is a classic of Mystical Theology.	1588
St Catherine of Siena	1347–1380	A Dominican mystic actively engaged in public life and responsible for returning the Papacy from Avignon to Rome. Her works, including her letters and *Dialogue of Divine Providence*, emphasised a spiritual disposition of complete abandonment to God.	1970
St Cyril of Alexandria	376–444	Patriarch of Alexandria from 412 to 444; he was a central figure in the Council of Ephesus in 431 and key opponent of the heresy of Nestorianism. Cyril's theology emphasised that the Incarnation had a reconstitutive effect on the nature of the human person – Christ was something more than a moral exemplar. His Christology explained the legitimacy and necessity of Mary's title *Theotokos* – God-bearer.	1883
St Cyril of Jerusalem	315–386	Bishop of Jerusalem who was active during the Arian heresy. His treatises on Mystagogy for catechumens remain influential works. He participated in the Ecumenical Council in Constantinople in 381.	1883

(*Continued*)

Name	Dates	Contribution to Theology and the Catholic Church	Promoted
St Ephraem	306–373	Known as the prophet of the Syrians. He wrote a wide variety of hymns, poems and sermons in verse, as well as biblical exegesis in prose. Particularly influential were his *Hymns Against Heresies*, which warned the faithful of the divisive consequences of heresy for the Church.	1920
St Francis de Sales	1567–1622	Bishop of Geneva known for his opposition to Calvinism and writings on spirituality, especially the vocation to holiness of the laity, as in the *Introduction to the Devout Life* and the *Treatise on the Love of God*. His short pamphlets dealt with the authority of the Church, faith and the Petrine Office.	1877
St Gregory the Great	c.540–604	A key figure in the history of ecclesiology, especially relations between Western and Eastern Christianity, and in the history of monastic theology and Church liturgy, including liturgical music. He was also famous for sending missionaries to convert the Anglo-Saxon tribes, under the leadership of Augustine of Canterbury.	1298
St Gregory of Narek	951–1003	An Armenian monk and poet who was distinguished for his reflections on the Incarnation and Mariology.	2015
St Gregory Nazianzus	329–389	Archbishop of Constantinople and one of the 'Cappadocian Fathers' (along with St. Basil the Great and St Gregory of Nyssa). He was renowned for his theological reflections on the Trinity, especially the importance of the Holy Spirit, whom he designated 'consubstantial' with the Father and the Son.	1568
St Hilary of Poitiers	300–367	An opponent of Arianism, he was exiled by Emperor Constantius II. During his exile, he wrote extensively on the Trinity. He also produced exegetical works on the Gospels.	1851
St Hildegard of Bingen	1098–1179	A Benedictine founder and visionary, known as 'the Sibyl of the Rhine'. She wrote on liturgy, music, theology, philosophy, pharmacy and botany. She was invited by bishops and abbotts to tour the Rhine preaching Church reform.	2012

Name	Dates	Contribution to Theology and the Catholic Church	Promoted
St Isidore of Seville	560–636	Archbishop of Seville who converted the Visigoths from the Arian heresy. In his *Etymologiae,* he attempted to compile a summa of universal knowledge. His works were vastly influential in the preservation of classical knowledge and they also influenced later medieval methods of historiography.	1722
St Jerome	c.347–420	An ascetic hermit who was invited by Pope Damasus to translate liturgical texts and the Scriptures from Hebrew and Greek into Latin. He is featured in art with his pet lion.	1298
St John of Avila	1500–1569	Known as 'the Apostle of Andalusia'. He was an expert on the Sacred Scriptures and a dedicated preacher. He was influential in improving the formation of candidates for the priesthood and he is also regarded as a significant influence upon St. Teresa of Ávila, St. John of God, St. Francis Borgia and Ven. Louis of Granada.	2012
St John Chrysostom	347–407	Patriarch of Constantinople renowned for his powerful preaching and theology of marriage and family life. He condemned the abuse of authority by ecclesial leaders, and promoted ascetic sensibilities and the monastic life.	1568
St John of the Cross	1542–1591	A Carmelite friar and collaborator with Teresa of Avila in the reform of the Carmelite Order whose Mystical Theology is comparable to the apophatic theology of the Christian East. His work *The Dark Night of the Soul* remains a spiritual classic. His works are also a rich source of nuptial theology.	1926
St John Damascene	676–749	Known for his strong defence of the Tradition of religious iconography, his works contributed to law, theology, philosophy and music. His Mariology paid particular attention to Mary's Assumption and he wrote extensively against heresy, including Nestorianism and Manichaeism.	1890

(Continued)

Name	Dates	Contribution to Theology and the Catholic Church	Promoted
St Lawrence of Brindisi	1559–1619	A Capuchin friar and gifted linguist responsible for a great many conversions during the Counter-Reformation, especially in Germany and Austria. He also led an army against the Ottoman Empire to reclaim parts of Christian Hungary and is renowned for his bravery at the Battle of Stuhlweissenburg. He is also known as the 'Apostolic Doctor'.	1959
St Leo the Great	400–461	The pope who confirmed the doctrine of the Incarnation. His *Tome of Leo* was foundational for the debates of the Ecumenical Council of Chalcedon in 451. He wrote extensively against heresy, especially Pelagianism and Manichaeism. He is also known for persuading Attila the Hun to turn back from his invasion of Italy.	1754
St Peter Canisius	1521–1597	A Dutch Jesuit priest active during the Counter-Reformation, who was renowned for his catechism. He is credited for adding the line 'Holy Mary, Mother of God, pray for us sinners' to the Hail Mary prayer.	1925
St Peter Chrysologus	406–450	Archbishop of Ravenna renowned for his oratory and dedication to the corporal and spiritual works of mercy. His works focus on Mary's perpetual virginity, the penitential value of Lent, Christ's real presence in the Eucharist and the primacy of St Peter and his successors in the Church.	1729
St Peter Damian	1007–1072	An ascetic monk and, later, cardinal and bishop of Ostia and Velletri who was committed to reform within the Church. He especially targeted the moral corruption of the clergy. He wrote many sermons and biographies, and his writings are known for their narrative style.	1828
St Robert Bellarmine	1542–1621	An Italian Jesuit cardinal who wrote extensively on the controversies of his day, including the temporal power of the pope and that of various monarchies in Europe. He was a major figure in Counter-Reformation history and theology.	1931

Name	Dates	Contribution to Theology and the Catholic Church	Promoted
St Teresa of Avila	1515–1582	A mystic and reformer of the Carmelite Order. Her magisterial *Interior Castle* is a great classic of Christian spirituality. Throughout all her mystical writings, there is a focus on the soul's ascent to God in prayer. She was a major influence in the conversion of Edith Stein/St. Teresa-Benedicta of the Cross.	1970
St Therese of Lisieux	1873–1897	A French Carmelite whose writings espouse a deep spirituality of filial trust. Her simple faith and focus on abandonment to Christ made her theology a strong antidote to the influence of Jansenism and contemporary forms of nihilism and unbelief.	1997
St Thomas Aquinas	1225–1274	Known as 'the Angelic Doctor', he was an Italian Dominican who was by far the most influential of the scholastics, famous for his integration of philosophy and theology, his 'rescue' of Aristotle from Muslim commentators, his Scripture commentaries and Eucharistic hymns.	1568

Bibliography

André-Vincent, Ph. I., 'Les Théologies de la liberation', *Nouvelle Revue Théologique* 98 (1976), pp. 109–25.

Barron, R., *Exploring Catholic Theology: Essays on God, Liturgy and Evangelisation* (Grand Rapids: Baker Academic, 2015).

Barth, K., *Gespräche 1959-62* (Zurich: TVZ, 1995).

Bauerschmidt, F. C., *Holy Teaching: Introducing the Summa Theologiae of St. Thomas Aquinas* (Grand Rapids: Brazos, 2005).

Bauerschmidt, F. C., *Thomas Aquinas: Faith, Reason and Following Christ* (Oxford: Oxford University Press: 2013).

Baum, G., 'Vatican II's Constitution on Revelation: History and Interpretation', *Theological Studies* 28 (1967), p. 62.

Benedict XVI, 'Address during Meeting with Organizations involved in interreligious Dialogue', Auditorium of Notre Dame Center in Jerusalem, 11 May 2009.

Benedict XVI, *Verbum Domini* (2010).

Bennett, Z., 'Action is the Life of All: The Praxis-based Epistemology of Liberation Theology', in Dawson, C. (ed.), *The Cambridge Companion to Liberation Theology* (Cambridge: Cambridge University Press, 2007).

Bergoglio, J. M., 'El Pluralismo Teológico', *Humanitas*, no. 79 (2015), pp. 458–75.

Blondel, M., 'The Latent Resources in St. Augustine's Thought', in Burns, T. (ed.), *A Monument to Saint Augustine* (London: Sheed and Ward, 1930), pp. 317–55.

Boeve, L., *Edward Schillebeeckx and Contemporary Theology* (London: T & T Clark, 2010).

Boeve, L., *God Interrupts History: Theology in a Time of Upheaval* (London: Continuum, 2007).

Boeve, L., *Interrupting Tradition: An Essay on Christian Faith in a Postmodern Context* (Louvain: Peeters Press, 2003).

Boff, C., 'Teologia da Libertação e volta ao fundamento', *Revista Eclesiástica Brasileira* 67 (2007), pp. 1001–22.

Boff, L., 'Is the Cosmic Christ Greater than Jesus of Nazareth?' *Concilium* 1 (2007), pp. 57–63.

Boff, L., *Jesucristo el liberado: Ensayo de cristolgia critica para nuestro tiempo* (Buenos Aires: Latinoamerica Libros, 1975).

Bonino, S-T., 'To Be a Thomist', *Nova et Vetera* 8 (2010), pp. 763–75.

Borella, J., *The Sense of the Supernatural* (Edinburgh: T & T Clark, 1998).

Borgman, E., *Edward Schillebeeckx: A Theologian in his History, Volume 1: A Catholic Theology of Culture (1914-1965)* (London: Continuum, 2004).

Borgman, E., '*Gaudium et spes*: The Forgotten Future of a Revolutionary Document', *Concilium* 4 (2005), pp. 48–56.

Borgman, E., "'Theology as the Art of Liberation": Edward Schillebeeckx's Response to the Theologies of the EATWOT', *Exchange* 32 (2003), pp. 98–108.

Bouyer, L., *Cosmos: The World and the Glory of God* (Petersham: St. Bede's Publications, 1988).

Brighenti, A., 'Church, Theology and Magisterium in Latin America', *Concilium* 2 (2002), pp. 39–43.

Butler, C., 'On the Value of History', *Downside Review* 68 (1950), pp. 290–305.

Caldecott, S., 'The Science of the Real: The Renewal of Christian Cosmology', *Communio: International Review* 25 (1998), pp. 462–79.

Candelaria, M. R., *Popular Religion and Liberation: The Dilemma of Liberation Theology* (New York: State University of New York Press, 1990).

Candler, P., *Theology, Rhetoric, Manuduction, or Reading Scripture Together on the Path to God* (London: SCM Press, 2006).

Carr, A. E., 'The New Vision of Feminist Theology', in Mowry La Cugna, C. (ed.), *Freeing Theology: The Essential of Theology in Feminist Perspective* (San Francisco: Harper, 1993), pp. 5–31.

Chapp, L., 'Revelation', in Oakes, E. T. and Moss, D. (eds), *The Cambridge Companion to Hans Urs von Balthasar* (Cambridge: Cambridge University Press, 2005).

Coffey, D., 'The Whole Rahner on the Supernatural Existential', *Theological Studies* 65 (2004), pp. 95–118.

Comblin, J., 'The Holy Fathers of Latin America', *Concilium* 5 (2009), pp. 12–23.

Comblin, J., 'The Signs of the Times', *Concilium* 4 (2005), pp. 73–85.

Cooper, A. G., *Naturally Human, Supernaturally God: Deification in Pre-Conciliar Catholicism* (Minneapolis: Fortress Press, 2014).

Copleston, F., *A History of Philosophy, Vol III* (New York: Doubleday, 1985).

Cordes, P. J., 'Not without the Light of Faith: Catholic Social Doctrine Clarifies Its Self-Understanding'. Address at the Australian Catholic University, North Sydney, 27 November 2009.

D'Arcy, M., *The Sense of History: Secular and Sacred* (London: Faber and Faber, 1959).

Davis, C., 'Theology and Praxis', *Cross Currents* 2 (1973), pp. 154–68.

de Lubac, H., *La Révélation Divine* (Paris: Cerf, 1968).

de Lubac, H., *Meine Schriften im Rückblick* (Einsideln: Joannes Verlag, 1996).

de Lubac, H., *Scripture in the Tradition* (New York: Herder and Herder, 2000).

de Lubac, H., *Surnaturel: A Controversy at the Heart of Twentieth Century Thomistic Thought* (Naples: Ave Maria Press, 2009).

Di Noia, J. A., 'American Catholic Theology at Century's End: Postconciliar, Postmodern and Post-Thomistic', *The Thomist* 54 (1990), pp. 349–518.

Di Noia, J. A., 'Thomism after Thomism: Aquinas and the Future of Theology', in Hudson, W., et al. (eds), *The Future of Thomism* (Mishawaka: University of Notre Dame Press, 1992).

Doran, R. M., 'System and History: The Challenge to Catholic Systematic Theology', *Theological Studies* 60 (1999), pp. 652–78.

Douthat, R., 'Will Pope Francis Break the Church?' *The Atlantic* 1395 (2015), pp. 31–50.

Dru, A., 'From the *Action Française* to the Second Vatican Council: Blondel's "La Semaine sociale de Bordeaux"', *Downside Review* 81 (July 1963), pp. 226–45.

Dupré, L., *Marx's Social Critique of Culture* (New Haven: Yale University Press, 1983).

Ernst, C., 'The Concilium World Congress', *New Blackfriars* 51 (1970), pp. 555–60.

Fabro, C., *La Nozione Metafisica di Particepazione Secondo S. Tommaso d'Aquino* (Torino: Società Editrice Internatiozionale, 1950).

Feingold, L., *The Natural Desire to See God According to St. Thomas and His Interpreters* (Naples: Sapientia Press, 2010).

Gałkowski, J. W., 'The Place of Thomism in the Anthropology of Karol Wojtyła', *Angelicum* 65 (1988), pp. 181–2.

Gallagher, M. P., 'Realisation of Wisdom: Fruits of Formation in the Light of Newman', in Keating, J. (ed.), *Entering into the Mind of Christ: The True Nature of Theology* (Omaha: The Institute of Priestly Formation, 2014), pp. 121–41.

Garaudy, R., 'What Does a Non-Christian Expect of the Church?' *Concilium* 35 (1968), pp. 44–5.

Geiger, L-B., *La participation dans la philosophie de saint Thomas d'Aquin* (Paris: Vrin, 1953).

Gilson, E., *Letters to Henri de Lubac* (San Francisco: Ignatius, 1988).

Gilson, E., *The Christian Philosophy of St. Thomas Aquinas* (South Bend: University of Notre Dame Press, 1994).

Glendon, M. A., 'Foundations of Human Rights: The Unfinished Business', *American Journal of Jurisprudence* 44 (1999), pp. 1–14.

Gnilka, C., *Die Methode der Kirchenvater im Umgang mit der Antiken Kultur* (Basel: Schwabe & Co Ag-Verlag, 1993).

Grygiel, S., *Discovering the Human Person: in Conversation with John Paul II* (Grand Rapids: Eerdmans, 2014).

Guardini, R., *Freedom, Grace, Destiny: Three Chapters in the Interpretation of Existence* (Westport: Greenwood Press, 1975).

Guardini, R., *The Spirit of the Liturgy* (New York: Aeterna Press, 2015).

Guardini, R., *Welt und Person* (Würzburg: Werkbund, 1939).

Guarino, T., 'Postmodernity and Five Fundamental Theological Issues', *Theological Studies* 57 (1996), pp. 654–90.

Gutiérrez, G., *Liberación de la teologia* (Buenos Aires: Ediciones Carlos Lohle, 1975).

Habermas, J., *Protestbewegung und Hochschulreformen* (Frankfurt: Suhrkamp Verlag, 1969).

Hall, D. J., 'The Great War and the Theologians', in Baum, G. (ed.), *The Twentieth Century: A Theological Overview* (New York: Orbis, 1999), pp. 3–13.

Hanby, M., *Augustine and Modernity* (London: Routledge, 2003).

Hankey, W., 'From Metaphysics to History, from Exodus to Neoplatonism, from Scholasticism to Pluralism: The fate of Gilsonian Thomism in English-speaking North America', *Dionysius* 14 (1998), pp. 157-88.

Hankey, W., 'Making Theology Practical: Thomas Aquinas and the Nineteenth Century Religious Revival', *Dionysius* 9 (1985), pp. 85-127.

Healy Jr, N. J., 'Henri de Lubac on Nature and Grace', *Communio: International Catholic Review* 35 (2008), pp. 535-65.

Healy Jr, N. J., '*Preambula fidei*: David L Schindler and the Debate over "Christian Philosophy"', in Schindler, D. C. and Healy, N. J. (eds), *Being Holy in the World: Theology and Culture in the Thought of David L Schindler* (Grand Rapids: Eerdmans, 2011), pp. 89-123.

Healy Jr, N. J., 'Natural Theology and the Christian Contribution to Metaphysics: On Thomas Joseph White's Wisdom in the Face of Modernity', *Nova et Vetera* 10 (2012), pp. 539-62.

Hennelly, A. T., 'Theological Method: The Southern Exposure', *Theological Studies* 38 (1977), pp. 709-36.

Henrici, P., 'The Philosophy of Hans Urs von Balthasar', in Schindler, D. L. (ed.), *Hans Urs von Balthasar: His Life and Work* (San Francisco: Ignatius, 1991).

Hinze, B. E., 'A Prophetic Vision: Eschatology and Ethics', in Schreiter, R. J. and Hilkert, M. C. (eds), *The Praxis of Christian Experience: An Introduction to the Theology of Edward Schillebeeckx* (San Francisco: Harper and Row, 1989).

Horn, G. R., *The Spirit of Vatican II; Western European Progressive Catholicism in the Long Sixties* (Oxford: Oxford University Press, 2015), pp. 131-46.

Hoskins, G., 'An Interview with Lieven Boeve: "Recontextualizing the Christian Narrative in a Postmodern Context"', *Journal of Philosophy and Scripture* 3 (2006), pp. 31-7.

Hovey, C., 'Alasdair MacIntyre's Hermeneutics of Tradition', in Hovey, C. and Olsen P. Cyrus (eds), *The Hermeneutics of Tradition: Explorations and Examinations* (Eugene: Cascade, 2014), pp. 144-73.

Huby, J. 'Henri de Lubac, *Surnaturel: Etudes Historiques*', *Etudes* 251 (1946), pp. 265-8.

Imhof, P. and Biallowons, H. (eds), Egan, H. D. (trans.), *Karl Rahner in Dialogue: Conversations and Interviews 1965-1982* (New York: Crossroad, 1986).

International Theological Commission, *Unity of the Faith and Theological Pluralism*, 7 (1972), Vatican City.

John Paul II, *Fides et Ratio* (St. Pauls: Sydney, 1998).

John Paul II, '"The Old Testament is Essential to Know Jesus", Address to the Pontifical Biblical Commission', Published in *L'Osservatore Romano*, 23 April 1997.

Jordan, M. D., *Rewritten Theology: Aquinas After His Readers* (Oxford: Blackwell, 2006).

Journet, C., *The Primacy of Peter* (Westminster, MD: Newman Press, 1954).

Keating, J., 'Theology as Thinking in Prayer', *Chicago Studies* 53:1 (2014), pp. 70-83.

Kennedy, A., 'Christopher Dawson's Influence on Bernard Lonergan's Project of "Introducing History into Theology"', *Logos* 15 (2012), pp. 138–65.

Kerr, F., *After Aquinas: Versions of Thomism* (Oxford: Blackwell, 2002).

Kerr, F., 'Ambiguity in Thomas Aquinas: Reflections After Aquinas', *Providence: Studies in Western Civilisation* 8 (2003), pp. 1–20.

Kerr, F., 'Knowing God by Reason Alone: What Vatican I Never Said', *New Blackfriars* 91 (2010), pp. 215–28.

Kołakowski, L., *Main Currents of Marxism Vol III* (Oxford: Clarendon Press, 1978).

Kozinski, T., *The Political Problem of Religious Pluralism: And Why Philosopher's Can't Solve It* (New York: Rowman and Littlefield, 2010).

Krieg, R. A., *Theologians in Nazi Germany* (London: Continuum, 2004).

Kucer, P. S., *Truth and Politics: A Theological Comparison of Joseph Ratzinger and John Milbank* (Minneapolis: Fortress Press, 2014).

Küng, H., *Disputed Truth: Memoires* (London: Bloomsbury, 2008).

Kupczak, J., *The Human Person in the Philosophy of Karol Wojtyła/John Paul II: Destined for Liberty* (Washington, DC: Catholic University of America, 2000).

Lambert, B., '*Gaudium et spes* and the Travail of Today's Ecclesial Conception', in Gremillion, J. (ed.), *The Church and Culture since Vatican II* (Indiana: Notre Dame University Press, 1985).

Lescoe, F., *Philosophy Serving Contemporary Needs of the Church* (New Britain: Mariel Publications, 1979).

Levering, M., *The Feminine Genius of Catholic Theology* (London: Bloomsbury, 2012).

Lonergan, B. J., 'Functional Specialities in Theology', *Gregorianum* 50 (1969), pp. 485–505.

Lonergan, B. J., *Grace and Freedom: Operative Grace in the Thought of St. Thomas Aquinas* (London: Darton, Longman and Todd, 1970).

Lonergan, B. J., *Insight: A Study of Human Understanding* (London: Darton, Longman and Todd, 1958).

Lonergan, B. J., *Philosophical and Theological Papers: Collected Papers (1958-1964)*, Crocken, R. C., et al. (eds) (Toronto: Toronto University Press, 1996).

Lonergan, B. J., *The Way to Nicea: The Dialectical Development of Trinitarian Theology* (London: Darton, Longman and Todd, 1976).

Lonergan, B. J., *Verbum: Word and Idea in Aquinas* (Indiana: University of Notre Dame Press, 1946).

Long, S. A., *Natura Pura: On the Recovery of Nature in the Doctrine of Grace* (New York: Fordham University Press, 2010).

Lossky, V., *Orthodox Theology: An Introduction* (New York: S. Vladimir's Press, 2001).

Lynch, P. J., 'Secularisation Affirms the Sacred; Karl Rahner', *Thought* 61 (1986), pp. 381–93.

MacIntyre, A., 'Aquinas's Critique of Education', in Rorty, A. O. (ed.), *Philosophers on Education: New Historical Perspectives* (London: Routledge, 1998), pp. 95–109.

MacIntyre, A., *Three Rival Versions of Moral Enquiry* (London: Duckworth, 1990).

Markham, I. S. (ed.), *The Student's Companion to the Theologians* (Chichester: Wiley-Blackwell, 2013).

Martinez, J., 'Christ of History, Jesus of Faith', in Pabst, A. and Paddison, A. (eds), *The Pope and Jesus of Nazareth* (London: SCM Press, 2009), pp. 21–50.

Mascall, E. L., *Christ, the Christian and the Church: A Study of the Incarnation and its Consequences* (London: Longmans, 1946).

McGregor, P., 'Spiritual Christology of Joseph Ratzinger' (unpublished doctoral dissertation, Australian Catholic University, 2013).

McLean, G. F., 'Karol Wojtyła's Mutual Enrichment of the Philosophies of Being and Consciousness', in Mardas Billias, N., et al. (eds), *Karol Wojtyła's Philosophical Legacy* (Washington, DC: The Council for Research in Values and Philosophy, 2008), pp. 15–33.

Melina, L., 'Christ and the Dynamism of Action: Outlook and Overview of Christocentrism in Moral Theology', *Communio: International Catholic Review* 28 (2001), pp. 112–40.

Melina, L., *Sharing in Christ's Virtues* (Washington, DC: Catholic University of America Press, 2001).

Milbank, J., 'On "Thomistic Kabbalah"', *Modern Theology* 27 (2011), pp. 147–85.

Milbank, J., 'The New Divide: Classical versus Romantic Orthodoxy', *Modern Theology* 26 (2010), pp. 26–38.

Milbank, J., *Theology and Social Theory: Beyond Secular Reason* (Oxford: Blackwell, 1990).

Millare, R., 'The Primacy of *Logos* over *Ethos*: The Influence of Romano Guardini on Post-Conciliar Theology', *Heythrop Journal* 54 (2013).

Moleski, M. X., *Personal Catholicism: The Theological Epistemologies of John Henry Newman and Michael Polanyi* (Washington, DC: Catholic University of America Press, 2000).

Montag, J., 'The False Legacy of Suárez', in Milbank, J., Ward, J. and Pickstock, C. (eds), *Radical Orthodoxy* (London: Routledge, 1999), pp. 38–64.

Mrówczyński-Van Allen, A., *Between the Icon and the Idol* (Oregon: Cascade Publications, 2014).

Müller, G., *The Hope of the Family: A Dialogue with Gerhard Cardinal Müller* (San Francisco: Ignatius, 2014).

Newman, J. H., *Essay on the Development of Christian Doctrine* (London: Longmans, Green & Co, 1903).

Nichols, A., *Discovering Aquinas: His Life, Work and Influence* (Grand Rapids: Eerdmans, 2003).

Nichols, A., *Lovely Like Jerusalem: The Fulfilment of the Old Testament in Christ and the Church* (San Francisco: Ignatius, 2007).

Nichols, A., *Scribe of the Kingdom* (London: Sheed and Ward, 1994).

Nichols, A., *The Shape of Catholic Theology: An Introduction to its Sources, Principles and History* (Collegeville, MN: Liturgical Press, 1991).

Nichols, A., *Beyond the Blue Glass: Catholic Essays on Faith and Culture* (London: St. Austin Press, 2002).

Nielsen, K. B., 'Bernard Lonergan', in Kristiansen, S. J. and Rise, S. (eds), *Key Theological Thinkers from Modern to Postmodern* (Farnham: Ashgate, 2013), pp. 239–49.

Norris Clarke, W., *The Creative Retrieval of Saint Thomas Aquinas: Essays in Thomistic Philosophy, New and Old* (New York: Fordham, 2009).

Norris Clarke, W., 'The Integration of Person and Being in Twentieth Century Thomism', *Communio: International Review* 31 (2004), pp. 435–47.

Novotný, D. D., 'In Defense of Baroque Scholasticism', *Studia Neoaristotelica* 6:2 (2009), pp. 209–33.

Oliver, S., Kilby, K. and O'Loughlin, T. (eds), *Faithful Reading: New Essays in Theology in Honour of Fergus Kerr OP* (London: T & T Clark, 2012).

Ormerod, N., 'Faith and Reason: Perspectives from MacIntyre and Lonergan', *Heythrop Journal* 46 (2005), pp. 11–22.

Ouellet, M., *Divine Likeness: Towards a Trinitarian Anthropology of the Family* (Grand Rapids: Eerdmans, 2006).

Ouellet, M., *Mystery and Sacrament of Love: A Theology of Marriage and Family for the New Evangelisation* (Grand Rapids: Eerdmans, 2015).

Ouellet, M., 'The message of Balthasar's theology to modern theology', *Communio: International Catholic Review* 23 (1996), pp. 270–99.

Pacepa, I. M., 'Former Soviet Spy: We Created Liberation Theology', *Catholic News Agency*, Published Online 5 May 2015.

Paul VI, 'Address to the International Congress on Theology of Vatican II', *AAS* 58 (1966), p. 891.

Peddicord, R., *The Sacred Monster of Thomism: An Introduction to the Life and Legacy of Reginald Garrigou-Lagrange* (South Bend: St. Augustine's Press, 2005).

Pieper, J., *Leisure as the Basis of Culture* (San Francisco: Ignatius, 2009).

Pinckaers, S-T., in Berkman, J. and Titus, C. S. (eds), *The Pinckaers Reader: Renewing Thomistic Moral Theology* (Washington, DC: Catholic University of America Press, 2005).

Pope Benedict XVI, *Porta Fidei* (Sydney: St Paul's, 2012).

Portier, W. L., 'Does Systematic Theology have a Future?', in Collinge, W. J. (ed.), *Faith in Public Life* (New York: Orbis, 2007), pp. 9–36.

Portier, W. L., 'Interpretation and Method', in Schreiter, R. J. and Hilkert, M. C. (eds), *The Praxis of Christian Experience: An Introduction to the Theology of Edward Schillebeeckx* (San Francisco: Harper and Row, 1989).

Queiruga, A, T., 'Vatican II and Theology', *Concilium* 4 (2005), pp. 21–33.

Rahner, K., *Karl Rahner: I Remember, An Autobiographical Interview with Meinrod Krauss*, Egan, H. D. (trans.) (New York: Crossroad, 1985).

Rahner, K., *Theological Investigations*, Harrison, G. (trans.) (Darton: Longman and Todd, London, 1972).

Rahner, K., 'Towards a Fundamental Theological Interpretation of Vatican II', *Theological Studies* 40 (1979), pp. 716–28.

Ratzinger, J., *Daughter Zion* (San Francisco: Ignatius, 1983).

Ratzinger, J., 'Dogmatic Constitution on Divine Revelation: Origin and Background', in Vorgrimler, H. (ed.), *Commentary on the Documents of Vatican II* (London: Burns & Oates, 1967-9), pp. 155–98.

Ratzinger, J., 'Guardini on Christ in our Century', *Crisis Magazine* 14 (June 1996), pp. 14–15.

Ratzinger, J., *Images of Hope: Meditations on Major Feasts* (San Francisco: Ignatius Press, 2006).

Ratzinger, J., 'Interreligious Dialogue and Jewish-Christian Relations', *Communio: International Catholic Review* 25 (1998), pp. 29–41.

Ratzinger, J., *Jesus of Nazareth* (New York: Doubleday, 2007).

Ratzinger, J., *Jesus, the Apostles and the Early Church* (San Francisco: Ignatius, 2007).

Ratzinger, J., *Mary: The Church at the Source* (San Francisco: Ignatius, 2005).

Ratzinger, J., *Nature and Mission of Theology* (San Francisco: Ignatius, 1995).

Ratzinger, J., *Principles of Catholic Theology* (San Francisco: Ignatius, 1982).

Ratzinger, J., *Principles of Christian Morality* (San Francisco: Ignatius, 1986).

Ratzinger, J., *Revelation and Tradition* (New York: Herder and Herder, 1966).

Ratzinger, J., *Salt of the Earth: The Church at the End of the Millennium* (San Francisco: Ignatius, 1997).

Ratzinger, J., 'Sources and Transmission of the Faith', *Communio: International Catholic Review* 10 (1983), pp. 17–34.

Ratzinger, J., 'The Dignity of the Human Person', in Vorgrimler, H. (ed.), *Commentary on the Documents of the Second Vatican Council* (London: Burns & Oates, 1967-9).

Ratzinger, J., *The Nature and Mission of Theology: Approaches to Understanding Its Role in the Light of Present Controversy* (San Francisco: Ignatius, 1995).

Ratzinger, J., *Truth and Tolerance: Christian Belief and World Religions* (San Francisco: Ignatius, 2004).

Rees, M. J., 'Latin American Women: "We are leaving behind patriarchal constructs and pushing toward something new"', *Concilium* 3 (2009), pp. 86–94.

Reiser, M., *Der Unbequeme Jesus* (Neukirchen-Vluyn: Verlag Neukirchener, 2013).

Rowland, C., *The Cambridge Companion to Liberation Theology* (Cambridge: Cambridge University Press, 2007).

Rowland, T., 'A Schallian Guide for the Perplexed', in Guarra, M. D. (ed.), *Jerusalem, Athens and Rome: Essays in Honour of James V Schall* (South Bend: St. Augustine's Press, 2013), pp. 235–61.

Rowland, T., 'Tradition', in Adams, N., Pattison, G. and Ward, G. (eds), *Oxford Handbook of Theology and Modern European Thought* (Oxford: Oxford University Press, 2013).

Sadler, G. B., *Reason Fulfilled by Revelation: The 1930s Christian Philosophy Debates in France* (Washington, DC: Catholic University of America Press, 2011).

Sala, G. B., *Lonergan and Kant: Five Essays on Human Knowledge*, Spoerl, J. and Doran, R. M. (eds) (Toronto: University of Toronto Press, 1994).

Sarah, R. C., *God or Nothing: A Conversation on Faith with Nicolas Diat* (San Francisco: Ignatius, 2015).

Scannone, J. C., 'Das Theorie-Praxis Verhältnis in den Theologie der Befreiung', in Rahner, K. (ed.), *Befreiende Theologie: Der Beitrag Lateinamerikas zur Theologie der Gegenwart* (Stuttgart: Kohlhammer, 1977).

Scannone. J. C., 'El papa Francisco y la teologia del pueblo', *Razon y Fe* 1395 (2014), pp. 31–50.

Scannone, J. C., 'Popular Culture: Pastoral and Theological Considerations', *Lumen Vitae* 32 (1977), pp. 157–74.

Schaab, G. L., 'Feminist Theological Methodology: Toward a Kaleidoscopic Model', *Theological Studies* 62 (2001), pp. 341–65.

Schillebeeckx, E., *Christ: The Experience of Jesus as Lord* (New York: Crossroad, 1980).

Schillebeeckx, E., 'Critical Theories and Christian Political Commitment', *Concilium* 4 (1973), pp. 48–61.

Schillebeeckx, E., *God the Future of Man* (London: Sheed and Ward, 1969).

Schillebeeckx, E., 'The Role of History in What is Called the New Paradigm', in Küng, H. and Tracy, D. (eds), *Paradigm Change in Theology* (London: T & T Clark, 1989), pp. 307–19.

Schillebeeckx, E., *The Understanding of Faith: Interpretation and Criticism* (London: Sheed and Ward, 1974).

Schindler, D. C., *Hans Urs von Balthasar and the Dramatic Structure of Truth: A Philosophical Investigation* (New York: Fordham University Press, 2004).

Schindler, D. C., *The Catholicity of Reason* (Grand Rapids: Eerdmans, 2013).

Schindler, D. L., *Heart of the World, Center of the Church: Communio Ecclesiology, Liberalism and Liberation* (Edinburgh: T & T Clark, 1996).

Schüller, B., 'Die Bedeutung des natürlichen Sittengesetzes fur den Christen', in Teichtweier, G. and Dreier, W. (eds), *Herausforderung Kritik der Moraltheologie* (Verlag: Würzberg, 1971).

Schüssler Fiorenza, E., 'For Women in Men's Worlds: A Critical Feminist Theology of Liberation', *Concilium* 171 (1984), pp. 32–9.

Schüssler Fiorenza, F., 'Political Theology: An Historical Analysis', *Theological Digest* 25 (1977), pp. 317–34.

Scola, A., *The Nuptial Mystery* (Grand Rapids: Eerdmans, 2005).

Segundo, J. L., *Our Idea of God* (Dublin: Gill and Macmillan, 1980).

Segundo, J. L., *The Liberation of Theology* (New York: Orbis, 1976).

Segundo, J. L., *Theology and the Church: A Response to Cardinal Ratzinger and a Warning to the Whole Church* (New York: Winston Press, 1985).

Sicari, A., 'For a Reflection on the Ideals of Communio', *Communio: International Catholic Review* 16 (1989), pp. 495–8.

Sillem, E., *Ways of Thinking about God: Thomas Aquinas and some Recent Problems* (London: Darton, Longman and Todd, 1961).

Sliuzaite, V., *The Notion of Human Experience in the Thought of Karol Wojtyła: A Study of the Notion of Experience in the Light of an Adequate Anthropology* (Roma: Pontificiam Universitatem Lateranensem, 2013).

Sobrino, J., *Christology at the Crossroads: A Latin American Approach* (New York: Maryknoll, 1978).

Spaemann, R., *Philosophische Essays* (Stuttgart: Reclam, 2008).

Spinello, R. A., 'The Enduring Relevance of Karol Wojtyła's Philosophy', *Logos* 17 (2014), pp. 17–48.

Strauss, L, 'What is Political Philosophy?', *Journal of Politics* 3 (1957), pp. 343–68.

Tracy, D., 'The Uneasy Alliance Reconceived: Catholic Theological Method, Modernity and Post-Modernity', *Theological Studies* 50 (1989), pp. 548–70.

Trower, P., *Turmoil and Truth: The Historical Roots of the Modern Crisis in the Catholic Church* (San Francisco: Ignatius, 2003).

Van Erp, S., *The Art of Theology: Hans Urs von Balthasar's Theological Aesthetics and the Foundation of Faith* (Leuven: Peeters, 2004).

Venard, O-T., 'On the Religious Imagination and Poetic Audacity of Thomas Aquinas' in Bugliani Knox, F. and Lonsdale, D. (eds), *Poetry and the Religious Imagination* (Ashgate: Aldershot, 2015), pp. 67–91.

Vigil, J. M., 'The Pluralist Paradigm: Toward a Pluralist Re-reading of Christianity', *Concilium* 1 (2007), pp. 31–9.

Vincelette, A., *Recent Catholic Philosophy: The Twentieth Century* (Marquette University Press, 2011).

Voderholzer, R., 'Dogma and History: Henri de Lubac and the Retrieval of Historicity as a Key to Theological Renewal', *Communio: International Catholic Review* 28 (2001), pp. 648–68.

von Balthasar, H. U., 'Current Trends in Catholic Theology Today', *Communio: International Catholic Review* 5 (1978), pp. 84–5.

von Balthasar, H. U., *Explorations in Theology: Vol. 1 The Word Made Flesh* (San Francisco: Ignatius, 1989).

von Bathasar, H. U., *Henri de Lubac: Sein organisches Lebenswerk* (Einsiedeln: Johannes Verlag, 1976).

von Balthasar, H. U., *Prayer* (San Francisco: Ignatius, 1986).

von Balthasar, H. U., *Romano Guardini: Reform from the Source* (San Francisco: Ignatius, 1995).

von Balthasar, H. U., *The Moment of Christian Witness* (San Francisco: Ignatius, 1994).

von Balthasar, H. U., *The Office of Peter and the Structure of the Church* (San Francisco: Ignatius, 1986).

von Balthasar, H. U., *The Theology of Karl Barth* (San Francisco: Ignatius, 1992).

von Balthasar, H. U., *Truth is Symphonic: Aspects of Christian Pluralism* (San Francisco: Ignatius, 1987).

von Balthasar, H. U., *Wer ist ein Christ?* (Einsiedeln: Johannes Verlag, 1965).

von Speyer, A., *Erde und Himmel. Ein Tagebuch: Zweiter Teil. Die Zeit der grossen Diktate*, von Balthasar, H. U. (ed.) (Einsiedeln: Johannes Verlag, 1975).

Wagner, K., Naumann, I. and McGregor P. J. (eds), *Mariology at the Beginning of the Third Millennium* (Eugene: Pickwick Publications, 2017).

Wainwright, E., 'Many Have Undertaken ... and I too Decided: The One Story of the Many', *Concilium* 2 (2006), pp. 45–52.

Walker, A., 'Christ and Cosmology: Methodological Considerations for Catholic Educators', *Communio: International Catholic Review* 28 (Fall 2001), pp. 429–49.

Walker, A., 'Love Alone: Hans Urs von Balthasar as a Master of Theological Renewal', in Schindler, D. L. (ed.), *Love Alone is Credible: Hans Urs von Balthasar as Interpreter of the Catholic Tradition: Volume 1* (Grand Rapids: Eerdmans, 2008), pp. 16–41.

Weinandy, T., 'Doing Christian Systematic Theology: Faith, Problems and Mysteries', *Logos* 5 (2002), pp. 120–39.

White, T. J. (ed.), *The Analogy of Being: Invention of the Antichrist or the Wisdom of God?* (Grand Rapids: Eerdmans, 2011).

Wierciński, A. *Between Friends: The Hans Urs von Balthasar and Gustave Siewerth Correspondence 1954-1963* (Verlag Gustave Siewerth Gesellschaft: Konstanz, 2005).

Wojtyła, K., 'Thomistic Personalism', in Sandok, T., OSM (trans.), *Person and Community: Selected Essays* (New York: Peter Lang, 1993).

Zanatta, L., 'Un papa peronista?', *La Rivista il Mulino* 2 (2016), pp. 240–9.

Zimmermann, J., *Incarnational Humanism: A Philosophy of Culture for the Church in the World* (Downers Grove: IVP Academic, 2012).

Author Index

Subject Index